"*The Reparative Impulse of Queer Young Adult Literature* is a treatise on queer futures, pasts, and presents, an homage to queer texts that represent the hurts alongside the optimism. In this stylish and astute study, Matos asks us to consider what it means to consume queer YA literature and culture within frameworks of pain, suffering, and the reparative possibilities open to us when we acknowledge past wounds and tragedies. Above all, this book asks us to make room for all the messy underpinnings of queer YA literature: the pain, hurts, and even happiness. Urging readers to embrace these contradictions, Angel Daniel Matos offers a refreshing approach to the study of queer YA cultures and literature."

—**Dr. Cristina Herrera,** *author,* Welcome to Oxnard: Race, Place, and Chicana Adolescence in Michele Serros' Writings *(2024) and* ChicaNerds in Chicana Young Adult Literature: Brown and Nerdy *(2020)*

"*The Reparative Impulse of Queer Young Adult Literature* artfully challenges the melancholic and often normative roots of queer YA literature by engaging with reparative frameworks that seek out hope as an act of resistance. Matos's deft inclusion of film and video games alongside more traditional texts is a breath of fresh air and positions *The Reparative Impulse* to be required reading for any who wish to keep up with the field."

—**Dr. Cristina Rhodes,** *Associate Professor of English, Shippensburg University*

"Matos approaches this reparative reading of queer YA through a complex look at how these texts refer to, move away from, or both at once, a queer past that that has often included harm. Reading queer YA is personal and often messy for Matos and all queer readers, and he shows this through a nuanced analysis of YA texts in multiple forms. This analysis is especially poignant when Matos discusses how he responded as a queer Latine to texts with queer Latine main characters."

—**Dr. Summer Melody Pennell,** *author,* Queering Critical Literacy and Numeracy for Social Justice: Navigating the Course *(2019)*

The Reparative Impulse of Queer Young Adult Literature

The Reparative Impulse of Queer Young Adult Literature is a provocative meditation on emotion, mood, history, and futurism in the critique of queer texts created for younger audiences. Given critical demands to distance queer youth culture from narratives of violence, sadness, and hurt that have haunted the queer imagination, this volume considers how post-2000s YA literature and media negotiate their hopeful purview with a broader—and ongoing—history of queer oppression and violence. It not only considers the tactics that authors use in bridging a supposedly "bad" queer past with a "better" queer present, but also offers strategies on how readers can approach YA reparatively given the field's attachments to normative, capitalist, and neoliberal frameworks. Central to Matos' argument are the use of historical hurt to spark healing and transformation, the implementation of disruptive imagery and narrative structures to challenge normative understandings of time and feeling, and the impact of intersectional thinking in reparative readings of queer youth texts. *The Reparative Impulse of Queer Young Adult Literature* shows how YA cultural productions are akin to the broader queer imagination in their ability to *move* and *affect* audiences, and how these texts encapsulate a significant and enduring change in terms of how queerness is—or can be—read, structured, represented, and felt.

Angel Daniel Matos is an Assistant Professor of Gender, Sexuality, and Women's Studies at Bowdoin College (Maine, USA), where he teaches courses on queer youth literature, queer Latinidades, teen cinema, and video game culture. His work has appeared in *Children's Literature, Research on Diversity in Youth Literature, The ALAN Review, Queer Studies in Media and Popular Culture,* among other journals and edited volumes. He co-edited *Media Crossroads: Intersections of Space and Identity in Screen Cultures* (2021) with Pamela Robertson Wojcik and Paula J. Massood.

Children's Literature and Culture

Jack Zipes, *Founding Series Editor*
Philip Nel, *Series Editor, 2011–2018*
Kenneth Kidd and Elizabeth Marshall, *Current Series Editors*

Founded by Jack Zipes in 1994, Children's Literature and Culture is the longest-running series devoted to the study of children's literature and culture from a national and international perspective. Dedicated to promoting original research in children's literature and children's culture, in 2011 the series expanded its focus to include childhood studies, and it seeks to explore the legal, historical, and philosophical conditions of different childhoods. An advocate for scholarship from around the globe, the series recognizes innovation and encourages interdisciplinarity. Children's Literature and Culture offers cutting-edge, upper-level scholarly studies and edited collections considering topics such as gender, race, picturebooks, childhood, nation, religion, technology, and many others. Titles are characterized by dynamic interventions into established subjects and innovative studies on emerging topics.

Speech and Silence in Contemporary Children's Literature
Danielle E. Price

Family in Children's and Young Adult Literature
Edited by Eleanor Spencer and Jade Dillon Craig

Lying, Truthtelling, and Storytelling in Children's and Young Adult Literature
Telling It Slant
Anita Tarr

Children's Literature in Place
Surveying the Landscapes of Children's Culture
Edited by Željka Flegar and Jennifer M. Miskec

Risk in Children's Adventure Literature
Elly McCausland

Detective Fiction for Young Readers
Full of Secrets
Chris McGee

The Reparative Impulse of Queer Young Adult Literature
Angel Daniel Matos

For more information about this series, please visit: https://www.routledge.com/Childrens-Literature-and-Culture/book-series/SE0686

The Reparative Impulse of Queer Young Adult Literature

Angel Daniel Matos

LONDON AND NEW YORK

Designed cover image: Paper cutting art by MicKenzie Fasteland

First published 2025
by Routledge
605 Third Avenue, New York, NY 10158

and by Routledge
4 Park Square, Milton Park, Abingdon, Oxon, OX14 4RN

Routledge is an imprint of the Taylor & Francis Group, an informa business

© 2025 Angel Daniel Matos

The right of Angel Daniel Matos to be identified as author of this work has been asserted in accordance with sections 77 and 78 of the Copyright, Designs and Patents Act 1988.

The Open Access version of this book, available at www.taylorfrancis.com, has been made available under a Creative Commons Attribution-Non Commercial-No Derivatives (CC-BY-NC-ND) 4.0 license.

Any third party material in this book is not included in the OA Creative Commons license, unless indicated otherwise in a credit line to the material. Please direct any permissions enquiries to the original rightsholder.

Open Access funding provided by Bowdoin College.

Trademark notice: Product or corporate names may be trademarks or registered trademarks, and are used only for identification and explanation without intent to infringe.

ISBN: 9780367482060 (hbk)
ISBN: 9781032886848 (pbk)
ISBN: 9781003038627 (ebk)

DOI: 10.4324/9781003038627

Typeset in Sabon
by Deanta Global Publishing Services, Chennai, India

To JSLM. May your impression continue to live through us.

Contents

Acknowledgments		*x*
Preface		*xiii*
1	The Politics of Critique and Repair	1
2	More Sad Than Not?	32
3	The Haunting Presence of AIDS	59
4	On Mortality and Permalife	89
5	Catastrophic Comforts	122
6	The Limits of Repair	155
References		*179*
Index		*192*

Acknowledgments

This book started as my doctoral dissertation, which I developed during my PhD studies in English and Gender Studies at the University of Notre Dame. Susan Cannon Harris and Pamela Robertson Wojcik were instrumental in helping me develop many of the theoretical foundations and methods used in this book. They pushed me to examine teen cultural productions drawing from broader conversations on queer theory and cultural studies, and they gave me the space and means to explore youth literature and media in an academic context. Thank you for your support and guidance. Susan, I want to especially thank you for working with me even when you were on sabbatical, and for welcoming me to your home to discuss texts and ideas. I would also like to thank Kinohi Nishikawa, who continued to work with me even when moving to another academic institution. Thank you for seeing value in my thinking and for pushing me to engage deeply with matters of materiality, time, space, kinship, and identity. I owe a thank you to Barry McCrea, who raised important insights on gaps present in the dissertation during its defense.

During the first stages of this project, so many friends helped me to develop readings and approaches. So many of them proofread, introduced me to methods and texts, helped me with English prepositions (my nemeses), challenged my ideas (over and over again), and offered insight and reprieve during moments of need. Ana M. Jiménez-Moreno—thank you for the heart-to-hearts during train rides to Chicago, your friendship, and for your helpful feedback on the early stages of this project. Robin Murphy, your razor-sharp feedback really helped me to develop my voice as a writer. I especially want to thank Leanne MacDonald, Suzi F. García, Lo, Eric Lewis, Margie Housley, Dani Green, Deborah Forteza, Amanda Bohne, Dan Murphy, and Linnie Caye for being there for me. A special thank you to Peter Holland, Jim Collins, Tim Machan, Patrick Clauss, John Duffy, Erin McLaughlin, and Chris Abram for their support during graduate school. Although this book looks very different from my dissertation, its core remains intact.

Acknowledgments xi

Thank you to my friends and colleagues in the fields of youth literatures and cultures. Pete Kunze, a.k.a. my favorite plantain, thank you for being such a thoughtful friend and for believing in my work back when I was an anxious grad student terrified of presenting at MLA. I'm forever grateful for your support and friendship. Cristina Rhodes, thank you for inspiring me and for pushing me to develop work that is hopefully thought-provoking and transformative. I look forward to more obnoxious singing, heart-to-hearts, and freezing treks through a blizzard-covered NYC. Derritt Mason, Katharine Slater, Josh Coleman, Victoria Ford Smith, Sarah Park Dahlen, Brigitte Fielder, Laura Jiménez, Kristin Arnold McIlhagga, Cristina Herrera, Trevor Boffone, Naomi Hamer, Annette Wannamaker, Brie Owen, Summer Pennell, Cody Miller, Kate Capshaw, Emily Rose Aguiló-Pérez, Victor Malo-Juvera, Crag Hill, Melissa McCoul, Leah Phillips—some of my favorite memories involve our times together thinking, laughing, cooking, eating, co-writing, debating, encountering the "ghostly gay child" and unruly children in elevators, and running around rented homes in mermaid tail blankets. Thank you for your friendship, and for igniting my imagination and corazón. Kenneth Kidd and Elizabeth Marshall—thank you for suppport, trusting in my work, and for inviting me to submit my monograph to the *Children's Literature and Culture Series*.

Thank you to my colleagues at Bowdoin College. You've been such major supporters of my work and teaching, and you always inspire me with your research, thinking, and generosity. Special thanks to Keona Ervin, Jay Sosa, Irina Popescu, Samia Rahimtoola, Belinda Kong, Hilary Thompson, Marilyn Reizbaum, Beth Hoppe, Carmen Greenlee, Adanna Jones, Aaron W. Kitch, Emma Maggie Solberg, Morten Hansen, Elizabeth Muther, Katie Byrnes, Tamis Donovan, Katy Stern, and Elizabeth Palmer for their insights, support, guidance, and constant kindness. Thank you to my outstanding editorial assistants, Corey Schmolka and Paloma A. Aguirre, for providing thoughtful feedback on Chapters 3 and 5 of this book. Special thanks to Dharni Vasudevan, Jennifer Scanlon, Ann Ostwald, and Bowdoin College's Faculty Development Committee (FDC) for helping me secure the means to publish this volume both in print and as an open-source digital text. The open-access distribution of this book was funded by a FDC Grant and the generosity of Bowdoin College.

Thank you to other colleagues for their support, encouragement, and mentorship throughout the years: Nandita Batra, Jocelyn A. Géliga Vargas, Ellen Pratt, Hoang Nguyen, Jessica Pressman, Phillip Serrato, Joseph Thomas, Michael Borgstrom, Shenila Kohja-Moolji, Roshaya Rodness, NanVan Vicente, Rosita Rivera, William Nericcio, Nick Haydock, and José Irrizarry.

Thank you to Sara Schwebel and the Center for Children's Books at the University of Illinois, Urbana-Champaign, and Vanessa Joosen, for providing me with opportunities to share the preliminary stages of Chapters 1 and 2 after the COVID-19 pandemic. I would also like to thank the four anonymous reviewers who provided thoughtful and constructive feedback for this project. The insights I gained from these experiences and people were fundamental in revising and restructuring this book.

Thanks to MicKenzie Fasteland for designing the paper cutting art used on the book's cover, which pays homage to many of the ideas and texts explored in this volume. I'll never forget the time, love, and attention to detail you put into this piece. I'm so glad my book can spotlight your work.

I owe a thank you to Bryony Reece, who was incredibly patient as my writing and research was continuously delayed due to unforeseen circumstances. Thank you for your persistence, understanding, and flexibility. Thank you to Lillian Woodall and the editorial team Deanta Publishing for their work and queries during the production stages of this volume.

A heartfelt thanks to my family—Angel, Rosa, Robbie, and Alyssa—for their encouragement and patience. Thank you for always supporting me, even when you don't always understand where I'm coming from, what I do, or what I'm writing about. Los quiero muchísimo.

Above all, I thank Alex, Terra, and Petra for being a constant source of care, laughter, love, and purpose as I struggled through health issues and other crises while writing this book. Thanks to you, "I know I can make it through."

Preface

As a teen, I had little language to understand feelings, thoughts, desires, and orientations emerging in and around me. While waiting for the school bus to pick me up from middle school, one of my friends looked me straight (or not so straight) in the eye and asked: "¿Alguna vez has sentido atracción hacia un hombre?" An electric and enthusiastic response reverberated through my throat and jolted out my mouth: "YES! ¿Y tú, has sentido attracción?" I didn't think twice. I didn't look to see who was around. The answer was impulsive, not subject to overthinking, not taking my context into account. I didn't have a fully developed language to discuss, much less understand queerness at the time. But queerness was embedded in my body. I felt it regardless of being unable to express it in either English or Spanish. It *existed*.

As usual, the bus was too overcrowded, so my friend and I didn't continue the conversation that day. As I sat in the bus, the loud music blaring from the speakers faded away. Memories, feelings, images, and sensations took over. The scent of cologne, the swelling stir in my chest when Ricky Martin forgot to button up most of his shirt, images of flesh and glistening skin in reruns of *Baywatch* dubbed in Spanish, a group of nearly a dozen boys relentlessly throwing rocks at me, one sleepover where our barely hairy legs remained touching as we played with Hot Wheel cars—these fragments burst in and through me. In a way, I'm trying to capture that moment of bursting through this book—that instant infused with fear, hope, angst, imagination, history, ambiguity, and impossibility. In so many senses, this book addresses the assurances I made to myself as a teen who refused to acknowledge straightness as the only pathway forward. Imagination illuminated that pathway.

My first (purely accidental) encounter with queerness in a Young Adult (YA) novel occurred soon after my friend asked me that pivotal question. My parents gave me a copy of Stephen Chbosky's *The Perks of Being a Wallflower* (1999), oblivious to the queer content embedded in its pages. My reaction to this moment of queer representation was deeply emotional.[1] Instinctual. I remember reading the moment protagonist Charlie encounters his friends, Patrick and Brad, kissing in a bedroom during a party. Picture it: a young queer teen reading a chartreuse colored book in the middle of the night, his heart beating at an accelerated pace, his body overcome by sensations of simultaneous joy and fear. Every couple of pages, I would pause and glance at my bedroom door—anticipating that at any moment, someone would barge into my space, rip the book away from my hands and uncover my queer affinities. Reading queer YA was a profound, inspiring, and frightening experience at the time. Fear and comfort couldn't be separated in my engagement with queer YA culture.

Sure, encounters such as these might seem slightly unremarkable today with the booming presence of queer content and representation in YA literature and media in 21st-Century Western contexts. But for a queer teen growing up in Aguada, Puerto Rico, in the early 2000s, *The Perks of Being a Wallflower*, despite its now obvious representational issues, significantly altered how I thought about queerness and sexuality. It pushed me to feel differently about myself and my place in time. Like graphic artist Alison Bechdel's experience of encountering queer literature when she was a young teen, as represented in her seminal graphic novel *Fun Home* (74), this question led to an instant sense of recognition and joy that further compounded the feelings stirred by my friend's question. A book further encapsulated and materialized thoughts and feelings that I believed were inexpressible, never to be represented. It pushed me to visualize a concrete future where queerness was a likelihood rather than a mere abstraction, intangible desire, or something that could never be expressed.

To say that this moment developed an obsession would be an understatement. I remember secretly researching queer teen literature at the computer lab of my school, making sure to delete the web browser's history. My undercover identity had to be protected, after all. I recall saving allowance money to visit the now-defunct Borders bookstore in Mayagüez—I would get my hands on any of the novels I learned about during my research. I remember taking deep breaths and hoping the cashiers wouldn't pay too much attention to my purchases. They almost always did. I developed significant strength and resilience by reading YA novels such as Nancy Garden's *Annie on My Mind* (1982), Ellen Wittlinger's *Hard Love* (1999), Alex Sánchez's *Rainbow Boys* (2001), Brent Hartinger's *Geography Club* (2003), Julie Anne Peters' *Keeping You a Secret* (2003), David Levithan's *Boy Meets Boy* (2003), and Brian Sloan's *A Really Nice Prom Mess* (2005), to mention a few. Some of these texts are rarely discussed today and didn't necessarily revolutionize queer representation in YA literature. Most of them are dated. But they connected me to a romanticized imagined community—a broader network that felt good but that was ignorant of the "hierarchical social and structural features" that mark queer lives as different, as Other (Acosta 640).[2]

I cherished the stories present in these scavenged books: stories where queer teens made other queer friends, held hands, went out on movie dates, challenged antiqueer attitudes, had first kisses, and were able to come out to their parents and friends in bold, sometimes terrifying, and exciting ways. These books were vastly different from my life as a teenager. Through queer YA literature, I encountered both realistic and fantastical stories that imagined futures that circumvented the normative parameters that restrict who we are, what we feel, who we love, and how we express a sense of our inner selves to the outside world. As the late José Esteban Muñoz would put it, queer YA literature gave me the primary means to latch onto a sense of queer futurity. This genre of literature pushed me to look and feel beyond the trouble of the present and to imagine a time and place different from my circumstances (*Cruising Utopia*). It taught me to survive. Even more importantly, it showed me how my pain connected me to broader systems, communities, and narratives of hurt. This hurt, even when we feel like we've overcome it, continues to move, evolve, and assume different forms. It haunts us.

This sense of queer futurity nourished and sustained me for many years—it filled me with a sense of relief that was inaccessible to me in my cultural and geographical context. Over time, however, this sense of joy and optimism dwindled, mainly because my realities as a queer Latine[3] teen started to clash with those represented in the YA novels published then. I remember, for instance, being so moved and inspired to come out to my friend/crush after reading a copy of *Annie on My Mind* I found at a used bookstore. My aforementioned friend—who asked *the* question—provided further encouragement and pushed me to be bold. "Things are different now. We're not living in the 1980s," I told myself after reading that hopeful ending. "I can do this!" I sat with my crush behind the music classroom. Inhale. Exhale. "Soy… gay. Me gustan los hombres. Like a lot." His hazel eyes widened so much—his face twisted in ways I don't want or need to describe here. "Espera un momento," he responds after a long silence. "If you had to choose between Jennifer Lopez and Ricky Martin, who would ya pick?" I'm sure you're well aware of my feelings for Ricky back then. We stopped being friends shortly after.

While I continued to read queer YA novels and engage with queer youth media, over time, I grew weary of how these stories represented outcomes that were so different from my circumstances and the realities of many other queer teens who I knew at the time. While many of these texts captured the joys and pleasures of queer life, many of them didn't touch upon the hardships that my peers and I experienced when growing up queer in Puerto Rico during the late 90s and early 2000s. My relationship with queer YA, and my own queerness, was saturated with tension and fear. I'd purposely keep my room messy to discourage people from snooping around it and discovering the queer treasures hidden all over the place. That didn't deter my sibling and cousin from digging into my drawers. I still hear the bewildered screams and laughter coming from my bedroom. I saw them hunched over my drawer, holding a rainbow-painted cardboard cigar box I had hidden. The rainbow box contained letters, trinkets, magazine clippings, and even expired breath mints connected to queer memories, experiences, and desires. I don't remember all of the subsequent events, but my body still recalls intense images and emotions. Impressions of me flushing the smaller trinkets of the rainbow box down the toilet, burning some letters and clippings. I don't remember what happened to the cigar box.

Queer youth narratives and media can now be accessed with a few clicks, taps, or swipes. I'm grateful for this development. However, the processes of scavenging, concealment, hope, and pain that were formative to my sense of being will always remain with me and will continually inflect how I understood, and continue to understand, queer youth culture. I was being told over and over again that it's okay not to be straight, but my feelings, body, and realities felt at odds with these narratives. I destroyed pieces of my history, of my past, because shame and normative aspirations were still ingrained in my flesh.

This sense of dissonance perhaps reached its peak as I tried to develop work on queer YA for my MA degree at the University of Puerto Rico, Mayagüez Campus. I was excited about this project and I had a whole team assembled to guide me. I remember my graduate methods course, where Dr. Jocelyn A. Géliga Vargas introduced me to intersectional frameworks and the term queer, and she guided me in creating a proposal focused on examining heteronormativity in queer YA. As I was developing this proposal, I was still processing the murder of 19-year-old teen Jorge Steven López Mercado. The links between queerness and mortality felt more palpable to me—to us—than ever before. Hell. When I found out I shared a surname with the person who murdered him, I remember nearly throwing up. I wanted to erase my name—disconnect myself in every way possible from this unbearable violence. We were so sad, so terrified, so aware of the dangers of putting our bodies out in the world. Everyone around me had a take and opinion on this hate crime, ranging from sympathy to others downright claiming that his brutally violent death was warranted. I still remember the words uttered by one of the police agents that was investigating Jorge's case: "Este tipo de personas cuando se meten a esto y salen a la calle saben que esto les puede pasar" (Primera Hora).[4] I couldn't escape those words. I'm haunted by them. Many of us still are.

I didn't end up writing that thesis. I remember telling people that I wanted to write my thesis on something "more serious" that would increase my chances of getting into a PhD program. Lies. I just didn't have it in me to write it. I was too overwhelmed. But the seeds of this book started during this moment.

After a break from queer YA, I revisited it again during my doctoral studies. My proposed project started as an examination of the relationship between YA and "adult" queer literature. But in doing so, I reinforced the differences between the two rather than focusing on the more comprehensive cultural work they mobilized. The project later evolved into an examination of hope and utopian sentiments in contemporary queer YA culture, inspired by the representation of queer Latine adolescence in Benjamin Alire Sáenz's *Aristotle and Dante Discover the Secrets of the Universe* (2012). Hope and progress were the guiding principles of this original project. However, the emotional parameters of my thinking warped and twisted due to events that occurred as these ideas matured: the 2016 Pulse nightclub shooting, Donald Trump's election, the mainstream attention given to queer teen suicide in the early 2010s, the rise of white supremacist ideologies and practices in different sociocultural domains, the censoring of books for young readers with queer content, the COVID-19 pandemic, and the increase of antiqueer and antitrans legislation regulating everything from public restroom use to the presence of drag culture in youth spaces. And this is just within the context of the United States.

During such moments of heartbreak and sorrow, the ideological and assimilative traits present in so much queer YA literature started to feel particularly fictional and bizarre. The hope so many people yearn for in engaging with these books draws its vigor and strength from normative aspirations that echo the desires of primarily white, middle-to-upper-class communities. Indeed, there was a future developing for the queer teen in the youth literature and media industries, but many of us were barred from that future. This sense of futurism was founded upon excluding voices, experiences, and bodies that can't—and, in many cases, *refuse* to—bend to the whims and mandates of normative cultures.

In more contemporary times, the field has become more diverse regarding representation, genre, and storytelling conventions (see Jenkins and Cart; Corbett; Booth and Narayan). Texts became more comprehensive in their depictions of queernesses and gender variance; they became bolder in terms of using different narrative and generic devices to mobilize different forms of queer futurism, queer reading practices, and queer alternatives to kinship and belonging. During a flight in 2016, I read Adam Silvera's *More Happy Than Not*. When I finished the last page, I started weeping. *Sobbing.* I covered my face with the book in embarrassment (in hindsight, I'm thankful this was before everybody started documenting everything with their cameras). The novel was devastating yet hopeful. It didn't shy away from the pain and the cultural hurt that's always connected to queer thought and the imagination. It channeled this pain to expose the cracks of baseless utopian thinking, the queer connections between the past and present (a divide that in and of itself is a sociocultural construct), and the ways we try to sideline—rather than witness—the hurt and pain tied to our bodies, minds, and psyche. It filled me with that sense of hope and fear I felt back as a teen.

The Reparative Impulse of Queer Young Adult Literature is, on the one hand, a love letter to queer YA literature and a recognition of how these texts use words, images, and narrative devices to encapsulate new ways of envisioning futures that are queer—or that at least defy the normalizing impulses toward gender and sexuality present in Western contexts. On the other hand, this book has an unabashed critical goal founded in the emotional politics of queer YA. What shapes do queer YA stories assume, and how does this shaping make us feel? What's the role of historical hurt in examining queer culture and representation, especially in genres and media produced during a time in which the sociocultural circumstances of sexuality and gender are supposedly "better"? How can we love and appreciate queer YA literature and culture for its future-oriented scope and its reparative bent toward social ills, while simultaneously holding these texts accountable for addressing the needs, desires, and hurt of teens who don't fit the norm, who aren't white, or who don't approach sexuality as a binary? What about those who are growing up in conservative or oppressive contexts in which a "happily ever after" is nearly impossible to envision, let alone *relate* to?

This book is my first comprehensive effort to answer these questions. I recognize that there are gaps in this book due to the limitations of my scholarly background and training—especially in terms of this volume's emphasis on United States cultural productions, its emphasis on YA novels and prose fiction, and the fact that the study of youth literature and cultures encompasses contradictory ideologies, goals, and discursive practices from different fields such as literary studies, critical theory, library science, education, and the publishing industry. This book can't conciliate the critical tendencies, expectations, and trajectories of these fields, which are composed of contradictory approaches, attitudes, and political affiliations. It's not meant to be an exhaustive exploration of the reparative impulse of queer YA literature and culture. Instead, it's focused on further animating existing conversations on how we read, critique, and give shape to queer youth cultural productions. The answers are imperfect, but in seeking them, I'm working towards envisioning more open ways of understanding youth literature and cultures. We need approaches to queer youth literature that deconstruct and build, that admire and denounce, that anticipate yet are grounded in the past. In attuning ourselves to the reparative impulse of queer YA, we do more than lament what queer youth literature has or hasn't accomplished. We build the space to rethink, challenge, and push the boundaries of what it could be, and more significantly, what it can *do*.

In her now classic exploration of queerness, politics, and emotion, Eve Kosofsky Sedgwick connects the broader work of queer studies to notions of youth, claiming that our research and creative thinking often connect to "vividly remembered promises made to ourselves in childhood" (*Tendencies* 3). Queer examinations often focus on making the invisible and silenced perceptible and, even more so, challenging "queereradicating impulses frontally where they are to be so challenged" (3). This book is a gesture toward—not the fulfillment of—the vivid (and, in hindsight, not-*so*-vivid) promises I made to myself as a teen. Promises that have imprinted on my body and that endure through my imagination.

Notes

1 Notably, Michael Cart approaches Chbosky's novel as one of the "most significant titles in all the [queer YA] canon" due to how it shifted the representation of gay teens in the field (Cart, "What a Wonderful" 50).
2 Benedict Anderson approaches nations as imagined political communities, stressing that they are imagined because "the members of even the smallest nation will never know most of their fellow-members, meet them, or even hear of them, yet in the minds of each lives the image of their communion" (6).
3 I use Latine [laˈtiːnɛ] as a queer, gender-neutral alternative to terms such as Latina and Latino—mainly since I discuss characters and practices that deviate from heterosexual, binary, and cisgender modes of thinking and language expression. While I acknowledge the term Latinx has gained currency in academia and US popular culture during the late 2010s, Latine is currently gaining more colloquial traction in Spanish-speaking communities across the globe. Latine is more straightforward regarding pronunciation and cultural access, and it also honors both of the languages I grew up speaking.
4 Roughly translates to "These types of people know that when they do these things and go out into the street... they know this can happen to them."

1 The Politics of Critique and Repair

When we historically examine texts with queer themes and characters published throughout the 20th Century, words like "hope," "optimism," "futurity," and "happiness" usually aren't the first to come up. These texts encompass an archive filled with stories of oppression, violence, and discrimination that have wounded queer communities for decades. These stories summon the cultural phantoms of the past, inviting us to acknowledge how their influence, failures, aspirations, hurt, and impressions continue to haunt us. We're akin to these phantoms. They won't and can't leave. The queer past—encoded not in historical records but in cultural artifacts—is a testament to the reparative and transformative legacies of queer writers and artists.[1] Words and images twist and bend, compelling audiences to interrogate the burdens of hegemony and normativity. Fictive worlds push us to dream, but these dreams are permanently sewn into our bodies, contexts, material realities, and critical moods. The ghosts of queerness haunt these dreams. There's too much unfinished business.

A quick examination of queer fiction highlights histories of sorrow and despair, in that queer people "have been thought of as inherently tragic figures" and that their narratives "almost invariably ended in murder or suicide" (Woods 359). In her exploration of the narrative and emotional parameters of HIV and AIDS narratives, Monica B. Pearl argues that the ties between queer literature and negative affect have been fundamental in shaping an imagination that moves beyond the scope of normativity: "If it is literature that is in significant part formative of the imagined gay community, it is also precisely the sadness in the literature that" was instrumental in shaping it (8). All queer texts—regardless of their emotional goals or aims—are unsettled by histories of tragedy, loss, sadness, illness, and death. Whether they document or imagine the difficulties of coming out of the closet, the disruptive and countercultural bent of queerness, the feelings of failure projected onto queer and trans practices, or the disastrous ramifications of HIV and AIDS from the 1980s onward, cultural productions focused on nonnormative sexualities and gender practices

DOI: 10.4324/9781003038627-1

This chapter has been made available under a CC-BY-NC-ND license.

2 The Politics of Critique and Repair

became an archive forged by the emotional resonances of pessimism and despair. This foundation of negativity has substantial effects on how we, readers, critics, and teachers of YA culture, approach queer texts crafted for younger audiences today—*especially* when said texts are celebrated for being happy, optimistic, utopic, and future-oriented in scope.

Since its indeterminate but palpable emergence, queer fiction has exposed broad audiences to the personal and systemic injustices that haunt people and communities on an everyday basis. By using clandestine narrative strategies, visceral and emotionally charged imagery, and the malleability of language and imagery, creators found ways to weave queerness into the structures and feelings of their creations. In this archive, we can identify how imagined queer persons—and the authors who flesh them out through words and images—envision these injustices. The sociocultural circumstances of gender, sexuality, and queerness have shifted drastically in the last decades, partially paving the way for different stories to be told about queer youth, their cultures, and their communities that move beyond the scope of sadness or despair. Nevertheless, given the literary and cultural ties between queer literature and feelings of shame, aversion, agony, and misery, how do we even begin to understand how hope and positive feelings—especially those championed in contemporary YA cultural productions—affect our interpretations of the historical foundations of queer literature? If we're to read queer youth literature in search of hope, optimism, and (dis)comfort, we must do so while keeping a critical, historical purview—and matters of survival—intact.

I want to explain my use of the term *queer* in this book, especially since the concept is used, framed, and applied in diverging ways in different fields. I'm first and foremost drawn to the reparative bent of the term. Queer is aligned with other reclaimed terms that started as slurs or negatively charged labels but are now used as terms of empowerment. Like "the words Chicano, Pocho, and Nuyorican," this term "entered the vernacular with decidedly negative connotations, which were then appropriated and transformed within these communities" (Rodríguez, *Queer Latinidad* 25). I use the interdisciplinary and deliberately open term queer when referring to nonheterosexual and noncisgender people and communities, or people who don't fit neatly within socially and state-recognized identities and categories. This use echoes Michael Warner's approach to the term, who frames it as a "capacious way" of discussing the "many ways people can find themselves at odds with straight culture" (38). In utilizing this term, I avoid the issues of inclusion and exclusion present in using acronyms such as LGBTQ+ and LGBTQIAA, among others. However, I recognize that this sometimes comes at the cost of specificity regarding gender and (a)sexual practices. Different embodiments of queerness categorized under the queer umbrella exist "within different proximities of violence and marginalization, different articulations of pleasure and vulnerability," not to mention legibility and visibility (Rodríguez, "Queer Politics" 179). I'll sometimes use specific terms and labels when referring to certain characters, identities, practices, and communities, especially if the characters apply such labels on themselves, or if the term is vital in conveying intersecting forms of power and control.

The term queer is generative in the study of youth cultural productions because many of them represent characters with nonnormative sexualities, affinities, desires, and gender identities, yet never bestow an *overt* identity category or label to these characters' practices and orientations. Many of these characters don't have a language or framework to label their desires and orientations, and they often identify alternative avenues for existing within the parameters of a given sociocultural context. YA literature and media represent beliefs, pathways, forms of kinship, and practices that disobey normative and dominant understandings of identity and sexuality. These representations, however, don't always fit neatly within dominant and neoliberal categories of identity—a notion I explore with more nuance in the following chapter of this volume. Queerness provides a framework to critically examine nonnormative practices and lives without engaging in the prescriptive practice of imposing a category of identity onto a character, community, or relationship.

In addition to being an expansive way of examining nonnormative practices, queerness denotes a method of critiquing, deconstructing, and contextualizing cultural productions. As Juana María Rodríguez frames it, queerness challenges heteronormative frameworks and "creates opportunities to call into question the systems of categorization that have served to define sexuality" (*Queer Latinidad* 24). In addition to systems of classification that delineate identity, this volume interrogates the emotions, categories, standards, and norms often implemented in the critique and creation of queer YA cultural productions. Finally, this volume wants to center on queerness' roots in notions of survival and livability. Gabrielle Owen approaches queerness as a method of persisting and enduring in a normative world, of finding solace and relief in a culture and society that rarely offers such affordances to queer folk and youth: "the urgency of challenging the boundaries of reality is the same urgency as finding pathways to be and to stay alive" (1). My use of the term queer channels this ethos of urgency. I move within and beyond the problematic and sometimes redundant binary of "good" or "bad" representation. Instead, I interrogate how texts and media disrupt and potentially reconfigure normative understandings of joy, triumph, kinship, and collectivity. The term queer and its multiple applications help us to focus on matters of survival and to develop a countercultural attitude towards the normalizing tendencies of YA literature and criticism.[2] It gives critics, readers, and educators space to be more upfront about a YA text's potential to heal and challenge dominant understandings of identity and kinship rather than solely focusing on a text's potential to hurt, misrepresent, or make readers feel inadequate.

Contemporary YA literature and culture operate within aesthetic, affective, and ideological frameworks constituted by positive feelings and optimism. This notion seems to contradict and, at times, erase the gloom and despair commonly found in the "primordial" queer canon. Queer YA literature, media, and culture present us with cases in which a field characterized and cultivated by negative feelings and emotions has transformed into one meant to instill a sense of hope, optimism, and resilience to its younger, target queer audiences—at least according to many critics of YA culture. Even older, non-target readers (such as myself, in my current age) frequently engage with queer YA texts as a means of escapism, of living vicariously through a character's experiences, or as an exploration of ideas and practices that were inaccessible to them as they came of age. My processes of reading queer YA are cultivated by the hope these texts gave me as a teen, the sadness in imagining what queer YA could've accomplished, the amusement I feel when engaging with contemporary YA texts that represent ideas and practices that were deemed unrepresentable years ago, and the simultaneous ambiguity, fear, and delight in thinking about what the future of these texts has in store.

This book explores how different representations and narrativizations of queer YA thought, experience, and community negotiate the tension between the foundations of negativity that led to the proliferation of queer literature and the positive emotions and outcomes often celebrated in YA cultural productions. In many senses, this project mirrors the historical and narrative goals of Tom Sandercock's *Youth Fiction and Trans Representation* in that it situates post-2000s queer YA literature and culture into conversation with broader frameworks and histories that move beyond the scope of contemporary adolescence and queer teen cultural production. Too often, criticism and analyses of queer youth literature and cultures sideline the broader conversations taking place in other fields regarding literature, identity, and relationality, thus reinforcing the constructed divisions between our fields—and between ideological constructs of childhood and adulthood—that prevent us from exploring political networks and coalition practices. Marah Gubar, in her exploration of models of relationality as applied to the study of youth literature and cultures, argues that "children and adults are akin to one another, which means they are neither exactly the same nor radically dissimilar. The concept of kinship indicates relatedness, connection, and similarity without implying homogeneity, uniformity, and equality" (453). Eric L. Tribunella further raises the stakes of Gubar's arguments in considering how YA narratives construct an oppositional relationship between youth and adulthood. Tribunella has shown how these narratives perpetuate the notion of childhood as "sacred," "comfortable," and "innocent," leading children to feel the transition into adulthood as "increasingly traumatic" due to what is sacrificed in the process (127). What happens if we acknowledge how pain, trauma, sadness, and despair transcend the barriers of age and developmental categories we normatively impose on them through law, fiction, and representation?

Queer YA is tethered to the broader queer cultural imagination. I don't view the project of queer cultural production to be one that obeys the strict binaries and hierarchies imposed by the dominant culture. Nor do I view the cultural or ideological frameworks of queer YA to be entirely removed from those espoused in the "sadder" and "gloomier" queer texts published with older audiences in mind. Gubar's work echoes prominent frameworks in queer, Black feminist, and trans studies—particularly the notion of transformative manifesting, or *tranifesting*, a healing framework focused on creating forms of coalition that move beyond the restrictions of normative identity categories and practices: "To tranifest is to mobilize across the contradictions, divisions, and containment strategies produced by the state and other large-scale organizations of power that work to limit our capacity to align ourselves across differences" (Green and Ellison 222). This approach doesn't ignore or sideline cultural hurt or suffering, but rather, it channels this hurt to spark further repair. Tranifesting is a way of thinking and deconstructing that "takes place at the crossroads of trauma, injury, and the potential for material transformation and healing" (Green and Ellison 223). How can we elevate queer YA's potential to heal and transform when so many people have problems recognizing that cultural hurt still exists, and that queer damage is *anything* but a relic of the past? What roles does this hurt play in literature meant for younger readers—literature that is designed for them to feel good about themselves and their place in society? To answer these questions, we must venture through these crossroads.

I map out points of convergence between a supposedly distant, negative, and impossible queer past and a supposedly free, open, and encompassing queer present. My focus here isn't to emphasize what makes queer YA different from a broader queer literary genealogy. Katie Schwab has deeply explored the differences between queer literature written for teen and adult audiences, especially in terms of their marketing, their embrace of diversity, and their implementation of trendy elements. Schwab's examination does an excellent job of tracing the transformation of queer YA vis-à-vis the publishing industry. I want to supplement this history by showing how queer literature for adult and teen audiences connect—both in terms of content and form—through their emotional and affective aims.[3] Queer YA is *akin* to the emotional and political frameworks of earlier queer texts despite their differences in scope, narrative form, audience, and connection to the market. I take the dialectic relationship between pain and healing, hope and despair seriously, especially when examining cultural productions generated from queer experiences and contexts. As I'll discuss in more detail later, we're seeing an uptick in queer YA criticism invested in distancing contemporary queer representation from the sadness and violence that was foundational to the broader queer imagination, with the goal of creating a more hopeful and supposedly *realistic* YA archive. Of course, these critical attitudes embody postgay, homonormative, and utopian sentiments that assume the conditions of queer life have undoubtedly improved for everyone (not true, of course) and echo a lot of the ideological frameworks found in practices such as whitewashing—they attempt to align history with supremacist narratives and national myths, erasing the realities of the marginalized and oppressed (see Montaño 60). Such attitudes ignore how the queer past and present are intimately connected and how queer youth and queer adults (and their stories) share surprising emotional, stylistic, and literary aims notwithstanding their surface and noticeable audience differences.

This project considers the generative outcomes that futurity and hope produce in the narrativization and interpretation of queer YA works and, even more so, how certain forms of interpretation can help us scavenge for happiness, survival, and futurity in ways that disrupt normative thinking and reading practices. Given conversations regarding the failures and pitfalls of optimistic thinking, mobilized by critics such as Lauren Berlant in the early 2010s, I argue that it would be too easy (and suspicious) to assume that we're dealing with an instance where queer YA culture offers readers a deceptive sense of futurism that avoids recognition of issues that cause some lives to be "unlivable." This method of thinking has some merit, primarily since countless YA works use hope and optimism to conceal rather than critique heteronormative and cisnormative foundations. However, such an approach leaves little room to explore how the positive feelings and narrative devices implemented in YA productions mark imaginative and deeply political ways of using words and images to foster a sense of affect—of *feeling*—that draws connections between a damaged queer history, our current moment, and potential futures.

José Esteban Muñoz has pointed out that affect

> is not meant to be a simple placeholder for identity… it is instead, supposed to be descriptive of the receptors we use to hear each other and the frequencies on which certain subalterns speak and are heard or, more importantly, felt.
>
> ("Feeling Brown" 677)

The affects present in YA cultural productions possess a critical potential to not only create a sense of historicity and futurity for present queer generations, but also to encapsulate an enduring change in how the intersection of youth and queerness is (or can be) read, perceived, and felt when channeled on the page and screen. Contemporary queer YA assumes different shapes than other kinds of literature, and it also conveys content that other genres of YA shy away from. Part of this has to do with how much the circumstances of youth have changed in Western contexts and how queer activism, trans emancipation, and changes in narrative tendencies have altered the cultural landscape for teens (Sandercock 171). I do more than trace these potential changes and moments of hope: I also determine how contemporary, mainstream queer YA works respond to, reject, or potentially reconfigure their ideological frameworks vis-à-vis the sadness, despair, and negative affect that was partially responsible for the flourishing of queer literature in Western contexts. Are queer YA cultural productions attempting to establish a reparative connection with the history of cultural hurt and violence that has influenced the queer imagination throughout the decades? Or, are they severing themselves from history in the hope of creating a utopia? What are the aesthetic, emotional, and political repercussions of either of these approaches?

Through the analysis of the emerging and increasing presence of positive emotions and hope in queer YA cultural productions, *The Reparative Impulse of Queer Young Adult Literature* also partakes in further examining a trajectory of queer progress through the analysis of works crafted for teen audiences. However, careful attention will be given to the relationship that this progress has with an anxious sociocultural framework that informs the creation and reception of queer content in YA works. Derritt Mason's theorizations on the anxieties of queer YA have called for the importance of embracing the field's ambiguity and penchant for redefinition and reinterpretation, pushing for the generation of nonnormative ways of interpreting YA texts. More specifically, Mason contends that queer YA becomes an incredibly stimulating and noteworthy site of study when titles are not scorned "for their association of queerness with loneliness and despair but are rather mined for the queer relations they represent" (*Queer Anxieties* 25). In line with Mason's sensibility and critical gestures toward repair, this book isn't an attempt to critique queer YA according to arbitrary standards of how queer teens should or shouldn't be represented on the page or screen. It's instead an attempt to examine the queernesses, hauntings, anticipations, and dreams that manifest in YA texts and how they help us to understand the risks and rewards that come with different models of hope, happiness, collectivity, kinship, and futurity.

This volume considers strategies on how to negotiate feelings of hope in the creation and reception of queer YA without dismissing the historical and contemporary realities that queer communities have faced—and will continue to face—despite how "better" things may seem today. It examines and deconstructs queer YA texts with the goals of worldbuilding, futurism, and repair in mind rather than focusing solely on the hermeneutics of suspicion or mining of texts for problematic content or issues. The hopeful, utopian critical drive to examine texts despite their glaring issues, gaps, and ideological tensions is informed by the tenants of reparative reading. This method invites people to acknowledge how texts can be helpful, meaningful, and emotionally sustaining for specific reading communities despite their issues, gaps, or omissions—or even though all texts that we read and teach are generated and created by people imbricated in hetero-and-homonormative, capitalist, and racist systems that all of us are complicit in. Melanie Ramdarshan Bold highlights this imbrication in *Inclusive Young Adult Fiction*, drawing attention to YA's connection to capitalist logics of production and tokenization, and its fixation on the values and aspirations of white, middle-class audiences (34–35). In reading reparatively, we're not attempting to fix the text. Instead, we engage with how the text makes us feel, think of unorthodox ways of engaging with the ideas it represents, and allow it to orient us towards queerer understandings of relationality and existence.

Influenced mainly by the work of Eve Kosofsky Sedgwick in the field of queer studies in the 1990s, reparative approaches traditionally focused on redeeming texts with heteronormative and antiqueer elements by showing how readers drew comfort and solace from them *notwithstanding* the presence of these elements. It arose in part due to the severe issues of queer representation and historicization that have haunted our culture. Reparative interpretations often rest on the promises of hope "to organize the arguments and part-objects" readers encounter to provide a sense of relief from the conditions and hardships of contemporary life (Sedgwick, *Touching Feeling* 146). Reparative strategies were later nuanced through intersectional inquiry. They were advanced with the work of theorists such as Gloria Anzaldúa, Juana María Rodríguez, José Esteban Muñoz, Rita Felski, and countless others. Reparative engagement can broadly be approached as a counterpoint to the hermeneutics of suspicion that has dominated literary (and particularly children's and YA) criticism, one that considers how queer communities obtain "sustenance from the objects of a culture—even a culture whose avowed desire has often been not to sustain them" (Sedgwick, *Touching Feeling* 150–151).

Sedgwick questions the centrality of suspicion in many humanistic and literary approaches. Suspicion leads to the creation and distribution of scholarship that anticipates something faulty in a text even before examining it. This critical impulse leads to instances in which criticism has become more of a prescription rather than a diagnosis (*Touching Feeling* 125).

Sedgwick breaks down the components of "paranoid reading," a method of interpretation that is anticipatory and based on negative emotions. We've all been there, and all done it. We avert being surprised and generous with what a YA text can accomplish and instead conduct readings in which "bad news" is "always already known" (*Touching Feeling* 130). A simple perusal of scholarship in children's and YA literature and media highlights a concerning trend. Many critics assume there's something *already wrong* about the implementation of future-oriented thinking in these texts, and much critical attention is given to dismissing texts that represent queernesses and identities in "bad" ways. This tendency has been spotlighted in Jennifer Miller's exploration of transformation in queer youth picture books, which identifies the normative panic narratives that dominate the discourse of queer youth literary studies, and how said discourses obscure the political possibilities present in queer youth texts (Miller). I in no way deny the critical validity of youth scholarship and approaches focused on exposing the issues of a text, especially when addressing the normative ideologies and practices that inform scholarship in these fields. This volume, nonetheless, will move within and beyond the impulse to vigilantly judge texts according to a determined set of binaries or dominant categories to promote the identification of underexplored queer epistemologies in youth fiction and culture.

Through their preventative nature, suspicious forms of reading are an application of strong theory—theory that is universalist, that holds as long as the presence of certain variables remains constant, and tautological, in that it reinforces the "very same assumptions with which it began" (Sedgwick 135). I'll be upfront: you can take virtually any queer YA text or media generated in a mainstream context and identify a slew of ways in which it upholds normative values, or how it is or isn't as queer as it seems on the surface, or how it upholds or refutes conservative ideologies, or how it reinforces a homonormative agenda. It's much more challenging to examine what a text attempts to accomplish through the intersection of queer and youth cultures, and to interrogate a text's potential to create a sense of queerness focused on solace, relief, and repair despite the obvious limitations of doing so.

Context *and* imagination matter. Take, for instance, a critical trend in queer and trans youth studies that critiques portrayals of trans characters as fantastic or magical creatures because it undermines the real-life experiences of trans youth—a notion I explore with more depth in Chapter 4. This discourse is connected to even broader narrative trends that link trans life and agency with animality and the nonhuman, further perpetuating discourses of otherness and monstrosity that have the potential to be dehumanizing when handled irresponsibly (Henderson). However, in completely dismissing fantastic representations of trans life in our efforts to craft so-called realistic fiction, we fail to acknowledge the strengths of speculative fiction from the perspective of queer worldbuilding and the emotional potentialities that the fantastic can summon. Alexis Lothian, for instance, has pointed out how queer speculative narratives and the past futures they represent "open possibilities for thinking and living the present in different, deviant ways" (20). Others like Ramzi Fawaz have highlighted the potential for fantastic, otherworldly, and nonhuman creatures to "capture the imagination, spark pleasure and wonder, and offer new ways of seeing the interrelations" between people, communities, experiences, and worlds (28). By engaging in a normative practice of labeling all fantastic and nonhuman trans representation as problematic or as a representative failure in youth literature, critics undermine what a text can accomplish beyond, and more importantly, *within* the parameters of language and the limitations of neoliberal frameworks. This is precisely why feeling, healing, pain, and history are so central in this discussion.

Reparative reading is less of an alternative and more of a challenge to suspicious reading practices. It's not meant to replace the hermeneutics of suspicion entirely. Sedgwick characterizes repair as a generous method of critiquing texts that considers emotions seriously. This practice focuses on undoing or healing the damage imparted by homophobia and heteronormativity rather than engaging in the suspicious practice of identifying how texts bolster heteronormative ideologies and/or hinder queer representation. Drawing from the work of Melanie Klein, Sedgwick ultimately contends that to read reparatively is to open oneself up to hope and surprise because it pushes us to rethink our relationship with a queer past and future (*Touching Feeling* 146). To read reparatively is to read a text with a plurality of times and temporalities in mind. In reassembling a deconstructed text with a sense of hope and reparation, we're not attempting to deny or undo the harsh realities that queer communities have and will continue to face. Instead, we're trying to understand our place in time, our relationship to a past that didn't need to be as heteronormative and antiqueer as it was, and what an ambiguous, ever-unknown future can potentially mean.

Rita Felski's work on the limitations of literary criticism further fleshes out the stakes of repair by bringing in the concept of *mood*, which broadly refers to a critic's overall relationship and positionality vis-à-vis a text or media: "whether our mood is ironic or irenic, generous or guarded, strenuous or languorous, will influence how we position ourselves in relationship to the texts we encounter and what strikes us as most salient" (21). Mood is both an individual and collective phenomenon. It connects to, but rests beyond, the domain of the particular reader or critic. Orientations toward texts can become so ingrained that it's hard to generate ideas and ways of reading that resist the time's critical norms, expectations, demands, and ideologies. Furthermore, let's not forget about the added layer of finding ways to contextualize this scholarship when it's informed by fields with conflicting attitudes and approaches, including but not limited to literary studies, queer studies, education, library science, childhood studies, cultural studies, and so on. As Felski puts it, the language and methods implemented in literary studies develop a sense of fossilization that forces people to generate anticipated forms of knowledge (note the parallels to Sedgwick's framework) and to possess particular inclinations towards a text that leave little room for alternative ways of thinking and reading: "like any other repeated practice, it eases into the state of second nature, no longer an [unfamiliar] or obtrusive activity but a recognizable and reassuring rhythm of thought" (21).[4] This sense of critical normativity is undoubtedly present in the study of youth literature and culture, where institutions and voices normalize the field and make it "difficult to think and imagine alternative possibilities" regarding representations of youth sexualities and gender practices (Wickens 161). The reparative impulse of this volume brings a hopeful yet countercultural mood into the interpretation and critique of queer YA literature and culture—a confluence that is anticipatory and resilient in scope but that doesn't undermine the effects that pain and hurt continue to have in the lives of queer people and queer teens.

Reparative approaches can sometimes come at a cost. While they indeed center notions of survival and comfort often disregarded or underplayed in suspicious critique, reparative aims usually enter YA criticism as an afterthought. As we grapple with different and emerging forms of interpreting youth literature, we must be especially mindful of the cultural expectations that come along with varying modes of critique. We must repeatedly remind ourselves that all critics examine texts with certain moods, emotions, prior experiences, frameworks, field expectations, and labor demands in mind. Do we feel a responsibility to salvage queer texts that are generally beloved by the reading public or that we've personally found comforting and emotionally nourishing? What compels us to poke holes in any narrative and try to expose that, deep down, something has been wrong with a text all along? Patricia Stuelke argues that most forms of reparation and critique fixated on generosity have "historically been implicated in short-circuiting rather than successfully realizing attempts to break with the world as it is to create equality" (29). Indeed, reparative reading can provide a sense of comfort to a reader. Still, there are legitimate concerns about the ability of these forms of comfort to provoke social change or to push us to align ourselves against existing forms of cruelty or injustice. Even more so, and as I'll discuss in Chapter 6, certain forms of reparative reading fail to consider historical and cultural realities, or attempt to read a text reparatively by ignoring its sociocultural, political, and intersectional contexts.

When I examine queer YA cultural productions from a reparative standpoint, I'm especially mindful of how these works push readers, viewers, and critics to decode the past. I also assess how an awareness of queer time and context influences our perspectives, moods, and feelings toward our place in time and history. I show how queer cultural productions can gather elements from the past and present to frame and enable hopeful readings of futurity. The merger between the negativity that shaped our queer past and the hope that lies in the unknown is instrumental in shaping our queer future. Shane T. Moreman has brought attention to queer YA's potential to create a sense of futurism that's historically oriented in that authors "devise lessons from the past to negotiate better messages for our present queer selves and queer communities" (187). Many positive emotions, particularly hope, rest in future-oriented domains and frameworks, for they're feelings structured on the very premise that the conditions of the future can be different from our contemporary circumstances. José Esteban Muñoz—echoing the sentiments behind Sedgwick's reparative drive—has gone as far as to claim that queerness inhabits the realm of futurity: "queerness is not yet here but it approaches like a crashing wave of potentiality. And we must give in to its propulsion" (*Cruising Utopia* 185). Temporal approaches to narrative, queerness, and aesthetics inform my understanding of how queer youth productions navigate the tension present between the negativity of the past and present and the positive emotions often glorified in YA culture. As I'll demonstrate in this volume, some of the most delightfully complex and politically viable queer YA cultural productions are those that use narrative, aesthetic, and temporal innovations to channel a painful (and at times forgotten) past for readers and viewers, while nonetheless being optimistic, future-oriented, and emotionally sustaining. As Jon M. Wargo and James Joshua Coleman have put it, a reparative orientation toward queer youth texts offers opportunities "to reinterpret the wounds of history, generating hope for a future divorced from the homonormativity of the present" (88). It entails thinking seriously about the roles of (dis)comfort, pain, pleasure, and joy in orienting ourselves toward unknowable and open futures.

Hurtful Histories, Utopic Aspirations, and Contemporary YA Criticism

This book's exploration of the emotional dimensions of queer YA literature and culture is mindful of the role of history and the past in the implementation of an optimistic stance towards queer youth, queer community, and queer politics. In a reflection on the evolution of queer literature, author and critic Colm Tóibín has suggested that queerness is slowly being detached from negative connotations "to the extent that the phrase 'post-gay' is slowly becoming current. Therefore, how we read the past, and read into the past, and judge the past are likely to become matters of more open debate" (11). Tóibín is correct in pointing out how current developments influence how we read and interpret the queer past and, in some ways, create a mood or disposition towards a particular archive of texts. I'm eager to determine how more recent cultural productions interpret, channel, or refute potential connections to queer affective and narrative histories. However, we must take a moment to scrutinize postgay sensibilities that frame the world as one liberated from discrimination and oppression. After all, more than two decades after the publication of Tóibín's *Love in a Dark Time*, and regardless of institutional changes observed globally, people still encounter discrimination, violence, injustice, and death because of their gender identities and kinship practices. We don't need to look too far back to fully understand how and why such utopian sentiments can be so troublesome when examining queer teens, young adults, and the texts created for them.

In the 2010s, for instance, the United States received global attention with the rise of a narrative centered on queer and trans teen suicide. This development saturated news outlets and social media sites at the time. An upsetting number of teens and young adults who engaged in queer practices and embodied queer identities died by suicide after facing bullying, ridicule, and harassment. One of the most widely publicized cases connected to this narrative is that of Tyler Clementi. A student at Rutgers University, he tragically took his own life in September 2010 upon learning that an intimate moment with another man had been broadcast live without his consent. Although this incident garnered significant attention in the early 2010s, its effects continue to be felt today. Almost a decade later, fifteen-year-old Nigel Shelby, a teen of color, died by suicide in 2019 after experiencing depression, which stemmed from antiqueer bullying. Throughout our recent past, other pressing issues have affected "postgay" notions that suggest we live in a more open, queerer present, including a rise in acts of violence toward queer and trans communities, the banning of drag performance and story time hours across the country, and the continuous banning of books with queer content from public institutions. The stakes of queer livelihood and safety become even more pressing when considering how Donald Trump and his administration purposefully enacted an "antiqueer animus through the appointment of openly homophobic and transphobic individuals to prominent positions" in his cabinet (Moreau 639). This profoundly altered the political landscape for queer communities in the US. Last but unfortunately not least, recall that in 2016, the Pulse nightclub shooting took place in Orlando, which had incredibly destructive consequences for both queer and Latine communities. How can we bask in the hope, optimism, and future-oriented promises of queer YA cultural productions when both the queer past and present are so riddled with hurt, cruelty, and violence?

Matters become trickier when considering the activist and political responses generated by these heartbreaks. The most visibly circulated response that connected directly to youth cultures was the *It Gets Better* campaign, a digital activist project spearheaded by columnist and pundit Dan Savage and Terry Miller in the early 2010s in response to this wave of queer teen suicides. This initiative encouraged adults—from professionals in various fields, celebrities, and prominent cultural figures, to everyday folk—to share videos and stories where they discuss bullying and the issues they experienced due to their nonnormative sexualities and gender identities. As Dan Savage and Terry Miller put it, "gay, lesbian, bisexual, and transgender adults all over the country—*all over the world*—were speaking to LGBT youth. We weren't waiting for anyone's permission. We found our voices" (6). Amusingly, Savage's claims disregard the fact that queer adults had already been speaking to queer youth, as seen through the increasing number of texts adults were writing for children and teens. Regardless, *It Gets Better* created a universalizing narrative hellbent on showing how the lives of queer people improve with time and age. Despite the noble intentions and the widespread effects of this campaign, there are significant issues present in its vision and ideological frameworks. After all, queer youths were repeatedly being assured that their lives would improve in the future. Still, these assurances were projected by adults who survived, adults who were fortunate and *privileged* enough to have successfully surmounted a period of potential bullying, harassment, violence, and oppression. Note that this sentiment is emphasized when Savage claims that "we," meaning queer adults, "found our voices," and again reinforces a hierarchy of knowledge and experience that sometimes casts queer youth as voiceless or powerless—a tendency Tribunella and Gubar challenge in their work.

It's painful to observe the recording and distribution of *It Gets Better* videos coming from straight adults and celebrities with little understanding of queer communities and contexts, and even more so, how the creation of these videos becomes more of a normative demand rather than a gesture toward queer futurism. One of my particular favorites is the one crafted and shared haphazardly by Stephen Colbert in 2012, which begins with, "I have a message for any gay and lesbian teens out there... okay, and I'm being told also bisexual and transgender... really, anyone who's been picked on" (It Gets Better, YouTube Channel). The comments section of this video is, at the moment of publication, unsurprisingly disabled. The project envisions very normative subjects sharing messages of hope. What about the queer people who can't or don't want to succeed and thrive within the parameters of a normative culture? What about those queer children and teens whose lives haven't gotten better with time? How about the stories of past queer children and teens that were never told or circulated? Where are their stories represented, and how do they complicate the promises and expectations of *It Gets Better*?

This project had colossal ramifications for queer YA texts and media that surfaced from the 2010s onward, especially when it came to the infusion of hopeful discourse in queer coming of age texts. Many texts published during and after this period, directly or indirectly, responded to the central tenets of *It Gets Better*—further amplifying the sense of hope and optimism embodied by this archive. These aspirations, however, are tricky given how the widespread coverage and panic regarding queer teen suicide contradicted the narratives of progress disseminated in mainstream and queer outlets. Jasbir K. Puar exposes the project's alignment with neoliberal sensibilities that echo the frameworks espoused in bootstraps immigrant mottos, and proposes that the outrage felt by these deaths was "based precisely on a belief that things are indeed supposed to be better, especially for a particular class of white gay men," reinstating the centrality of "white racial privilege" (151). Mason has further suggested that both the project and queer YA are characterized by elements of impossibility in that they exemplify "the messy ways in which adult authorship, fantasies, desires, and anxieties are inextricably enmeshed with how children's literature produces meaning" ("On Children's Literature" 98–99). This is especially true when we consider that most YA cultural productions are generated by adult authors, leading to what Mike Cadden identifies as the paramount irony with YA texts: "Novels constructed by adults to simulate an authentic adolescent's voice are inherently ironic because the so-called adolescent voice is never—and can never be—truly authentic" ("The Irony" 146). YA culture and its narrativization rely on hierarchies of power and an adult's understanding of what it means to be a teenager. In this sense, most YA literature is ironic, a fantasy of youth filtered through adult consciousness. Jennifer Miller augments the stakes of this irony even further by considering the histories that authors pass down to young readers and how the narratives that are ultimately available to them through queer youth literature and culture "represent versions of the past considered inheritable by a vast network of adult gatekeepers" (187).

This project is less interested in critiquing this network of adult gatekeeping and in exploring questions of authenticity, and instead is more interested in examining: a) the narrative strategies that authors use in constructing a deliberately ironic queer narrative and how they negotiate differences between the "bad" queer past and "good" queer present; b) the moods that we adopt when we create, read, and critique queer YA texts; and c) the narrative, aesthetic, temporal, and political strategies authors use to address cultural hurt, critique normative understandings of happiness, and construct queer knowledges. I closely examine how YA fictive worlds are built for younger audiences using words, images, and narrative conventions, and as Sonia Alejandra Rodríguez highlights in her exploration of conocimiento narratives, how creative practices and expressions "offer both an opportunity to challenge and transform existing epistemologies and the possibility to create new, more liberating ones" (11). This is precisely why this book closely examines the fantasies that queer YA cultural productions circulate through their narratives and how they transform current queer YA critical epistemologies and forms of knowledge production. Given how central hopeful discourse was in the creation and distribution of queer YA literature and media during 2010-2020, the primary texts deconstructed and examined in this volume were originally published during this timeframe. With the rise of the COVID-19 epidemic and the contemporary development of artificial intelligence technologies, more time is needed to see how the emotional, visual, representative, and narrative boundaries of post-2020s queer YA culture will change, congeal, or expand.

The dominant critical mood of queer YA is fixated on hope, (cruel) optimism, and post-gay sentiments. The discourses generated by this dominant mood attempt to demolish associations between teen queer life and negativity, reinforcing many of the ideological trappings present in the *It Gets Better* campaign. Of course, this critical tendency can be traced to the fact that early YA novels espoused negativity and despair, and they narrativized gruesome outcomes that painted a "dismal picture" of queer being and life (Pennell 335–336). The critical move away from pain and negative affect has been popularized and reinforced by the work of Christine Jenkins and Michael Cart, two foundational scholars in the field of queer YA criticism. In their latest book, *Representing the Rainbow*, Jenkins and Cart have argued that writers and critics of queer YA must "abandon the traditional and too-easy equation between homosexuality and violent death" (222). In an even more telling claim, Jenkins and Cart suggest that many earlier and some recent queer YA novels

> perpetuate stereotypes by characterizing [queer people] as lost souls doomed to either premature death or the solitary life of exile at the margins of society. Others—most, though not all, of a more recent vintage—present gay and lesbian characters in a more *realistic* light.
>
> (xii, emphasis mine)

Other critics such as Caroline T. Clark and Mollie V. Blackburn align queer YA criticism with a normative agenda and determine that novels focused on adverse outcomes can lead young readers "to understand that to be LGBTQQ is a lonely life, devoid of sex and love but full of violence." They caution readers to be wary of YA novels that include violence if not balanced with "scenes that portray individual agency and healthy intimacy" (883). While Clark and Blackburn acknowledge how discourses of violence in YA are important in that some queer teens continue to be victims of it, they highlight how such narratives can pose "damaging consequences," and later align the frameworks of queer YA with the *It Gets Better* project (883). Damaging consequences for whom, exactly? Adrienne Colborne and Vivian Howard go as far as to position contemporary YA against—rather than within or alongside—the emotional frameworks of early queer YA literature, especially in terms of mood: "New stories are needed to combat the trends from earlier decades in which queer characters were rarely shown having positive life experiences. The world is changing for people who are LGBTQ+, and young adult literature should reflect that social change" (6). What about the old stories and histories that were suppressed and not allowed to be told? What about how the world hasn't changed for queer youth? Are these critics' understandings of positive representation the same as mine, the same as yours, or the same as a teen's, for that matter?

A particular mood informs the criticism these scholars mobilize, which directly or indirectly promotes the sidelining of negative outcomes and emotions in favor of supposedly more "realistic" and "grounded" representations that mesh more with the circumstances of queerness today. There are already concerns when it comes to realistic and grounded representation in YA, given the paradox that it captures the voice and ideas of an *adult* and presents them under the guise of a teen voice. Not to mention that even "realistic" literature follows a set of norms and narrative conventions meant to convey a *sense* of reality—but this reality is still fabricated, constructed, imagined, and shaped by adult and institutional forces. What's concerning here is that there's a monolithic mood that elevates itself as crucial in the study of queer YA, one that sidelines "gloomy" and "negative" literary viewpoints because things are supposedly better for queer teens today. Mason encapsulates this critical shortcoming succinctly when stating that YA critics aspire for versions of queer YA that "will provide young readers with the fictional role models ostensibly necessary to their thriving" (*Queer Anxieties* 14). Mason contends, however, that this utopic approach assumes that the queer anxieties that have haunted our culture have been treated, understood, and resolved (14). A critical mood that sidelines pain and cultural hurt to instead focus on the possibilities and joys queer teens have access to today eventually prolongs a normative and hegemonic "history of willful forgetfulness" akin to ideological colorblindness often present in the critique of queer literature and film (Kohnen 20).

Matters become more charged when we consider that a queer approach toward youth literature and culture requires consideration of a plurality of viewpoints that go beyond the aims of progress-driven narratives. Instead of eliminating narratives of death and despair in queer YA, Katelyn R. Browne argues we should instead consider how representations and treatments of death "can expand to include queer characters as surviving *subjects* of death narratives rather than the sanctified and deceased *objects* upon whose graves developmental work is performed" (8, emphasis in original). Browne compellingly suggests that death and despair shouldn't be segregated from queer YA narratives, for doing so forecloses opportunities to consider how understandings of youth overlap or conflict with notions of survival, grief, and remembrance. Queer YA literature and criticism should be attuned to the varying emotions, practices, and feelings connected to queer lives. They shouldn't be limited to elevating happy, normalizing, and utopic narratives regardless of how turbulent the history of queer representation has been. As Michelle Ann Abate and Kenneth Kidd have distinctively argued in their volume, *Over the Rainbow*, understanding and examining youth literature from a queer perspective "means embracing trajectories and tonalities other than the lesbian/gay-affirmative and celebratory" (9). My critical mood considers the place and role of sadness, violence, doom, and loneliness in the field by connecting YA to a broader queer literary and affective legacy. I don't try to undermine or undo queer cultural hurt or pain in YA, but as David L. Eng would put it, I attempt to *work through* it. Such a disposition "presents us with the possibility of love and the creative impulse that loss, grief, and forgetting might be temporally cojoined with new ideas" (Eng 196). It helps us to identify fresh and affectively complex avenues for understanding queer youth, the literature adults craft for them, and the merger between a negative queer past and a supposedly more positive present.

I don't want to entirely dismiss the claims that some critics mobilize in their efforts to promote queer YA literature and culture imbued with hope. These critics are calling for a range and multiplicity of stories—novels that challenge the negative emotions and deathly connotations present in the larger tradition of queer literary representation. Indeed, narratives that immortalize the link between queerness and death have been overly saturated in contemporary culture and media, thus stressing the need for queer stories that present multiple ways for queer teens to live, thrive, and exist in the world. We don't need to look hard to find a slew of queer narratives that reinforce the infamous "bury your gays" trope, a narrative pattern in which one of the lovers in a queer romance "must die or otherwise be destroyed by the end of the story" (Hulan 17). However, I draw an issue with how these arguments are framed, especially in how they characterize violence, death, and loneliness as "too easy" and "unrealistic" forms of representation. What makes a queer YA novel realistic or unrealistic? What makes representation "too easy" or "harmful" given the irony that people in positions of privilege and power are the ones who craft YA narratives for teens, reinforcing the hierarchies and power binaries spotlighted in Tribunella and Gubar's work? My resistance to these claims lies in their failure to interrogate gloom and violence as it manifests through different and constantly changing junctures of culture, class, history, and geographic context.

Moreover, the expectation that representations of violence should be buffered with "healthy" representations of sex and intimacy limits what queer YA can accomplish from an ideological perspective. It centers a normative outlook toward what constitutes "good" or "wholesome." Think about how decades ago, queer representation was considered unhealthy. Such normative attitudes reduce the overall scope of what a queer YA text can or should explore. Instead, we should question what teens are privileged enough to explore these intimacies and disconnect from the negativity and violence attached to queer life and its representation. When considering the death, violence, homelessness, bullying, despair, and oppression that many queer and trans youths continue to confront every day, perhaps critics need to rethink what constitutes realism in the first place—or look beyond the parameters of dominant realities, moods, and histories.

We must think carefully about what queer teens are being imagined when claims are made in terms of what literature is or isn't realistic, suitable, happy, healthy, or appropriate: typically straight, cisgender, white, normative, "innocent," middle-to-upper-class subjects (see Kathryn Bond Stockton; Robin Bernstein; Ebony Elizabeth Thomas, Tribunella). From an emotional and empowerment perspective, there's value for both teen and adult queer readers to find relief in the literatures designed with them in mind. However, suppose queer YA literature downplays or abandons the negative emotions, structures, histories, and representations that shaped queer literature. In that case, it undermines readers and communities who can't escape the harms and deathly responses tied to queer life and representation that haunt all of us. Laura M. Jiménez reminds us that when it comes to queer texts, "the ways that emotions, experiences, and histories are told matter, especially when there are so few stories being told" ("PoC, LGBTQ" 438). The push for more positive representation and the downplaying of narratives focused on sadness and hurt is precisely the binary and hierarchical thinking that queer theories attempt to resist and challenge.

How we imagine our emotions, legacies, past, and engagement in an ongoing struggle matters. At the same time, there's no singular way to imagine them. I refuse to adopt a normative lens that erases or undoes a legacy of how we, as queer folk, convey our moods, emotions, and histories. Distancing queer youth content from negative affect and frameworks in service of mobilizing an artificial narrative of progress does little to help queer communities understand their place in history and time, and to understand the emotional, intellectual, and bodily labor involved in repairing a world ruined by normative forces. As Gloria Anzaldúa succinctly puts it,

> We must bear witness to what our bodies remember, what el corazón con razón experiences... [in doing so,] we revise reality by altering our consensual agreements about what is real, what is just and fair. We can trans-shape reality by changing our perspectives and perceptions.
>
> (*Light in the Dark* 21)

Feeling like reality can be different shouldn't be a privilege. However, working towards this new reality shouldn't happen by sacrificing the pain and anger that shaped our minds, communities, bodies, and spirits. Readers, young and old, must continue bearing witness.

The Ghosts of a Damaged Queer Past

Although an earnest attitude toward problems characterized YA novels from the late 1960s to the mid-1980s, contemporary texts have embraced an ironic stance toward social ills and issues, primarily due to ideological shifts in the postmodern period. Karen Coats suggests that while we now reject grand narratives and universal ideals, we typically don't recognize how remnants of these narratives remain embedded in our systems and how "archaic impressions from the unconscious push back against cognitive, rational determinations" (326). Because of the tensions caused by the simultaneous rejection and lingering of grand narratives, Coats argues that YA literature immerses contemporary teenagers into a double bind of potentiality that constantly highlights the importance of positive attitudes while simultaneously demonstrating their ineffectiveness. Young readers can notice parallels and inconsistencies that exist between the messages and ideologies emanating from the realm of the text versus the realm of the worlds they inhabit. Although youth texts tend to glorify and elevate hopeful narratives, these discourses of hope are always in conflict with the ways in which politicians and authority figures misuse them to reinforce hegemony and normativity (Coats 326). A palpable sense of dissonance can be felt when contrasting the hopeful scope of a YA novel with the elements of violence, death, and despair that have become virtually inescapable in our world. Today's youth particularly feel these tensions with the rise in armed conflicts across the globe, the rise of movements such as #MeToo and #BlackLivesMatter, and how the COVID-19 pandemic brought notions of death, inequity, and despair to the forefront of our collective consciousness. Youth see these realities. They know them in spite of our efforts to conceal them. They *feel* them.

Hope and comfort are to be found not through sidelining pain, but by painstakingly and ethically exploring how to cope and deal with said hurt.

They're not felt by omitting histories of hurt, but rather, by bringing these histories of loss, pain, and sadness to the foreground. Considering how YA novels and media push readers to read and channel the past and future is crucial when one explores the ties between queerness and emotion and when thinking through a text's potential to be interpreted reparatively. Negative emotions and feelings, as suggested above, have been deemed theoretically and politically vital in the development of earlier queer texts. In *Feeling Backward*, Heather Love exposes many ways in which progress-driven narratives are ignorant of the historical and cultural damage that has affected queer lives. *Feeling Backward* pieces together a history of 20th-Century queer representation that is framed through negative affect, or as Love calls it, "backwardness"—which includes emotions and feelings such as shyness, failure, loneliness, and self-hatred, among others. Using modernist queer texts that are framed through feelings of "backwardness," Love traces a long history of queer suffering and loss, arguing that negative emotions in queer texts function as lenses that focus on the pain that still lingers in our culture in an effort to connect the "bad" past to our present moment, while also spotlighting "the inadequacy of queer narratives of progress" (27). Negative or backward feelings help unpack how contemporary queer people still feel agony and shame when dealing with their sexualities and gender identities today—thus highlighting the importance of historical awareness and context in the interpretation of queer texts. Love is correct in pointing out that backward feelings "are closely tied to the realities of queer experience past and present" (147). Embracing one's queerness almost inevitably demands a personal, social, or cultural cost: "that, as much as anything, makes us queer" (Love 163). The precariousness of these costs has become even more palpable with the rise of social media, the spread of narratives on queer teen suicide, the surge in queer and trans murder victims, the contentious debates that *still* surface regarding the livability of queer communities, and the hateful rhetoric pushed forth by boisterous, conservative politicians in the news circuit.

The social, personal, and political costs of embodying queer identities and practices are still tangible in contemporary US cultures. They always will be, especially since the future contains queernesses, embodiments, and practices that we can't even begin to imagine today. As Love claims, we're still able to access the corporeal, spiritual, and historical remnants of a damaged, heteronormative, and antiqueer past that have lingered since and before increases in the visibility of queer representation. Love stresses the importance of paying attention to these historical burdens because they can provide respite in a supposedly postgay world: "In a moment where gays and lesbians have no excuse for feeling bad, the evocation of a long history of suffering provides, if not solace exactly, then at least relief" (146). Even more so, evoking such a history is vital in addressing how this

22 The Politics of Critique and Repair

cultural hurt still haunts us. Avery F. Gordon argues that the concept of *haunting* helps unpack the queer hurt of the past because it demonstrates how "abusive systems of power make themselves known and their impacts felt in everyday life, especially when they are supposedly over and done" (xvi). Through understanding how a damaged queer past haunts contemporary queer culture, "we are notified that what's been concealed is very much alive and present, interfering precisely with those always incomplete forms of containment and repression ceaselessly directed toward us" (xvi).

Understanding how YA literature and culture push us to channel a queer history of suffering is crucial in interrogating whether queer YA works can effectively conjure this haunted history while also embodying a sense of hope and *relief* that is not naïve or misguided. Beyond matters of relief, I think carefully about how healing and imagination play a role in these histories and narrativizations. Gloria Anzaldúa has reminded us that *imagination*—which she approaches as a system of thoughts, images, moods, and feelings—"offers resolutions out of the conflict by dreaming alternative ways of imaging/feeling/thinking... we need to envision a different reality, dream new blueprints for it, formulate new strategies for coping in it" (*This Bridge* xxxviii). When I thus refer to the "queer imagination," I'm not thinking about it monolithically. Instead, I approach it as an ever-growing combination of diverse and conflicting images, feelings, moods, dreams, and aspirations tied to sexuality, gender, and relationality.

This volume considers how queer YA literature and media are capable of surprising us through their implementation of positive affect, generative thinking, and connection to a queer history of hurt that has haunted our past and present. I share how creators of YA texts can (re)organize affective, aesthetic, and narrative elements in service of unforeseen futurity—or ways in which readers can potentially fragment and reorganize a text to generate different ways of thinking about concepts such as happiness and belonging. This volume embodies a generous and hopeful mood that sees a more countercultural future in YA literature and culture by addressing and challenging the normative ghosts that continue to haunt and possess us. It does not exorcise these ghosts, nor can it. However, it invokes them to push readers to acknowledge the broader histories and emotional/narrative genealogies that affect how we interpret and critique queer youth texts. This book recognizes how queer YA cultural productions problematically reinforce hetero-and-homonormative attitudes. Nevertheless, it highlights how these texts implement positive affect, optimistic thinking, and collective futurism to compel readers during times of crisis, unhappiness, and urgency. It also highlights shifting modes in how queerness is (re)envisioned in fictional works geared toward YA audiences.

In *The Promise of Happiness*, Sara Ahmed informs readers that they "need to think more about the relationship between the queer struggle for a bearable life and aspirational hopes for a good life" (120). Ahmed's notions of a "good life" are based on Aristotelean ideas that encompass the conditions necessary for happiness, and that today take the form of pathways, milestones, and hallmarks that are expected to induce joy and fulfillment: marriage, children, monogamy, and heterosexuality, to mention a few. However, rather than focusing on the normative parameters that come along with creating a "happy" and "good" life, Ahmed advocates for developing attitudes and practices that allow people to live a life that can be endured despite its inability to fulfill the promises and expectations of happiness: "A bearable life is a life where what must be endured does not threaten that life, in either the bare facts of its existence or in the sense of its aim, direction, or purpose" (97). Criticism oriented toward the reparative possibilities of queer YA literature and media inevitably assesses how these texts imagine a livable and bearable existence for queer people and communities despite the presence of antiqueer sentiments, ideologies, and practices in their cultural contexts. In reading reparatively, we reinforce life's bearings and find different ways to endure and survive.

By focusing on notions of livability and survival in our criticism of YA literature and culture, we also interrogate the conditions that allow imagined queer lives to not only achieve happiness but to *exist*: "I think the struggle for a bearable life is the struggle for queers to have a space to breathe. [...] With breath comes imagination. With breath comes possibility" (Ahmed, *The Promise* 120). While there's much value in highlighting how texts limit us, it's equally important to focus on how texts can liberate us and guide us to feeling solace, relief, freedom, and repair. In her examination of race and the imagination in contemporary youth literature, Ebony Elizabeth Thomas pushes us to interrogate what readers and critics expect through our relationship with imagined worlds. She pushes us to think critically about the moods we adopt when relating to and interpreting fictive universes, and to consider how readers who have been marginalized by their race or Otherness have had a long history of negotiating and understanding "the cartographies of the imagination" that have traditionally been shaped and regulated by White, heterosexual voices and institutions (152). Queer YA feels like it has more room to exist, thrive, and breathe. We're increasingly finding ways of reading that make life seem more bearable, pushing us to think of the different shapes our lives will assume in the future. We must be wary, however, of texts and perspectives that provide relief and catharsis by underplaying negative affect or by assuming that narratives of progress for queer and marginalized folk are singular and universal.

Scavenging Wounds

An examination of the emotional, narrative, and reparative possibilities of queer YA cultural productions—keeping both suspicious and generative methodologies in mind—facilitates the identification of potentialities that imagined queer teens experience as they face the tension between a bearable life and a good life. Queer YA texts may certainly reinforce the very heteronormative binds that it struggles to free itself from. However, it also presents us with cases in which queer teens fight, resist, love, and find solace and comfort in a world that refuses to sustain them through the tools of historical perspective and futurism. Queer YA possesses the potential to challenge the very standards of happiness, hope, and time that society enforces in the lives of young people today. A study of the reparative potentialities of queer YA works entails, as Sedgwick would argue, an openness to being surprised by the field—an intense and sincere desire to think carefully not only about what these texts want us to believe but even more so, what they want us to *feel*.

Each chapter of this book examines how emotions, generative thinking, time, and reparative strategies operate in our interpretations of queer YA texts—focusing primarily on queer YA novels but also briefly addressing other cultural productions such as teen films, video games, and webcomics. My approach to close reading and examining the political/emotional imagination of queer YA are centered on the practice of queer scavenging, which Jack Halberstam describes as a way of combining methods and forms of knowledge "that are often cast as being at odds with each other" and refusing "the academic compulsion toward disciplinary coherence" (*Female Masculinity* 13). My perspectives toward YA are influenced by a confluence of approaches from fields such as queer theory, narratology, children's literature, teen film and media, Latine studies, post-1945 US literature, critical youth studies, pedagogy, and affect theory. I don't always obey disciplinary boundaries, and even though the title of this volume emphasizes the word *Literature*, my discussions often move beyond the written word: "Traditional disciplinary boundaries become inadequate containers for subjects whose lives and utterances traverse the categories meant to contain them" (Rodriguez *Queer Latinidad* 30). Using close reading, reparative approaches, and a queer scavenger methodology, each chapter interrogates, either directly or indirectly, the tensions that exist between the "bad" queer past and the "good" queer present in YA texts and media. Given that YA literature and media are often generated with the goal of comforting readers and guiding them toward traditional pathways of success and adulthood (see Trites), particular attention will be given to how queer frameworks mesh with these aspirations. Each chapter demonstrates how queer YA narratives often challenge the emotional and narrative conventions of YA texts, and guides readers into understanding how the merger between hope and aesthetic innovation can lead us to envision alternative, queerer forms of being "happy," comfortable, and politically aware in a damaged world. Each chapter addresses the following set of questions:

1) To what extent do queer YA literature and media respond to, or connect to, the history of cultural hurt, oppression, and violence that has haunted queer communities? How do queer YA cultural productions (mis)align themselves with the sadness, despair, and backwardness that have been integral to the formation of the queer YA imagination?
2) What reparative strategies or outlooks are present in queer YA texts themselves? What narrative, affective, and aesthetic elements do texts implement in their attempts to address and provide proactive solutions to the hurt, violence, and oppression experienced by queer youth in the United States?
3) What are some of the tactics that we can employ in reading queer YA texts reparatively, given that they are produced within the confines of normative, capitalist, and neoliberal cultures? How can different ways of reading help us identify alternative strategies for understanding other forms of pain and hurt (personal, historical, cultural, temporal, and political) and their ties to notions such as hope, resilience, collectivity, and transformation?

Every chapter in *The Reparative Possibilities of Queer Young Adult Literature* examines queer texts that center on the intersection of "trauma, injury, and the potential for material transformation and healing" (Green and Ellison 223). I focus on how YA culture represents, negotiates, and creatively expresses these manifestations. Critics such as Jesus Montaño and Regan Postma Montaño have explored the potential that youth literature possesses to prompt "healing from the violence of racism, sexism, binarism, and other forms of exclusions and oppressions" (4). I center ideologically overloaded and, at times, contradictory texts in which negative emotions and pain are central in their representation of queer youth culture, and that channel different forms of hurt and suffering with a focus on repair. I then engage them in broader conversations on narrative, queerness, emotion, and queer YA cultural production. The texts I explore in this book thematically (and, at times, allegorically) focus on negatively charged events such as gay conversion therapy, the deathly ramifications of HIV and AIDS on queer communities, the end of the world, the necropolitics of trans and queer youth representation, and queer teen suicide.

"More Sad Than Not?" explores the uneasy relationship that queer YA cultural productions have with notions of unhappiness and ambiguity, and the difficulties that some authors have in negotiating the presence of pain and hurt in their texts. Beginning with an examination of Aurora Guerrero's film *Mosquita y Mari* (2012), segueing into a brief historical overview of unhappiness and queer literary production, and concluding with an examination of the publication (and subsequent revision of) Adam Silvera's *More Happy Than Not* (2015/2020), this chapter highlights how narratives of resistance and survival are always in tension with queer YA's impulse to reinforce normative perspectives on success and pleasure. I highlight how sadness was used as a way of overcoming queer censorship, and I draw connections between YA and broader queer archives to think about the emotional expectations audiences have when engaging with representations of queer teens on the page and screen.

"The Haunting Presence of AIDS" expands upon this discussion by examining queer AIDS literature—a literature often credited for permanently linking queerness to notions of death and sadness. In this chapter, I connect YA narratives on HIV and AIDS to broader affective and literary histories, paying close attention to how narrative techniques facilitate conversations between a damaged queer past and a supposedly better queer present. Here, I focus my attention on examining how David Levithan's YA novel *Two Boys Kissing* draws from the affective and formalistic structures of the NAMES AIDS Memorial Quilt (colloquially known as the AIDS Quilt) to construct a narrative that combines contradictory emotions, political inclinations, and histories in an effort to spark repair and transformation. I'm particularly invested in examining how Levithan's novel negotiates the place of happiness and futurity in a subset of queer literature explicitly centered on notions of death, illness, and loss. While I emphasize how the text historicizes the representation of AIDS in troubling ways, I also point out how Levithan uses ghostly narrative devices to weave political connections between past and current queer generations.

"On Mortality and Permalife" examines the deathly dimensions that inform the creation of YA literature and culture, and demonstrates how frameworks on the speculative and fantastic are used to contest them. Drawing from the video game concept of permalife developed by Bo Ruberg, a mechanic/rule that prevents a character from dying within the fictive universe of a video game, I examine the dialectic relationship between death and life as present in Anna-Marie McLemore's trans YA novel *When the Moon Was Ours*, Supergiant's roguelike video game *Hades*, and Patrick Ness' fictional meditation on queer teen suicide in *More Than This*. In doing so, I highlight strategies that these texts implement in infusing a queer YA narrative with logics of death *and* life, and in addressing the ties between contemporary youth and the negative feelings and structures that continue to haunt them. In turn, I also pressure normative critical attitudes present in the study of queer and trans YA culture that attempt to downplay the political and affective significance of imagination and the speculative, in favor of more "grounded" and "realistic" representation.

"Catastrophic Comforts" centers on how comfort, narrative closure, and hope are addressed in post-apocalyptic stories, and how elements of despair are addressed through a text's narrative closure or conclusion. Beginning with an examination of Suzanne Collins' *Mockingjay* (and its 2015 film adaptation) and concluding with an examination of Andrew Smith's YA novel *Grasshopper Jungle*, I interrogate the expectations of comfort and happiness that come along with the implementation of epilogues in YA narratives. Epilogues are unique in terms of narrative and emotion, in that they are designed to explicitly "fast-forward" into the future to show that characters are happy, successful, and comfortable. I highlight how *Grasshopper Jungle* thwarts the emotional expectations of epilogues in favor of a narrative resolution that decentralizes human authority over the world, while also exposing the limits (and harms) of representation. I especially explore the emotional and political effects of narrative closures that are designed to discomfort and disturb readers, rather than console and reassure them.

Lastly, "The Limits of Repair," which adopts the form of an afterword and addresses various issues raised through this book, examines the role of repair in our evaluation and critique of queer youth cultural productions. I draw from Tillie Walden's queer webcomic, *On A Sunbeam*, to think carefully about the role of history, repair, and reconstruction in our engagement with youth texts. I then segue into an examination of Benjamin Alire Sáenz's *Aristotle and Dante Discover the Secrets of the Universe*, and its sequel, *Aristotle and Dante Dive Into the Waters of the World*, with a particular emphasis on the first novel's omission of an AIDS narrative even though it takes place in the late 1980s. I consider the affordances and drawbacks that come along with certain forms of reading and critique, and I question the value of reparative readings that strip queer YA novels of their historical and political context to make them better comply with broader utopian, assimilative, normative narratives. I show the importance of implementing intersectional thinking in conducting reparative interpretations of queer youth cultures, and I also reflect on the desires, hopes, and aspirations that drive the impulse to read and create queer YA with a reparative mindset.

These chapters aren't meant to be exhaustive or complete explorations of queer YA literature and culture in any way, shape, or form. I see them more as a gesture toward the reparative drive found in queer YA texts. The ideas in this volume are designed to rouse, provoke, excite, and perhaps even inspire—but at the same time, they're devised to be expanded, modified, and built upon. It's impossible for any single volume to exhaustively chart the emotional contours of queer YA and a full scope of the possibilities and limitations that come along with reparative approaches. There are other sites of pain, hurt, hope, and joy to explore, and this book is just scratching the surface.

Hope and "feeling good" are prominent affective components of YA narratives, although, as discussed above, how these components are channeled and implemented in the field varies. I won't deny that there's a saturation of YA literature that fosters hope and positive affect in a naïve and earnest fashion—one that often ignores how the realities of the world negate the promises and expectations of hope. As I'll discuss in more detail in the next chapter, early queer YA literature often rejected the potential for positive outcomes to take place, demonstrating that early queer YA novels are more connected to the negative emotional frameworks that have characterized the 20th-Century queer imagination than we tend to acknowledge. I want to continue examining what effects these frameworks have in contemporary imaginings of queer teen life, and think of futurity not as a time removed from hurt and pain, but as a time where we're all better equipped to channel this pain in service of shaping new worlds, pathways, and affinities.

In many ways, YA literature and culture are especially amenable to reparative approaches centered on hope and futurism. After all, the criticism and examination of YA literature and culture have always been unique regarding the moods and attitudes commonly present in literary and cultural studies. Coats argues that YA literature and culture often require critics to develop countercultural and antiauthoritative stances towards accepted practices and attitudes. After all, we are part of a critical industry focused on examining texts and ideas that are supposedly not as "evolved" as those crafted for adult audiences. Thus, conducting criticism in the field of YA literature and culture often requires us to embody some of the stereotypical characteristics of adolescence itself: "Critics, like teens, will need to rebel against established theoretical orthodoxies and adult-inflected expressions of value, to be constantly attentive to innovation… to take risks, to be unapologetically presentist" (Coats 322). We can challenge and expand this critical ethos further, moving beyond the impulse to view adolescence as a presentist mode of being and acknowledging its ties to notions of futurism and history. Gabrielle Owen believes that while presentism is crucial in defining adolescence, we must also keep in mind that from a queer perspective, this life stage is characterized by its indefinability and elusiveness: "the notions of adolescence we encounter are not stable, not fixed in time, not objectively defined or even definable" (8). Furthermore, notions of futurism are already overloaded into the developmental category of youth, which in and of itself is founded upon the idea of unfulfilled time.

According to Clémentine Beauvais, young people possess "a longer future in which to act," in contrast to adults who have "a longer time past with its accumulated baggage of experience, knowledge, and therefore didactic legitimacy" (19). Beauvais refers to this potentiality, this longer future composed of unrealized time, as *might*, a power embedded in young people's "potent, latent future to be filled with unknown action" (19). It's precisely this attachment to the unknown, this ambiguity, that makes notions of futurism so provocative yet terrifying. It's hard to look backward and forward when the present is so overwhelming from a political and emotional perspective. Nevertheless, as Judith Butler reminds us in *Undoing Gender*,

> To live is to live a life politically, in relation to power, in relation to others, in the act of assuming responsibility for a collective future. However, to assume responsibility for a future is not to know its direction fully in advance, since the future… requires a certain openness and unknowingness.
>
> (226)

It's time for us to channel this openness and unknowingness to witness the possibilities present in this might, this ambiguity, and this lack of definition. To begin imagining and working towards a future and YA criticism that does not need to mirror our present. As José Esteban Muñoz reminds us, "The present is not enough. It is impoverished and toxic for queers and other people who do not feel the privilege of majoritarian belonging, normative tastes, and 'rational' expectations" (*Cruising Utopia* 27).

Many of us are exhausted by the presentism of the field. On a more personal note, I'm concerned with how neoliberal narratives of assimilation and normalization are met with cheer and applause at youth literature conferences and workshops. I'm troubled by critical attempts to reduce queer youth narratives down to normative and dominant understandings of what counts as happiness, fulfillment, pleasure, and success. I'm baffled by critics who think of queer YA solely as a happiness enterprise focused on protecting queer teens, rather than thinking about the other political, aesthetic, and emotional possibilities that these texts can foster.

For us to fully understand the cultural work queer YA and grasp and unlock the reparative potential of these texts, we must be unapologetically *futurist*. We must rebel against the idea that positive emotions and optimism serve as mechanisms for concealing issues or offering readers a naïve and false sense of hope. We must take risks and mobilize both suspicious and reparative reading practices to avoid falling into the habit of claiming that YA cultural productions represent queerness in either a "positive" or a "negative" way. We must take a moment to acknowledge the ghosts that continue to haunt the field and assist critics and readers in thinking through a collective future focused on *opening* rather than *excluding* different emotions, critical moods, and ways of being. This book embodies this spirit of rebellion and is ultimately an invitation to think about queer YA culture in surprising, complex, and at times, unconventional ways.

YA criticism focused solely on identifying the misgivings, pitfalls, and problematic features of YA literature and culture is limited in its capacity to transform. It restricts the moods that our criticism can assume. It's a suspicious practice. Much critical attention has been focused on demonstrating that queer YA texts offer readers and viewers a false sense of hope, that they possess trite literary or aesthetic quality, problematically depict progress by reproducing normative structures, offer uncritical depictions of adolescence, perpetuate heteronormative and damaging stereotypes, and provide assimilative perspectives while being unaware of historical struggles. Are teen readers and critics of queer YA thus forced to remain stuck in how we interpret texts, or is there a different outlook in store for YA criticism? The issue at stake lies both in what we read and *how* we read. E. Sybil Durand and Marilisa Jiménez-García have poignantly highlighted that in addition to the field demanding more diverse representation, it also needs to "examine how authors construct these literary representations and to what extent these representations reflect" more contemporary understandings of identity, intersectionality, kinship, and relationality (1). However, to think queerly involves thinking through how youth texts reflect contemporary understandings of being and how these reflections are tethered to broader histories, projects, and communities. As Cristina Rhodes compellingly argues, youth texts become particularly fascinating when they interpolate audiences into broader histories, stories, and communities, allowing them to envision different pathways for transformation and futurity ("Processes of Transformation" 466–467).

There are other ways of reading, understanding, and developing a relationship with the texts we encounter. There are ways to build pathways towards futurism and hope that don't involve a burial of hurt. I want to acknowledge some of the misgivings of queer YA literature and media while at the same time examining how they implement reparative frameworks to push readers to witness (and potentially put into practice) the affordances of generative thinking, historical awareness, collectivity, and activism. *The Reparative Impulse of Queer Young Adult Literature* is my endeavor to further shed light on queer and underexplored ways of thinking through these complex and layered issues. It's an attempt to consider how queer YA literature can gesture toward unfamiliar ways of understanding how queerness can be perceived, read, and felt in a normative place and time that still entirely denies queer teens, adults, and communities the possibility for livable, bearable existences. Queer YA culture, regardless of its emotional scope, is built upon the ashes and rubble that normativity has left—and continues to leave—behind.

Nevertheless, as Gloria Anzaldúa might put it, within these ashes we might find knowledges and forms of kinship that "glow like live coals illuminating our past, giving us sustenance for the present and guidance for the future" (*This Bridge* xxxv). Things have not fully gotten better for many queer youth, lives, and communities. The past has shown us repeatedly that practices, feelings, and orientations that we can't even begin to imagine or represent will be crushed and erased by normative pressures. There will constantly be emerging forms of youth, kinship, and fashioning oneself that exist outside of the dominant simply because they won't fit the narratives and frameworks espoused by institutions, critics, and the status quo. The past is connected to the present, and the future will have ways of living, being, and dwelling in the world that defy the limits of contemporary thinking and representation. There's a politically and emotionally viable kernel of excitement, fear, and pleasure to be found in contemporary queer YA culture that channels the hurt of the past to imagine queer coalitions, gestures, dreams, struggles, and futures.

Notes

1 In their exploration of queerness and comics, Darieck Scott and Ramzi Fawaz disclose how comic books can be approached as a form of queer history rather than a supplement to it. They approach comics as an "archival visual history" that provides insights into gender and sexuality in ways that historical records, and historians, often refused to (211). Given that queerness was often excluded from larger historical and narrative imaginings, comics help to address this critical gap. In many ways, I also approach queer YA literature as an archive of gender, sexuality, and countercultural thought that is connected to a broader legacy of queer thought.
2 In "Young Adult Novels with Gay/Lesbian Characters and Themes, 1969–92: A Historical Reading of Gender, Content, and Narrative Distance," Christine A. Jenkins discusses the trope of endangerment in the queer YA. While many characters discuss how stressful and dangerous it is to be queer in a heteronormative world, and while these novels discuss the detriments of being openly queer, they rarely tend to focus on "the strategies and skills minority group members develop in order to survive" (155).
3 Antero Garcia has pointed out how YA has had a major influence on both youth and adult cultural spheres and how it "drives cultural engagement for a large portion of literate America. Additionally, as more young adult authors work toward bleak and post-apocalyptic world-building, the novels that are consumed profitably by the book-buying audience are acting as a zeitgeist of the current climate in America" (3).
4 Felski's reading echoes Bahktin's reading about how certain genres and narratives congeal and lose their political bite through their recognition and overuse: "These generic forms, at first productive, were then reinforced by tradition; in their subsequent development they continued stubbornly to exist, up to and beyond the point at which they had lost any meaning that was productive in actuality or adequate to later historical situations" (16).

2 More Sad Than Not?

In an interview with Richard T. Rodríguez, director Aurora Guerrero explores the emotions and processes of repair that informed the creation of her film *Mosquita y Mari* (2012). The film centers on the close relationship between Yolanda (Fenessa Pineda) and her neighbor, Mari (Venecia Troncoso), as they deal with diverging economic, cultural, and social pressures while growing up in Southeast Los Angeles. When discussing the backstory behind the themes of silence present in the film, Guerrero emphasizes the importance of honoring history in constructing intersectional forms of queer representation. The film draws from her experiences as a Latina teen developing an emotional and physical attachment with another girl, all while not having the language or frameworks to communicate said intimacy and desire. The film pays tribute to these feelings and yearnings, an attempt to go against the grain in terms of how teen intimacies are imagined and visualized:

> There were never any labels used to identify this relationship, nor was it possible to speak directly about what was happening. I therefore wanted to honor that relationship that lacked a label. […] I wanted to capture the unspoken existence of their relationship and mine, and through the film give it a history.
>
> (Rodríguez, "Filmmaking Found" 265)

In picturing this unspoken history through film, Guerrero doesn't revise the past, nor does she erase the pain that she experienced in fictionalizing her negotiations of queerness as a teen. The film isn't designed to perpetuate a history of queer impossibility, but rather, to breathe life into practices and experiences that were deemed unrepresentable, unspeakable, and unthinkable. Guerrero undoubtedly embodies a healing agenda through the creation of this film. Nonetheless, this healing connects to the hurt and confusion she experienced growing up in a context that made little space for queerness, and much less provided her with a framework to discuss

DOI: 10.4324/9781003038627-2

This chapter has been made available under a CC-BY-NC-ND license.

it. This teen-centered film, situated in our contemporary moment, works within and through this pain, loneliness, and silence in attempts to materialize a story that wouldn't (and perhaps couldn't) circulate decades ago.

Mosquita y Mari follows narrative trajectories that harken back to a queer past imbued with pain, a lack of language and frameworks regarding sexuality, and uncertainty. The film initially follows the path of a coming-of-age movie, and we see Yolanda and Mari growing closer but struggling to label or understand their desires for each other. Although the intimacy between the two teens increases towards the film's conclusion, the narrative ends in a way that current critics of YA might label as "sad," "gloomy," "lonely," or that reinforces the connection between queer life and negative affect. Yolanda and Mari don't end up together, and their queer desires toward each other are never fulfilled or represented on the screen. Despite any hopes the viewer might have for their relationship to come to fruition, the queer potentialities between the two teen characters are "brutally cut short by pervasive heteronormative and violent sexualizations and the need to survive" (A. J. Aldama 126). Not to mention that this narrative outcome also undermines the expectations of critically "successful" queer YA narratives that represent sexualities and desires "grounded in visible and coherent sexual identity" (Mason, *Queer Anxieties* 18). *Mosquita y Mari* wasn't crafted to make audiences feel good. It was crafted to materialize emotions and histories using the very tropes of silence and ambiguity that led to the proliferation of queer culture in the early 20th Century. This materialization mirrors how silence has been used to encode queerness in early 20th-Century Western cultural productions. Antonio Sanna, for instance, argues that given the antiqueer laws that existed in Late-Victorian England, queer works of that time represented "silent actions and secret fulfillment of what society considered as sin and law condemned as illegal" as a form of resistance, in that they clandestinely circulated and represented the very elements that were silenced and regulated (36).

Despite the gestures and moments of intimacy shared by the two teens throughout the film, queer potentialities are short-circuited due to the countless economic, cultural, and familial pressures they encounter. Mari, in particular, faces financial burdens that push her to join the workforce at an early age, to engage in sex work, and to prioritize matters of survival over any desire she has for Yolanda. After the film clarifies that the two teens are heading toward two very different pathways, geographies, and futures, it concludes with Yolanda and Mari standing on opposite sides of a street in their neighborhood, gazing into each other's eyes (see Figure 2.1). There's no final goodbye. No final kiss. They're still determining what the future has in store for them. They haven't come out of the closet or labeled their sexualities. There's no assurance that they'll be together in the future. As the film's audience, we witness two Latina teens staring at each

34 *More Sad Than Not?*

Figure 2.1 Yolanda (above) and Mari (below) stand on opposing sides of the street, gazing at each other's eyes as the scene fades away into a memory of the two teens sharing a moment of intimacy in a vehicle. Note that the characters are never shown on the screen simultaneously, reinforcing the distance between them and the different paths they are walking down (Guerrero 2012). Scenes cropped and stitched for argumentative purposes.

other with nothing but futurity and ambiguity in store. The scene fades away into a memory of the two teens sharing a moment of tenderness in an abandoned car as they trace their initials on the dust settled on the windshield: "M y M" (Guerrero). A review published during the film's release critiqued the film for being "too coy" in its representation of Yolanda and Mari's relationship, and for not offering "much insight into the twosome's attraction, platonic or otherwise, to each other" (Fear). Guerrero's film, however, aligns with a countercultural ethos that contests the whims and expectations of normative viewership.

Mosquita y Mari's ending denies this insight deliberately. It instead invites us to be uncertain about the future that's in store for the teen characters—a gesture of particular importance given the film's concentration on queer Latinidades and its departure from white-centered narratives of progress. Guerrero's film refutes the celebratory tone found in so many contemporary queer YA cultural productions in favor of a more indeterminate one that exposes how closely homonormative representations of happiness in queer YA "are entwined with social norms and power" and "the possibilities and the liberation that arises from reworking the script" (Wayland 104). The film invites us to pause, turn, and look at the potentialities that await on the other side of the street rather than fixing our gaze on the straight and narrow path forward.

From a suspicious perspective, we can uncritically denounce this film because it reinforces the dynamics of loneliness and impossibility espoused in earlier forms of queer YA literature and culture (see Jenkins and Cart; Clark and Blackburn; Colborne and Howard). Immediate concerns might be raised regarding how *Mosquita y Mari* represents queerness as an unlikelihood and how its narrative closure refuses to provide a sense of contentment and ease to its viewership. It refuses to make us "feel good" about queerness, and it refutes positioning itself as a film that presents queer Latine kinship as a relationship meant to be consumed uncritically. Trevor Boffone and Cristina Herrera have suggested that representations of Latine teens on screen "offer a roadmap to understanding issues of representation, visibility, and the complexities of Latinidad, including racial politics that directly impact these communities" (6). However, what happens when critical roadmaps focused on naive aspirations and optimism become the expected and normative trajectories in the field? If we focus exclusively on this moment of representative "failure" rather than centering on the politics of class and race that have haunted queer Latinidades, we're denying the text the opportunity to disclose particular moods and explore practices that emerge in contexts that are not safe, happy, comforting, or definable. In a sense, a YA text emanates queerness when it pushes us "to reimagine the practice of knowledge production" (Rodriguez, *Queer Latinidades* 3), rather than assimilating teens into preexisting and normative institutions, practices, and understandings of identity (see Trites). In this sense, the aims of queer fiction are very much attuned to the affective dimensions of YA situation tragedies in that they "highlight the unfairness of the world and the attendant precariousness of unhappiness" while also challenging "dominant narratives of identity formation in young adult fiction" (Wayland 97). *Mosquita y Mari* may seem out of place and time in terms of how it harkens back to the codes of silence present in earlier forms of queer (YA) representation, and it embodies this temporality deliberately. In doing so, the film shows how these codes still haunt us, how people still have difficulties conciliating their desires with the need to survive, and how we might not always have the language and frameworks to understand our feelings, much less the feelings of others.

In her discussion of responses to the film's ending, Larissa M. Mercado-López argues that *Mosquita y Mari*'s closure has the potential to tell us much about our moods and engagements with broader conversations on queerness and what we yearn for through our engagement with queer teen cultural productions: "This vagueness and the film's lack of a happy ending are, I would argue, its best features; the vagueness of the ending resists the expected denouement, thereby revealing to the audience their (own) queer desires" (Mercado-Lopez 277). How does this ending make us feel? These feelings gesture towards our broader thoughts and desires regarding queer representation, kinship, and the emotional/political expectations we have of YA texts and media. It helps us understand the drive to approach any ending as emotionally nourishing or harmful, as happy or unhappy, healthy or unhealthy for younger audiences. It highlights normative YA narratives' obsession with providing answers, solutions, and clear pathways that can be followed and replicated.

While the final moment of contact between Yolanda and Mari invokes feelings of sadness, separation, and impossibility, it also paints a moment where we observe two teen characters "pivoting out of the present and looking to other possible worlds and ways of being" while also seeing how they "come into a self-knowing, assuredness, and a community of queer possibility and utopic futurity" (Ruiz 289). Rather than offering viewers a sense of resolution that consoles according to dominant understandings of happiness and kinship, Guerrero channels ambiguity as a challenge. The ending pushes us to question the normative impulse towards hope, success, and heteronormative comforts that many other YA texts glorify. Guerrero's silences, gaps, and omissions aren't critical fallacies that perpetuate notions of secrecy and loneliness, but rather, they're gestures that completely thwart our narrative and emotional expectations of queer YA texts and how they generate knowledge. Whitney Monaghan, for instance, has pointed out how *Mosquita y Mari* stands in opposition "to the confessional, dialogue-focused *coming out as coming of age* narrative" (104, emphasis in original). Viewers witness a representation of queer Latine teen life that doesn't present coming out or the identification and naming of one's sexual desires/practices as the driving force that helps queer teens to find fulfillment. This reading echoes Katharine Slater's work on lesbian geographies in queer youth texts, which highlights how queer youth narratives embrace the values of multiplicity and ambiguity in their efforts to challenge the "assumptive outcomes of heterosexual adolescence" present in coming of age trajectories (2). Plenty of relationships never reach fulfillment. Loneliness can still be a part of our lives despite sociocultural change. Sometimes, things don't get better. Queer YA's potential lies in its ability to not only demystify normative outcomes and trajectories, but to offer strategies for refuting them.

Because of *Mosquita y Mari*'s resistance against many of the narrative and emotional expectations of YA cultural productions, it's easy to see why this ending might be considered undesirable or discomforting. But as Mercado-López reminds us, "To be 'at ease' is a white, heterosexual luxury. [...] for queer people, especially queer people of color, the future is never certain" (Mercado-Lopez 277). The film could've headed down a more normative narrative trajectory and conclude with a "progressive" or "celebratory" ending similar to what we see in films such as Greg Berlanti's romantic comedy *Love, Simon* (2018). The film's falling action, for instance, focuses on its main characters sharing their first kiss atop a festival wheel as the entire school cheers for them from down below (see Figure 2.2). Of course, *Love, Simon* has a different scope and audience (and let's not forget budget), not to mention that it focuses on entirely different intersections of queer teen life. While *Mosquita y Mari* intends to visualize experiences of the past that couldn't achieve representation, *Love, Simon* situates a queer teen relationship "within the romantic conventions which have traditionally been oriented around heterosexual couples" (Haley 1). This framing of the film using heteronormative narrative structures pushes us to interrogate why this ending is so beloved and celebrated by audiences. Part of it has to do with the assimilative ideologies celebrated in YA circles, and how some critics attempt to approach bodies and practices through neoliberal lenses. Robert Bittner, for instance, has highlighted how critics in queer YA elevate narratives of normalization that sideline "the numerous intersecting identity politics that complicate" simplistic understandings of queer life, and the relationship between queer youth and the cultural dominant (201). Putting the endings of *Mosquita y Mari* and *Love, Simon* side by side emphasizes the stakes raised by Bittner, and invites us to think more deeply about the politics of YA representation and how they're inflected by different axes of power and oppression.

What would be lost if *Mosquita y Mari* were to follow a more "progressive" narrative blueprint? Does progress, comfort, happiness, and a feel-good celebratory kiss on top of a festival wheel come at the cost of history and the possibilities of ambiguity? If one's upset about the ambiguity and lack of definition present in Guerrero's ending, perhaps one must acknowledge they possess a normative understanding of the future, one overloaded with "race and class privilege, with imperial hubris, with gender and sexual conventions, with maldistributed forms of security both national and personal" (Duggan and Muñoz 276). It's worth questioning what outlooks we're striving for in narrativizing and representing queer youth, and what responsibilities teen cultural productions (and their creators and critics) must assume, given their temporal placement between a history of hurt and a future that can be different from today.

38 *More Sad Than Not?*

Figure 2.2 *Love, Simon* concludes with its main characters, Simon (Nick Robinson) and Bram (Keiynan Lonsdale), engaging in a Hollywood-screen kiss while riding a festival wheel at a school fair—a deed that is met with cheers by the Ferris wheel's spectators (Berlanti 2018). Scenes cropped and stitched for argumentative purposes.

Examining queer YA vis-à-vis a history of unhappiness and hurt invites us to further comprehend the negotiations that take place between YA's aspiration to comfort its readership, the cultural and historical hurt that has haunted queer life in the past and present, and the uneasy critical relationship that exists between negative affect and contemporary youth cultures. Considering the place of (un)happiness in the field of queer YA comes with various challenges. Divergences in critical perspectives regarding the use and value of youth literature (perspectives attached to different disciplinary expectations and demands) make it difficult to agree on common definitions of joy, happiness, and success. Furthermore, queer YA authors and creators oftentimes experience trouble in locating "progress and triumph set against the sad history of damage, loss, and trauma" (Robinson viii). Sure, witnessing two queer teens being cheered by a crowd as they kiss can invoke feelings of hope, joy, utopia, euphoria, and futurity. But what happens when such a celebratory representation contrasts with the more ambiguous, quiet, subdued, and unsettling way *Mosquita y Mari* renders its characters? It pushes us to question what we consider progressive, happy, or sad in the first place. To further nuance and examine these complexities, I expand upon the role of negative emotions and outcomes in the formation of a queer YA archive and the critical responses that arose from these representations. After overviewing this trajectory, I examine Adam Silvera's debut novel *More Happy Than Not* (2015)—a light science fiction novel and allegorical approach towards gay conversion therapy that centralizes the role of negative affect in the life of a lower-class Latine teen.

I examine how Silvera's text summons the cultural hurt, violence, and oppression that's historically been attached to queer Latine life—and juxtapose this narrative with debates on the emotional and narrative possibilities of queer YA. I then examine the publication of a deluxe version of *More Happy Than Not* published in 2020, one that revises the unhappy and ambiguous ending present in the original 2015 text. In a way, this novel's publication history offers us a unique case in which an author attempts to approach their work reparatively. This repair, however, sacrifices the political bite and countercultural attitude that made the novel's original version so profound from an emotional, historical, and narrative perspective. Through this examination, I explore the assimilationist practices that operate in the creation and reception of queer YA literature, and consider what we surrender in efforts to align queer YA narratives with normative models of happiness, comfort, and triumph. Concurrently, I view this chapter as a further opportunity to interrogate the emotional politics of queer YA and the compromises that we must go through in considering the role of survival and (un)happiness in these stories. Queer YA that hurts and goes against normative expectations of joy and success possesses political importance during a time in which the field uncritically elevates normative narratives of hope, progress, and joy at the cost of history and coalition.

Looking (and Feeling) Backward

In *The Promise of Happiness*, Sara Ahmed examines feelings of negativity and unhappiness projected onto queer narratives throughout history, and approaches unhappiness as an ironic political gift for queer cultural production. In her examination of Vin Parker's efforts to get her lesbian pulp novel published in the 1950s, Ahmed discloses how early queer fiction was only published under the condition that queer characters could not experience joyful or happy outcomes. There were fears that the publication of a queer book with a happy ending would be seen as an endorsement of queer lives and practices or, worse, as "an attempt to influence readers to become queer" (*The Promise* 88). These sentiments, eerily but unsurprisingly, echo the publication of the first YA novel with queer content, John Donovan's *I'll Get There. It Better Be Worth the Trip*. Harper, the book's original publisher, was apprehensive about disseminating the book's queer content in 1969. Employees in the publisher's publicity department downplayed and, at times, omitted mention of the text's queer elements for fear that it would affect its reception (Lodge). In a letter that Donovan wrote to Ursula Nordstrom—who at the time was the head of Harper's children's division—he discloses how another publisher of children's picture books refused to consider the novel because they only "see it as an adult book" (HarperCollins Publishers), therefore perpetuating the constructed wedge between the emotional parameters and content of youth and non-youth literature.

Notwithstanding the glaring issues overloaded with these representative demands, Ahmed argues that unhappiness provided the means for queer discourse to be published and circulated—it was a form of censorship that "provided a means for overcoming censorship" (88).[1] Ahmed implores us to focus on archives of unhappiness in queer literature because they help us to challenge neoliberal narratives of success and happiness, engage in "an active disbelief in the necessary alignment of the happy with the good," and acknowledge how notions of happiness are often rooted in normative aspirations (88). For both better *and* worse, unhappiness became the defining affective framework that informed the creation, marketing, and reception of queer YA literature from its inception until the mid-1980s.

Critics often frame Donovan's *I'll Get There. It Better Be Worth the Trip* as the epicenter of queer YA's foundational attachment to pain and negativity. This 1969 novel focuses on thirteen-year-old Davy, who befriends another teen named Altschuler during his time in New York City. As the bond between the two boys grows, Davy and Altschuler kiss and engage in potentially sexual acts that they're unwilling to disclose (either to themselves or to readers) explicitly. The ties between queerness and negative affect are reified near the novel's conclusion, where Davy's dog dies soon after the protagonist admits to his parents that he "made out" with Altschuler, thus leading him to link the dog's death to his budding queerness: "It wouldn't have happened if it wasn't for me. It is too my fault! All that messing around. Nothing would have happened to [my dog] if I hadn't been messing around with Altschuler. My fault. Mine!" (Donovan 172). The ending of this novel isn't surprising given its historical context. Both Davy and Altschuler agree to never act upon their queer desires ever again, and they maintain that they need to "respect each other" (189). Infused with melodrama and melancholia, Davy's narrative trajectory incarnates the disconnection between queerness and representations of adolescence in YA culture.

Donovan's novel was just the first example of a prominent trope in which queer characters experience negative outcomes or consequences after revealing their desires and practices to another person (or sometimes, even to themselves). In this respect, the emergence of the queer YA novel was very similar to the body of queer literature written for adults that was present during the time, in that negative affect, death, and sadness were deeply ingrained in the understanding of queer life. Part of this has to do with, as Michael Cart and Christine A. Jenkins argue in *The Heart Has Its Reasons*, the fact that queerness "was viewed by many at the time as a social problem," which led these characters to become a fixture in the subgenre of the problem novel and often "robbed homosexuals of individuality and perpetuated stereotypes" (18).[2] Cart and Jenkins have demonstrated that in addition to Donovan's text, early queer YA novels, such as Isabelle Holland's *The Man Without a Face* (1972), while ostensibly well-intentioned and reflective of the social attitudes of their time, "equate homosexuality with disfigurement, despair, and death," thus leading to the reinforcement of oppressive attitudes toward queer people and communities (22).

Queer YA wasn't removed from the emotional and political negotiations that other queer literatures underwent during their primordial years. The nationalization of queer literature and media in the United States (see Chasin) and the increasing visibility of queer youth cultures led to a palpable sense of dissonance developing between the hope that saturated narratives focused on straight characters and the despair that colored queer life at the time. In these early texts, characters often faced obstacles that weren't surmountable and, at times, not survivable. They were anything but unassailable during the emergence of queer YA narratives. On the one hand, we know that these negative representations could lead people to feel bad or tie their queerness to undesirable emotions and outcomes. On the other hand, we must reckon with the fact that this negativity allowed queer youth to be represented on the page in 1969—and haunts expectations of queer YA representation until this very day.

The portrayal of queerness in YA narratives remained predominantly negative until Nancy Garden's *Annie on My Mind* was published in 1982. Considered a groundbreaking novel at the time, it offered a more optimistic perspective on white lesbian adolescence and ended on a hopeful note, unlike many of its predecessors. Despite facing discrimination and separation, the two main characters' relationship remains relatively intact towards the end of the text—showing how their relationship endures beyond the temporal limits of youth. Cart and Jenkins have praised the book's "integrity" (The Heart 55), which has helped it become a classic in queer literature. However, I'm apprehensive of the term "integrity" here and wonder how this affects how we categorize texts with different narrative and emotional trajectories. It's worth noting that *Annie on My Mind* was written when problem novels were the most widely published genre in YA literature, with queerness often presented as *the* central issue to be resolved. However, does its alignment with notions of hope and success necessarily mean that it espouses more truth—more integrity—than texts focused on negative feelings and outcomes? How does the overloaded concept of integrity undo queerness' penchant for challenging viewpoints that mark certain ideas and practices as "bad," "(dis)honest," or "deviant"?

The late 20th and early 21st centuries marked the steady emergence of more traditionally hopeful and optimistic queer YA literature before the proliferation of the *It Gets Better* project, including but not limited to texts such as Francesca Lia Block's *Weetzie Bat* (1989), Stephen Chbosky's *The Perks of Being a Wallflower* (1999), and Alex Sánchez's *Rainbow Boys* (2001), a text critically and popularly celebrated for how it shifted queer representation in youth literature. As Thomas Crisp notes, few YA novels with queer content "have received the type (and quantity) of critical, scholarly, and popular acclaim and commercial success as has *Rainbow Boys*," and consequently, the novel "has become as close to a canonical work of [queer] fiction as any other book" ("The Problem" 237–238). Crisp acknowledges the influence of *Rainbow Boys* in shifting the representation of queerness in the field, especially when it comes to offering portrayals that "help young people to believe in themselves when those in society are telling them that what they feel is wrong" (243), thus demonstrating that the novel helped to challenge the emotional boundaries of the YA queer imagination. While *Rainbow Boys* was indeed revolutionary, Crisp interrogates the novel's popularity, claiming that it offers a progressive and assimilationist perspective on gay life by constructing its characters through the implementation of heteronormative frameworks. It reinforces binary thinking through the representation of "masculine" or "feminine" gay men, thus underpinning "heteronormative and stereotypical constructions of gender and sexuality" (259). Hence, it was only possible to infuse a queer YA narrative with positive affect and optimism by using heteronormative frameworks as a representative foundation, thus highlighting how optimism came at the expense of perpetuating heterocentric ideologies and aspirations.

From this perspective, *Rainbow Boys* and other queer texts published during this time exude an affective structure that Lauren Berlant would characterize as "cruel optimism," precisely because the novel's characters identify avenues toward happiness and success by embracing the very practices that mark them as different or as other. Berlant creates immense ties between normativity and hope, compelling readers to "think of normativity as aspirational and as an evolving and incoherent cluster of hegemonic promises about the present and future experience of social belonging" (167). While these hegemonic promises may provide comfort, they come at the expense of reinforcing the status quo and developing resistance against social change: "Optimism is cruel when the object/scene that ignites a sense of possibility actually makes it impossible to attain the expansive transformation for which a person or a people risks striving" (2). Berlant approaches certain forms of optimism as cruel because they're caught between the risky and the well-intentioned. For instance, a queer YA novel might try to portray an uplifting story in which queer characters can thrive. Still, this narrative aspiration might rely on attaching queer teens to the very heteronormative and capitalist legacies that mark queer teens as powerless rather than powerful, as victims rather than survivors. Optimism can thus be considered cruel when our desires prevent us from achieving the respite, revolution, or emancipation it promises.

Berlant's analysis of the emotional structures of cruel optimism helps us further nuance the heteronormative implications of *Rainbow Boys* and similar queer YA texts. Critics and academics laud Sanchez's novel for its positive portrayal of gay and bisexual characters. True, the novel draws attention to broader narratives of hurt linked to gay identity. One of the novel's three protagonists—as I will discuss in more detail in Chapter 3—has unsafe sex with a stranger he meets on an online dating site, which connects the novel to broader narratives on HIV and AIDS. The novel also discusses the discrimination and harassment that the protagonists face in their high school. However, as Crisp points out, the fact that many critics perceive this novel to be optimistic and affirming says much, especially when said optimism aligns with heteronormative frameworks. The protagonists' desire and hope for heteronormative comforts eventually hurt them. In a different exploration of genre in queer YA fiction, Crisp argues that authors "are the creators of worlds they ask their readers to accept and trust: every 'reality' constructed in YA literature relies on ideological assumptions about how the world looks and operates" ("From Romance" 339). The worlds crafted by these authors, according to the perspective of cruel optimism, can be both threatening and affirming. They're pleasurable in that they portray queer adolescents in ostensibly happy and comforting situations, but also threatening in that this happiness relies on the reinforcement of binary, hierarchical, and normative modes of thinking.

Some queer YA texts have complicated relationships with utopianism but strive to represent worlds in which queerness isn't an issue. Most notably, David Levithan's 2003 novel *Boy Meets Boy* marked a radical shift in queer YA fiction because it was one of the first novels to depict queerness as a utopic possibility—even though the novel, as Crisp points out, still adheres to heteronormative values such as monogamy and constructs queerness "as something *different* and therefore in relationship to some 'norm'" ("From Romance" 343).[3] The novel takes place in an alternate universe where queer thought, experiences, and practices are entirely accepted and integrated into the cultural dominant. For instance, Paul, the novel's protagonist, comes out to his best friend in second grade. One of the novel's most memorable characters, Infinite Darlene, is the high school's quarterback and homecoming queen, introduced as "a six-foot-four football player scuttling through the halls in high heels, [and] a red shock wig" (Levithan, *Boy Meets Boy* 15)—offering us portrayals of gender identity that were uncommon in mainstream queer YA, and dare I say, ahead of their time.

The novel deviates from the parameters of realism typical in early 2000s YA texts to envision a hopeful and bearable future. Still, unlike the positive emotions and optimism found in other works, the affective structures of *Boys Meets Boy* are not wholly reliant on heteronormative ideologies. As Corrine M. Wickens argues in an assessment of how queer YA literature challenges normative assumptions, Levithan's novel blurs genres and experiments with language in a way that allows it to undermine "heteronormative assumptions by presenting the unthinkable: children as sexual beings, [and] hegemonic masculinity as in fact non-hegemonic and detrimental to success" (156). William P. Banks has conversely pointed out that while many readers enjoy the narrative voice and attitude of *Boy Meets Boy*, they also consider the utopia represented in the text too unrealistic and far removed from the current social circumstances of queerness. He nonetheless appreciates how the text aims to create "a critical pedagogy for reenvisioning the options before us" (34). This reenvisioning was part of Levithan's goals in writing the book, for he *deliberately* wanted to contradict the trend of negativity commonly found in queer cultural productions.

In a reflection on the impact of *Boy Meets Boy* ten years after its initial publication, disseminated in *OUT* magazine, Levithan notes that he was disheartened but not surprised when he found out that people thought "it was a radical notion to have a happy romantic comedy about two boys" (Feeny). Because of this tendency, his YA works strive to demonstrate that "tragedy and miserabilism aren't prerequisites for a gay adolescence." Notably, Levithan's work deliberately tries to uncouple the relationship that exists between queer narratives and loss through the imaginative possibilities of fiction. While some may approach the hopeful and optimistic view of YA literature as moralizing and unrealistic, Levithan ultimately contends that compelling YA narratives necessitate some degree of hope while putting this hope in conversation with notions of livability and survival: "That's life, isn't it? [...] Shit hits the fan. The abyss opens up. But then you get through it. You wrestle it down. You find a way to survive" (Feeny). While Levithan's initial work was more naively utopic in scope and represented adolescence as an obstacle to overcome, his later works became more nuanced in their framing of hope. As I'll discuss in Chapter 3, Levithan's later works moved from more abstract representations of queer utopia to more historically grounded imaginings of queer life centered on still-existing inequalities and forms of oppression.

Contemporary YA texts don't always embrace the "happily ever after" attitude typically found in children's literature and media; however, the tensions and problems found in YA fiction are almost always portrayed as survivable. Crisp, however, questions the ability of future-oriented narratives to offer optimistic stories that aren't founded upon cruelty: "Texts that seek to imagine a brighter future or a better world ultimately feed the normative social order as well. To the extent that a better world is the reward of future generations [...], a dichotomous heterosexual/not distinction remains central" ("From Romance" 344). This perspective, however, exemplifies what Felski calls a suspicious reading in that it refutes the possibility of recognizing the potential for these narratives to sustain us emotionally and politically even though they're imbricated in a capitalist industry focused on normative approaches to comfort and wellbeing. A reparative mindset, however, will push us to be more open and mindful as to what texts are attempting to accomplish, given their historical and sociocultural context and limitations, and to examine how these texts attempt to create a historically grounded sense of queer futurism for their audiences.

Although immense pleasure can be found in the proliferation of happy queer YA narratives, this pleasure comes at a cost. For readers and critics to fully understand the cultural work of queer YA and grasp and further examine its emotional politics, we must be willing to rebel against the idea that negativity, violence, and despair have no place in the contemporary canon. We must also think about queerness within and *beyond* matters of representation. As Bo Ruberg succinctly puts it, moving beyond issues of representation "allows us to make new space for queer identities, desires, and ways of being within the medium across its past, present and future" while also disrupting "the neoliberal instrumentalization of LGBTQ content" (17). This doesn't deny the importance of representation, of seeing one's desires and experiences filtered through the page or screen. However, focusing on representation shouldn't and can't be the end goal in examining the negotiations of power connected to gender, sexuality, and identity. In reading and reviewing queer YA literature, readers must take risks and avoid falling into the habit of claiming that YA cultural productions represent queerness in either a "good," "bad," (un)healthy, or (in)authentic way, as seen in the work of queer YA critics such as Jenkins/Cart, Clark/Blackburn, and Colborne/Howard.

To think more deeply about these issues, I want to shift our focus and examine the notoriously unhappy work of Adam Silvera—a Puerto Rican queer YA author who grew up in the Bronx and who implements adverse events, outcomes, and feelings as central elements in his YA novels. The negativity of his works draws readers in. His books often top bestseller charts, and his reading communities "love how sad his books are," going as far as to post videos of their tears and reactions all over social media (Gates). A quick look at the titles he's published instantly demonstrates the affiliation of his YA texts with frameworks of negativity: *History is All You Left Me* (2017), *They Both Die at the End* (2017), and *The First to Die at the End* (2022) being just a handful of examples. This discussion will center on his first novel, *More Happy Than Not*, a YA novel I selected due not only to its popularity in critical YA circles but also due to its fixation on queer negativity and its curious publication trajectory. The story, for instance, doesn't shy away from exploring the connections between queerness and topics such as gay conversion therapy, suicide, class, masculinity, and antiqueer violence. Silvera published a revised edition of this novel in late 2020, a version that added an entirely new final chapter to the story. He revises the original, ambiguous ending and replaces it with one that meshes with normative expectations of happiness. This revised edition of the book demonstrates the negotiations and compromises that queer YA literature, and its authors, must undergo in overlapping queer life with certain emotions, practices, critical expectations, and frameworks. I hope to shed further light on the place of emotion in understanding the fraught political and ideological dimensions of queer YA texts, including their reception, production, and critique.

The Joywashing of *More Happy Than Not*

Published in 2015, Silvera's *More Happy Than Not* focuses on violence and negativity during a time when said violent and harmful representations of queer teen life began to fade away from queer YA representation. This was due, in part, to the increasing influence of the *It Gets Better* project, which I discuss in more depth in the introduction of this volume. In this speculative text, scientists have developed a costly medical procedure known as Leteo, designed to subdue people's harmful and painful memories. The reasons why characters decide to undergo the medical procedure vary: some want to forget past relationships, others want to forget losses that they've experienced, and controversially, some desire to forget evils, crimes, and acts of violence they've committed. Things take an upsetting turn as the novel's protagonist, Aaron Soto, desires to undergo this procedure to suppress his emerging queer desires—thus making *More Happy*

Than Not a text tethered ideologically and allegorically to the negativity imbued in gay conversion therapy practices and centered on how state and institutional forces regulate queer teen bodies (see Bittner, Pennell, and Miller).

Aaron Soto—a Latine teen from the Bronx—struggles between his love for his girlfriend Genevieve and his growing attraction toward his best friend, Thomas. Further complicating Aaron's story, we learn that his father not only died by suicide, but that Aaron also tried to take his own life before the novel's events. After coming out to Thomas and kissing him on the rooftop of a building, Thomas reveals that he's not attracted to men and that he can't reciprocate Aaron's affections. This rejection sparks such deep despair that Aaron views his queerness as *the* cause of his unhappiness, and consequently, Leteo as the key to his salvation and survival. But before he can go ahead with the procedure, he experiences brutal antiqueer violence from one of his childhood friends when he's caught hugging another boy in public. The visceral violence Aaron experiences triggers the unraveling of memories that he'd suppressed—an apt metaphor for how histories of hurt and violence are often suppressed in queer YA culture. In an unexpected twist, we're informed that Aaron had *already* undergone a Leteo procedure to suppress his queerness and forget that his father died by suicide because he was ashamed of Aaron. An act of antiqueer violence that Aaron experiences exposes his suppressed memories, and Aaron must then reconcile his suppressed past with his lived present. *More Happy Than Not* harkens back to a damaged queer past and to the negative emotional frameworks commonly found in early queer literature. This novel strengthens the ties between queerness and unhappiness while also echoing the deathly resonances often critiqued in queer YA scholarship. But rather than falling into the trap of framing this novel as one that reinforces the so-called "too-easy equation" between queerness and negative affect (see Jenkins and Cart), I first consider the intersectional dimensions present in this novel, i.e., the overlapping axes of power and oppression that complicate monolithic readings of this text, similar to Chrisman and Blackburn in their examination of Silvera's novel. I then explore how Silvera's text uses negative affect and the potential of ambiguity to provide a counternarrative against the normalizing tendencies of YA literature and criticism.

In many ways, Aaron departs from the representative conventions commonly present in YA literature that focuses on queer teens. Aaron's queerness is the central element explored in this story; however, his sexuality is influenced in significant and inextricable ways by his social class and his Latinidad. Aaron resides in a one-bedroom apartment with his widowed mother and brother, and he's also an active contributor to his home's economic livelihood. In an even more compelling example, Aaron contemplates how access to money would've helped both him and his family to secure forms of happiness that are inaccessible to them, which connects to the notions of privilege and economic mobility explored in other representations of queer Latine adolescence such as *Mosquita y Mari*. When reflecting on his father's suicide, Aaron speculates how Leteo might have helped save his father. However, he concedes that his family would never be able to afford the cost of the procedure (Silvera 7). The irony here being that part of the reason they are in such poverty is due to the cost of paying for Aaron's forgotten procedure in the first place. The psychic weight of his father's death can also be connected to matters of heteronormativity and machismo in that Aaron initially approaches his failure to live a straight life as the root of his unhappiness.[4] Silvera's novel meticulously illuminates the social, cultural, and systemic conditions that prevent Aaron from separating his queerness from the pain he experiences—conditions that are often emphasized in many Latine YA texts with queer themes and characters.

The ties between a Latine queer YA tradition and negative affect have been palpably present since the publication of Gloria Velásquez's *Tommy Stands Alone* in 1995, which centers on Tommy's complicated relationship with his parents due to the discomfort that his emerging queerness provokes within a religious, Latine household. The novel doesn't end on a traditionally positive note and emphasizes how Tommy's sexuality will always be at odds with his Latinidad. This narrative tendency continued well with the publication of novels such as Sánchez's *Rainbow Boys*, which concludes with an intense showdown between protagonist Jason Carrillo and his father (Sánchez 199). Other texts, such as Mayra Lázara Dole's *Down to the Bone*, show how queerness opposes traditional understandings of la familia upheld in Latine contexts. The protagonist's mother melodramatically grieves when her daughter comes out of the closet: "I don't understand how someone like you came out of me. I'm embarrassed about you, Laura. I can't have you being a *tortillera* in this house" (340, emphasis in original). *Down to the Bone* frames and structures queerness as a force capable of rupturing even the so-called indestructible bonds of biology and genealogy, reinforcing the notion that queerness has no place within Latine stories centered on youth.

Other texts focused on queer Latine adolescence such as Justin Torres' *We the Animals* use the structure of the *Bildungsroman*—which translates loosely to novel of development or education—to explore the affectively overloaded ties between notions of family, sexuality, and Latinidad across a large span of the protagonist's life. We witness the nameless teen protagonist—a lover of literature, drawing, and the creative arts—noticing the dissonance that exists between the aspirations held by his family and his own emerging queer desires. The protagonist's parents discover creative work that "exposes" the protagonist's sexual attraction to men—leading to a violent confrontation between the main character and his entire family. Jeremiah Zagar's 2018 adaptation of the film visualizes this confrontation in visceral, gut-wrenching ways through the use of close-up shots of the family's reactions of disappointment to the protagonist's art. Jonah—the name given to the protagonist in the film adaptation—stares at his family in disbelief as tears fall down his eyes. Images of the family's intervention are juxtaposed with first-person shots of Jonah's homoerotic drawings, musings, and poetry—putting viewers in a position where they momentarily inhabit Jonah's positionality and witness how he uses images and words to forge queernesses within normative contexts (see Figure 2.3). His family's mournful gazes foil and destroy the joy and desire clearly expressed

Figure 2.3 First-person close-up shots of Jonah's homoerotic art and drawings are juxtaposed with shots of the intervention staged by his family. Immense effort is made to contrast the queer possibilities embedded in creative and expressive work with the harms experienced in Jonah's real-world context. *We the Animals* exploits the affective tension between queer desire and traditional understandings of la familia (Zagar 2018). Scenes cropped and stitched for argumentative purposes.

through Jonah's art. The sorrow and disappointment conveyed through the family's gestures and reactions are akin to "a gravestone marking a death: the point at which one's future as a straight adult expired, along with parental plans for one's future" (Stockton 158). Representations of queer Latinidades must often negotiate the place of queerness within and around broader frameworks connected to other sites of power such as cultural heritage, the home, la familia, race, class, and machismo, among others. Negative affect becomes vital in narrativizing queer Latine experiences in YA cultural productions—and the dialectic relationship between pain and healing often explored in these texts.

Even though Silvera's text was published decades after this trajectory became prominent in narrativizations of Latine queer YA life, it nonetheless channeled how understandings of home, sexuality, and family were bound to negativity in earlier YA texts, returning once again to the problem novel's tendency of framing the character's queerness as the central issue the text explores. In an examination of issues of identity that emerge in queer Latine YA productions, Boffone argues that by "feeling like a problem, Latinx individuals often find a link that functions to help them belong within a society that openly and frequently discriminates against them" (148). In many ways, Aaron views the Leteo procedure as the link that will help him integrate into the very powers and norms that control his actions, thoughts, and desires. Leteo exudes cruel optimism. Aaron believes that suppression of his queerness is the solution needed to address most of the issues present in his life. In simpler terms, Aaron creates ties between assimilation and happiness, viewing integration and a sense of sameness as solutions to the pain that he constantly experiences as a queer Latine teen from a deeply underprivileged background. He's informed by an ingrained sense of normalization fostered by his environment and social interactions. Once again, Aaron's desires ironically echo some of the arguments present in assimilative YA scholarship, in that frequently, both integration and the normalization of queerness are seen as aspirational goals for the field.

Do we want queer teen characters to find fulfillment through normative means of happiness and success, or do we instead want them to question and challenge the causes of their unhappiness? To echo a question presented by Ahmed, does happiness for queer youth entail "a revolution in the organization of sexuality, desire, and the body, or does it simply make queers part of the same world, the world of 'happy folk,' even if we have to work to get there?" (*The Promise* 107). Readers must be critical of YA novels that reward their queer teen characters with happiness under the condition that they approximate "signs of straightness" (*The Promise* 115), and we should be even more cautious of critiques that celebrate novels for approximating such signs. *More Happy Than Not* disrupts these critical expectations by showing how Aaron fails to achieve happiness through assimilation. Aaron couldn't approximate such signs of straightness even with the assistance of a medical procedure eerily reminiscent of contemporary gay conversion therapy practices. Aaron assumes that forgetting the past would be the solution for eradicating the pain he experiences as a queer teen—yet an instance of antiqueer violence was enough to reinvigorate a past that he desperately tried to suppress.

As discussed in this book's introduction, Heather Love stresses the importance of memory in the construction of a queer political purview to show how not all queer folk have access to the same affordances: "the temptation to forget—to forget the outrages and humiliations of gays and lesbians and to ignore the ongoing suffering of those not borne up by the rising tide of gay normalization—is stronger than ever" (10). In many ways, *More Happy Than Not* can be approached as a direct critique of the assimilative, normative, and conservative ideologies that haunt the field of queer YA literature and criticism. After Aaron's suppressed memories return, he contemplates undergoing a second Leteo procedure to subdue his queerness again. However, the original procedure's failure has caused him to develop anterograde amnesia, which refers to the inability to form new memories. While Aaron anxiously awaits a reparative procedure for his anterograde amnesia, the novel ends ambiguously, with no guarantee that he'll recover from his condition. He ends up accepting his queerness and now approaches his memories as "a childhood friend who moved away for years and finally came back home" (Silvera 293). The teen who initially tried to erase his queer past can't shape a future—left only with the past intact. This conclusion sidelines the normative anticipation for a happy ending expected from contemporary queer YA novels and pushes us to dwell in ambiguity and the unknown. It forces readers to reckon with a history of hurt and violence constantly fading from cultural memory.

It should come as no surprise that Silvera has faced some criticism for the way he concluded the novel, criticism that he was swift to address on social media: "I will forever stand by *More Happy Than Not*'s rough ending; it's not called *More Happily Ever After*. Life's issues aren't resolved at 17" (Tweet, 5 January 2016). Despite its potential lack of resolution, *More Happy Than Not* suggests that happiness can still be found if we rethink its causes and sources. Aaron doesn't want readers to lament his current state. At the novel's conclusion, he's come to terms with his queerness and emphasizes the importance of holding onto his memories and past rather than trying to suppress them: "Happiness exists where I can get it" (293). Katlyn R. Browne has highlighted how *More Happy Than Not* reparatively approaches the narrative of queer teen unhappiness and suicide and challenges the trajectories typically found in queer stories with deathly resonances: "While suicide novels have historically removed the homosexual character from any possible future and reinscribed the idea that homosexuality is fundamentally incompatible with adulthood, [...the novel] sends Aaron into adulthood with *only* his [queerness], the most unkillable thing about him" (16).

In a sense, Aaron has learned how to be happily queer rather than viewing the concept of happiness through a normative, assimilative lens in that he is "happy to be the cause of unhappiness" (Ahmed, *The Promise* 115). He finds solace in not complying with the norm, finds pleasure in recalling his past despite the pain intertwined in it, feels delight in cutting ties with his homophobic peers, and is happy to disrupt the expectations of machismo that once haunted him. Aaron's happiness no longer relies on dominant understandings of what happiness entails, nor depends on distancing himself from the pain, violence, and deathly events he experienced. In the haunting final lines of the novel, Aaron addresses the reader directly and states: "I'm more happy than not. Don't forget me" (293). This direct addressing of the reader eerily reverberates with a narratively peculiar moment in Edmund White's seminal queer work *A Boy's Own Story* (1982). During a somewhat jarring instance in White's novel, the protagonist breaks the fourth wall and addresses the reader directly using a first-person voice, a rupture from the rest of the novel's narrative conventions:

> I say all this by way of hoping that the lies I've made up to get from one poor truth to another may mean something–may even mean something most particular to you, my eccentric, patient, scrupulous reader, willing to make so much of so little, more patient and more respectful of life, or a life, than the author you're allowing for a moment to exist again.
> (White 84)

Oversaturated with melodrama and deliberately out of place in the narrative, there's something to be said about how our engagement with the literature allows us to "make so much of so little." Through this narrative rupture, White highlights how our commitment with his words and feelings gives the protagonist a sense of recognition and legitimacy that was denied to the protagonist as he was growing up queer in the Midwest during the 1950s.

In a time when the allure of forgetting history and normalization become increasingly palpable, as pointed out by Love, these moments of narrative excess and rupture are a haunting and urgent call to action: Remember. Don't forget histories of queer hurt. It's a call for us to bear witness to the pain that was foundational to the formation of queer communities and literature and that continues to haunt the lives of many queer teens. To recall the words of Anzaldúa shared in this volume's introduction, we must continue to bear witness. To offer testimonio. In examining the novel's temporal frameworks, Cristina Rhodes argues that *More Happy Than Not* informs readers that the future depends "on accepting all memories, even those that are painful and especially those that are deeply about ourselves such as one's sexuality" (4). Unfortunately, the queer critiques elevated through this ending, and its reparative potentialities, were ultimately undone when Silvera published a revised version of the text five years later.

Soho Teen published a deluxe edition of *More Happy Than Not* in 2020, which enhanced the original text by adding an epilogue. Entitled "More Happy Ending," this epilogue jumps ahead one year after the novel's original ending to update readers on Aaron's life as he deals with the effects of anterograde amnesia. As Cadden has pointed out, epilogues are crafted with readers' comfort and happiness in mind—they're implemented "to reassure them that happiness 'sticks'" ("All is Well" 344). Happiness sticks, unsurprisingly, by attaching it to heteronormative ideals such as monogamy, relationships, and success. Although the 2015 novel challenged understandings of how positive outcomes are attained and questioned the normative contours used to define happiness in queer YA cultural productions, the deluxe version undoes the subversive queer potentiality. The revised version's ending provides a sense of closure that critics come to expect of most contemporary queer YA literature and shows the difficulties in negotiating the place of (un)happiness within this corpus.

The epilogue centers on Aaron's experiences coping with his anterograde amnesia. Readers witness Aaron's frustrations as he can't form new memories. He relies entirely on a journal to understand what he experiences and how his relationships with his friends and family have developed. Aaron then undergoes a surgical procedure that *cures* him of his amnesia, allowing him to form new memories once again. The boy with no future can suddenly see and feel one on the horizon. After this development, the epilogue painstakingly provides a sense of comfort to readers by assuring them that Aaron will be okay and has a bright future. He rebuilds his relationships with his friends and develops a close relationship with another queer Latine teen whom he meets in a group therapy session for people who underwent Leteo procedures. While this epilogue emphasizes how Aaron and his family still live in conditions of poverty and Aaron struggles to adjust to his recovered capacity to form new memories, it quashes the sense of uncertainty and ambiguity in the original version. Aaron is cured. He can create new relationships. He now has the means to find a happily ever after that complies with normative reader demands and expectations—one that mollifies the critical and political incisiveness of the 2015 version.

In the afterword to this revised edition, Silvera states his reasons for revising the book and for creating an ending that sidelines the sadness of the original text. While he believes that the original ending was "true" and "surprising," he felt compelled to change the text's ultimate outcome: "I was genuinely haunted by this ending, and I wanted to give Aaron a long overdue win" (Silvera, Deluxe Edition, 324). The text's capacity to stick, to haunt, to linger, is precisely what made the original version so compelling and so necessary. The original novel disturbs and dwells through our imaginations well after finishing it. So much is lost through how the revised ending elevates normative models of success, happiness, and development. The original novel not only exposes the negativity and violence found in diverse intersections of queer life but also pushes us to rethink the many different forms that (un)happiness can assume. As Alyssa Chrisman and Mollie V. Blackburn have pointed out in their analysis of this text, happiness tends to be aligned with privileged subjects. Thus, many marginalized readers "can find strength in rejecting those norms, even if it results in constructed unhappiness" (88). The original novel's politically powerful, ambiguous, and devastating ending dampens from a howl to a whisper to assure readers that happiness sticks and that it gets better. The revision *joywashes* the original text. It returns to the very normative constructs of happiness, memory, pleasure, and belonging that the first novel attempted to unravel.

Both endings are emblematic of tensions present in the broader realm of queer representation and the tensions rising in the critique and creation of YA texts. These tensions are overt when examining the paratextual elements present in the deluxe edition, especially when contrasting Silvera's somewhat baffling afterword with the new introduction to the novel written by Angie Thomas, the author of *The Hate U Give* (2017):

> with that gut-wrenching ending, Adam reminded me of something else—it's okay to have not-so-happy endings or rather, it's okay if things are less happy than not. Young people especially need to know that it's okay if they don't get their "fairy tale ending."
>
> (Silvera, Deluxe Edition, xiv)

Given the original version's impact in pushing other prominent YA novelists to rethink the politics and role of (un)happiness in YA literature, I have trouble fully understanding why this revised version exists. Chris Crowe has reminded us that the label "Young Adult" is implemented "mostly for marketing" purposes, in that teens are often repulsed by the notion of being approached as "something less than adult" (146). Of course, we also know how the YA market is capitalistically driven and how the deluxe edition can be seen as a ploy to drive further sales of an already successful queer YA title that has topped bestseller charts. It's unsettling to read an introduction to a novel that celebrates its "gut-wrenching ending" only to have the novel conclude with a new "More Happy Ending" that stalls the political drive that made the original version so queer and so effective in connecting queer YA literature to the sadness that has been central in the formation of a queer imagination.

Negotiating (Un)Happiness

At the National Council of Teachers of English Annual Conference in 1998, Judith A. Hayn and Lisa A. Hazlett offered a presentation where they reviewed queer YA published at the time. In this presentation, they shared a "wish list" of suggestions for future novels queer characters and themes. The top item on this list was: "Sexuality is not the central issue or problem to be overcome" (69). Years after making this claim, the authors determined that there was indeed an emerging body of YA "where being LGBTQ was not the plot's nucleus; rather, in many works, all characters are treated as adolescents living the teen experience, no matter their sexuality." Hayn and Hazlett approach this development as "the single most positive and defining movement towards LGBTQ adolescent works" (70). Nearly two decades after making this claim, we have *More Happy Than Not* being published—a text that frames queerness as *the* central issue the protagonist faces. Is this a problem? Are we going backward? How do the intersectional frameworks implemented in *More Happy Than Not* pressure Hayn and Hazlett's wishes, and expose the normativity, whiteness, and cruelty embedded in their aspirations?

There's a thin line between reparative and revisionist approaches, between wishful thinking and the realities of life. While repair wants to focus on matters of survival and emotional sustenance, the revisionist text sidelines hurt and history in the promise of a "better future." While *More Happy Than Not*'s revised ending endeavors to counteract the sadness and despair culturally attached to queerness and to help the novel's protagonist to find "success," it comes at the cost of the vagueness and ambiguity that made the original text so revolutionary, and at the expense of no longer interrogating the normative values and aspirations attached to constructs of happiness and joy. How can we celebrate the original text's potential to push us to interrogate normative happiness scripts when this potential is quashed by forcing readers to feel better about the novel's outcome? And given the novel's reconfigured affective aims, who is the revised book ultimately *written for*, given that comfort is a white, heteronormative luxury?

As a thought experiment, we can return to the ambiguous, countercultural ending of Guerrero's *Mosquita y Mari*. Suppose Guerrero was to revise the film's ending to align with normative parameters of success, happiness, and progress. We would probably witness Yolanda and Mari crossing the street, locking lips and basking in the future they'll share. Crowds would gather around the two teens as their queerness is celebrated and made palpable to the public. However, that isn't the story and history shared through that film. In representing queer Latine adolescence as a state of development that hinges on an uncertain future and in denying a celebratory outcome similar to what we've seen in countless other queer YA productions, we're shown how the world hasn't changed, how some forms of queernesses have been (and continue to be) omitted and suppressed, and the infinite ways in which queer life can be embodied and represented. In so many queer Latine texts, ambiguity mobilizes critique, transformation, and healing. Transformation is contingent on acknowledging, not undermining, the very real hurt and violence people can experience for engaging in nonnormative practices and desires. The queer Latine embrace of ambiguity, the indefinable, and the intangible poses a challenge to the cruel optimism that saturates queer youth cultural production.

I worry, however, about what the revision of Silvera's novel signals regarding the broader emotional politics of queer YA. Does unhappiness no longer have a place in contemporary queer YA? What does it mean that one of the most important "sad" queer YA texts published during our moment has backtracked on the very emotions and frameworks that made it so impactful? Echoing some of the notions discussed by López-Mercado in her examination of *Mosquita y Mari*, the revision of this novel leaves much to be said about our queer desires when engaging with youth cultural productions—and even more so about the attachment of queer YA texts and media to normative practices, institutions, and enterprises.

My colleague Jon Wargo and I have shed light on an ongoing predicament that we've encountered when evaluating queer YA literature and culture. There's so much pressure and impossibility that comes with keeping hope intact while also engaging with the "historical and contemporary realities that people have and will continue to face in a time that has yet to come" (Matos and Wargo 9). Just as Aaron implored us to remember his story and the pain he endured, I invite you to thoughtfully consider what constitutes a happy or unhappy YA novel and how these representations of emotion (mis)align with the principles of queer resistance. *More Happy Than Not* shows us how YA can channel the sadness, despair, violence, survival, and oppression that was foundational in the development of queer representation to challenge and transform. Its revised ending shows us how traditional and normative expectations can suppress the critical and radical aspects of queer thinking and representation. *More Happy Than Not*, and its revision, gesture toward broader disagreements and contradictions within contemporary youth cultures regarding the emotions, feelings, and orientations the archive should embody. Perhaps we can engage with the queernesses embedded in "the murky middle of the book" instead of focusing on the revised epilogue, as Nat Hurley might suggest ("The Perversions" 124). We could sideline the deluxe edition's conclusion and focus instead on the queer, ambiguous, and nonnormative practices present in the text's core. But such an attempt at repair comes at the cost of witnessing, working through, and working *alongside* the broader narratives and feelings of negativity that structure the queer imagination. The revised edition of Silvera's novel demonstrates how contentious hurt and sadness can be when conveyed in a YA text. However, as Gabriel Duckels notes in his analysis of YA AIDS literature, the "classic negative rhetoric of queer young adult literature will *always* have currency in the representation of queer lives, no matter how far the field ostensibly comes of age." We must continue to examine the "long histories and herstories and theirstories of oppression, whether allegorical or direct" ("Melodrama" 320). No form of reparative reading can undo the emotional and normative implications that haunt the revised ending.

If we desire a queer YA that meshes with the ethos of queer approaches and their penchant for disrupting norms, then we must think deeply about the affordances that queer YA novels provide to their readers, and the strategies for survival and happiness they accentuate. Although the sociocultural circumstances of queerness have advanced in Western contexts and beyond, we must make sure that queer youth literature (and its critics) focus beyond privileged reading subjects who don't *have to* think about the harmful ideologies that have marked queer life and history as violent or unspeakable. Frederick Luis Aldama has reminded us that "queer feelings, queer selfconcepts, queer social identities, and queer behaviors have been and continue to be inscribed within a binary" focused on excluding certain bodies and spaces for the benefit of dominant and hegemonic subjectivities (*Brown on Brown* 3). Queer YA texts can be compelling in their efforts to refute the notions of assimilation, socialization, and normalization circulated in YA critical discourse since they're couched in a capitalistically driven field obsessed with glorifying these comforts. Nevertheless, its capacity to do so becomes moot when we reinscribe queer youth texts into the very dichotomies we're trying to liberate them from. *More Happy Than Not* is emblematic of this process of reinscription—and the deluxe version of the novel offers us a version of hope and optimism that contains cruelty at its core.

Several critics and readers fail to recognize the immeasurable potential for emancipation that YA cultural productions can offer. As critics, creators, readers, and teachers of queer YA, we should attune ourselves to the broader themes of resistance, survival, and ambiguity that inform countercultural thought and that electrify the potentialities of queerness. Rather than prolonging a simplistic and overly optimistic narrative of progress, we need cultural productions, authors, critics, and readers who are willing to challenge the rigid constraints imposed by neoliberal ideologies and the "ossifying" portrayals of queerness prevalent in popular culture (Muñoz, *Cruising Utopia* 22). Rather than aspiring to develop a happy queer YA literature, we should instead endeavor to develop a literature that continues to question the normative values we attach to happiness, and the bodies, ideas, and experiences we sacrifice in the pursuit of fulfillment, belonging, and success.

Does queer YA maintain the status quo, or does it subvert the dominant norms of representation and storytelling by connecting itself to broader networks of survival, resistance, and hurt? We need to ensure that the processes of joywashing present in *More Happy Than Not*'s revision don't become a norm in the field, and that happiness continues to be interrogated, questioned, deconstructed, and reimagined. We must reject the idea that readers should be content with conventional happiness scripts. We need a queer YA literature and culture that provides us with fresh imaginings of what it means to exist, care, desire, suffer, and resist. We can create fictional worlds where queer representation and storytelling are not only embraced, but also allowed to tap into a range of emotions, memories, histories, feelings, and forms of imagining.

Notes

1 YA novels with queer content have faced many issues of censorship since the emergence queer sexualities in the field. The most notable of these cases occurred in 1993, when Nancy Garden's lesbian YA novel *Annie on My Mind* (1982) became the target of protests organized by religious fundamentalists in Olathe, KS. The fundamentalist groups engaged in a public burning of the book on the steps of the Kansas City School District headquarters, and the Olathe superintendent's decision to remove the book from the school library was followed by "Student petitions calling for the book's reinstatement, rancorous public hearings, and a lawsuit" (Miner).
2 Brian W. Sturm and Karin Michel describe the problem novel as a "subgenre of 'wayward children'—contemporary realistic fiction that exhibits a nearly unrealistic number of problems, poor quality of writing, pedestrian language, and formulaic plots" (40).
3 This echoes David V. Ruffolo's arguments in *Post-Queer Politics*. Ruffolo problematizes queer theories and queer approaches by pointing out how these methods of critique are reliant on a binary opposition between the queer and the heteronormative—a dichotomy that he considers fruitless given phenomena such as the rise of globalization and neoliberal capitalism. As Ruffolo argues, "such discourses are restricted by the endless cycle of significations that reposition subjects on fixed planes—bodies that are either resituated in predetermined significations (moving from one identity category/norm to another) or are represented through differentiated significations" (4).
4 In *Beyond Machismo: Intersectional Latino Masculinities*, Aída Hurtado and Mrinal Sinha discuss three dimensions that surface when defining machismo in Latine cultures. The first dimension, developed by Mexican philosopher Octavio Paz, comprises an ideological unwillingness to show signs of weakness and emotion. The second dimension, also developed by Paz, comprises a hegemonic hypermasculinity that depends on power exerted over supposed weaker people such as women and queer men. The third domain comprises men who eschew intellectual pursuits in favor of physical domination.

3 The Haunting Presence of AIDS

The queer imagination has been historically associated with a range of negative emotions, including shame and sadness. However, few cultural productions emphasized these emotions more than literature and media focused on HIV and AIDS. Fictional representations of AIDS are varied and focus on a range of moods and feelings. Nevertheless, this literature provides us with opportunities to witness historical legacies of suffering, loss, and community—and their connection to current narrative practices in queer YA cultural production. By exploring the interplay between the queer imagination (approached by Anzaldúa as a combination of images, sensations, and feelings) and the lived experiences of those affected by AIDS, we acknowledge how YA fiction can help us confront painful histories through the use of specific tropes, storytelling conventions, and narrative techniques.

Suzanne Poirier has argued all AIDS texts must confront and interrogate—either directly or indirectly—"a public mythology still committed to the belief that homosexuality = illness = death" (2). What happens when the deathly elements of queer literature centralized in HIV and AIDS narratives merge with the hopeful, upbeat sensibilities commonly fostered via YA texts? How do texts focused on AIDS negotiate the broader utopic aspirations of YA with the material realities that have haunted queer lives and communities? What place do these histories of negativity have within the YA archive, and how do authors weave these histories into their imaginings? This chapter explores the representation of HIV and AIDS in queer YA culture, with a specific focus on how literary techniques and tropes are used to channel histories of hurt and oppression. Throughout this exploration, I highlight the strategies YA novels implement in narrativizing and aestheticizing AIDS stories aimed at younger audiences, and even more importantly, I demonstrate how YA literature can exploit the special effects enabled by the literary imagination to channel a past that lives and breathes through us. YA literature can invoke AIDS as a powerful motif

DOI: 10.4324/9781003038627-3

This chapter has been made available under a CC-BY-NC-ND license.

for identifying and mending the historical, homophobic, and normative damage that continues to haunt contemporary society.

In the concluding chapter of M.E. Kerr's YA novel *Night Kites* (1986), Pete—a gay writer dying of AIDS-related complications—points out how people rely on the process of rearrangement to cope with a world of hurt: "Mom used to rearrange the furniture when she was unhappy. I'd be upstairs at my typewriter rearranging the world" (Kerr, *Night Kites* 216). Although Pete and his mother put the process of reorganization into practice through different means—one through the process of writing and one through the activity of manipulating her domestic space—both characters use the material affordances available to them to envision alternative forms of dwelling in the world. Although different sources influence their sadness, both characters view the activities of restructuring and reimagining as integral for identifying ways of coping with their respective predicaments.

When Kerr published *Night Kites* in 1986, she didn't believe that AIDS would continue to be a significant problem in the future: "*Night Kites* is still in print. I wish I could end by saying there wasn't a need for it anymore, that it was back in time when there wasn't a cure" ("Writing about AIDS" 67). These were Kerr's concluding words in a reflection on AIDS and YA literature written in 1993—seven years after the publication of *Night Kites*, which was the first YA novel to include a significant gay character diagnosed with AIDS. It should come as no surprise that Kerr was apprehensive about the publication of her book, since it focused on charged topics in the field throughout the mid-1980s: "If there are two subjects teens don't warm up to, one is homosexuality and the other is illness" (Kerr "Writing About AIDS" 66).

Despite Kerr's reservations, *Night Kites* remains relevant for this discussion because it sparked the representation of the pandemic and explored notions of reparation and rearrangement in YA AIDS narratives. The novel concludes with Pete expressing his desire to use writing to reshape the world, using the written word to frame his perspectives on society in an empowering and uplifting fashion. This desire for rearrangement echoes Sedgwick's notions of reparative reading in that by rearranging the world through writing, authors of AIDS literature attempt to envision a future where readers could extract substance from texts produced in a "culture whose avowed desire has often been not to sustain them" (*Touching Feeling* 150–151). The notions of reparation and memorialization implemented in *Night Kites* became crucial in later YA novels that thematically and structurally focus on AIDS; however, this penchant for reparative narration was strangely absent in many YA texts published soon after Kerr's text.

Despite the increasing number of YA novels published since 1986 that address AIDS, most of these novels focused on demystifying HIV transmission rather than offering a humanized, reparative representation of People with AIDS (PWAs). Melissa Gross has pointed out that the central tension in these early novels revolved around the issue of casual transmission, and how earlier examples of these novels pushed readers to develop empathy for PWAs. These representations were problematic in that the teens represented in the literature were never directly affected by HIV or AIDS, and even more so, in how HIV/AIDS was framed as "primarily the concern of adult males" (Gross 23). *Night Kites* fits this description, as the novel's narrator, Pete's younger brother Erick, doesn't view AIDS as a concern that can affect him. Erick's closeness with the PWA represented in the novel makes *Night Kites* exceptional, especially since protagonists of YA novels, for the most part, "do not have close relationships with the story's primary HIV/AIDS characters" (Gross 23), which augments the distance between teen characters and the disease.

Further intensifying these issues, Gabriel Duckels has pointed out how early YA novels that explored AIDS were more concerned with addressing how AIDS affected "the heteronormative American family—the citizen—rather than the cultural history of the crisis" ("From Heterosexualization" 428). Although contemporary representations of AIDS and their ideological scope have shifted in YA literature, we can still observe traces of these tendencies in present-day texts. The novel that this chapter will later focus on—*Two Boys Kissing*—particularly illustrates this disjuncture in that AIDS doesn't pose a tangible threat to its teen characters. Furthermore, given that the characters with AIDS in Levithan's novel are, for the most part, ghostly figures, it becomes virtually impossible for living characters to establish any concrete or tangible relationship with them. This narrative fissure in the novel was spotlighted by Derritt Mason, who points out how despite the text's communal aspirations, it partakes in a representative tradition that "anxiously keeps HIV/AIDS at a 'safe' distance from its young protagonists" (*Queer Anxieties* 71). Given that Levithan's novel narratively represents AIDS as a ghostly presence in contemporary culture, there's the risk of classifying HIV and AIDS as historical issues that have no effect on the present. And in many ways, I agree that the text deliberately represents the past and present as "unreconciled and unreconcilable" in order "to address the history of the AIDS crisis and recognize its ongoingness" (*Queer Anxieties* 78). This tense representation of temporality brings together the text's emotional and affective frameworks. How do narrativizations of AIDS in YA toy around with form and structure to tap into the hurt and oppression that has marked queer life as lesser, unhealthy, or deathly? How are these feelings important in establishing political, transgenerational bonds that move beyond discourses of blood, genealogy, and biology?

Judith Laurence Pastore has highlighted the emotional and political value of didactic texts in creating and legitimizing representations of AIDS.

Although she recognizes that didactic literature may seem outdated or unfashionable, she argues it has nonetheless been crucial in signaling when cultural values and ideologies need to adjust to new realities. The earliest AIDS-adjacent works preached safe sex practices and cleaner methods of drug use to combat "the multiple untruths and prejudices surrounding the disease" while also gaining "sympathy for the infected and their loved ones" (3). Given that both AIDS and YA literature are invested in didactic matters, the fact that this illness remains absent and underexplored in the field remains troubling. As Mason suggests, it signals the broader anxieties that inform the creation and critique of queer YA cultural productions. The field of queer YA literature and media has perplexingly sidelined or "fossilized" AIDS, a baffling notion given how this illness shaped the queer literary imagination beyond the scope of youth literary production.

Although Monica B. Pearl has suggested that loss and sadness have been central elements in the queer canon, she further argues that the emotional weight and resonances of these elements increased drastically in US literature with the emergence of AIDS narratives. Pearl proposes that the appearance of AIDS in queer literature facilitated the articulation of a "pre-existing, and mostly vague and inarticulable, sadness around unacceptance and loss of family bonds" (11). Pearl's assertion highlights the degree to which the themes of loss and death became central to literary treatments of queer subjects during the mid-1980s and early 1990s. It also shows how AIDS narratives epitomized queer literature's use of negative affect and nonnormative forms of narrative and structural organization—and it's precisely matters of form and structure that I want to focus our attention on.

The narrativization of AIDS, as pointed out by Pearl, shifted significantly in 1995, when the disease started to lose its ties with deathly associations due to the rise of protease inhibitors, combination therapies, and antiretroviral treatments. The shift of AIDS from a death sentence to a chronic and manageable illness had a serious impact on queer literature both from an ideological and formalistic perspective. The presence of effective treatments for HIV and increasing methods for preventing its transmission essentially prevented people from thinking about HIV and AIDS straightforwardly: "Because some people thrive on these new drug combinations and others cannot tolerate them—and for some, as these latter-day AIDS novels suggest, they have arrived too late—there are no more standard stories of what happens when you have AIDS" (Pearl 116). The "New AIDS Literature" that surfaced during the post-1995 era indeed resisted the tendency to universalize stories and experiences connected to HIV and AIDS. Many of these works dealt almost exclusively with matters of survival: how people cope with having lived through the peak of the epidemic and how the disease shifts understandings of queer experience and identity. While Pearl acknowledges that the fragmented and nontotalizing tendencies of New AIDS literature can broadly be attributed to tropes and trends in postmodern expression, she argues that they can more accurately be traced to how these works thematically "shift from mourning to melancholia" (162)—emphasizing the literature's ties to processes of memorialization.

Pearl argues that these changes in the sociocultural circumstances of AIDS led to a significant shift in how AIDS was represented, and how queer stories were structured. As a result of the increasing "normalization" of the disease, due in part to the development and effectiveness of antiretroviral drugs and preventive treatments such as Pre-Exposure Prophylaxis (PrEP), AIDS will no longer have to be the primary focus of the queer imagination. This doesn't imply, however, that AIDS should be forgotten, or that we should ignore the devastations and fundamental uncertainties that still rooted in the social psyche due to AIDS. Any novel that thematically or structurally implements AIDS-related themes will certainly summon the pain, confusion, fear, unpredictability, anguish, and violence imposed on queer people and communities—AIDS haunts queer cultures despite changes in the circumstances of people with HIV and AIDS (Pearl 118). AIDS reifies and intensifies the negative affect that haunts the queer literary archive, and it pushes us to witness societal failures that normative citizens would rather bury.

Changes in the narrative representation of AIDS had significant repercussions for YA literature, for it would prove difficult for HIV and AIDS to be discussed in the simple, straightforward, universalizing fashion that was typical of earlier novels in the field. Given the decentralization of AIDS in fiction and popular culture, how are these devastations and fundamental uncertainties of the social psyche channeled into and expressed in YA literature? For starters, AIDS no longer achieves representation as a core concern in problem novels. While there certainly may be a PWA present in the narrative or a character who suspects that they've contracted the disease, AIDS typically isn't the contemporary core issue present in queer YA stories. Other YA novels express this sense of destabilization by historicizing—or dislodging—the disease away from our contemporary moment. So many queer YA novels frame AIDS as a relic of the past, when it continues to have bodily and sociopolitical ramifications for queer youth today.

In Alex Sanchez's pioneering novel *Rainbow Boys*, for instance, one of its three main protagonists, Nelson Glass, has unprotected sex with an older man he meets in a gay chatroom. HIV realistically and overtly poses a threat to Nelson's sense of self and wellbeing, and the thought of getting infected creeps into his mind as the older man lies naked on top of him: "Then [Nelson] remembered the condom, or lack thereof. A new tide of gloom flooded him. He couldn't believe he'd been so stupid. He knew he'd just done—or, more accurately, let be done to him—the riskiest thing possible" (Sánchez 149). The novel, unlike the earlier works of YA literature that Gross analyzes, indeed depicts HIV as a threat to both adults and teens alike. *Rainbow Boys* includes an appendix that offers young readers information about organizations and agencies they can contact if they have any questions about HIV/AIDS, such as the Center for Disease Control. Although unsafe sex summons the specter of AIDS in Nelson's life, the text's overall form and structure overshadow its significance. *Rainbow Boys* focuses on the coming of age journeys of three queer teens, with each chapter focusing on one of their perspectives. The novel's focus on the experiences of two other teens, in addition to the fact that the HIV narrative arises towards the latter half of the book, inevitably results in the AIDS narrative competing for representation in a fictive universe that centers on other characters dealing with other issues.

Similar shifts could also be observed in AIDS literature found in the broader queer canon. James W. Jones, for instance, explores a body of AIDS narratives written after the genre reached its peak during the 1990s. After scrutinizing a set of AIDS texts, he noticed that many authors refused to refer to the illness explicitly. The refusal to refer to the disease by its full name or acronym alludes to a possible lack of acceptance or acknowledgment of the condition; even worse, it can allude to a blockage caused by fear in that the connotations of AIDS are so gloomy and dreadful that the word can't even be uttered. In a bold move, however, Jones views this lack of naming as a constructive practice. Echoing Poirer's ideas in the introduction of this chapter, Jones shows how AIDS produced an ideological link that still lingers in our culture that affirms that

> homosexuality = illness. Moreover, since illness = AIDS, it follows as a matter of course that homosexuality = AIDS. While other works within the growing genre of AIDS literature may indeed ultimately reinforce that link, [particular works...] break that chain of signification through the rejection of oppressive language and discourses.
>
> (Jones 240)

The unwillingness to refer to the disease by name in literature isn't act of omission but, rather, an act of resistance. By refusing to name the disease, subjects rebuffed the perpetuation of the linguistic constructs that reinforced normative associations between PWAs and the overloaded affects projected onto the disease. When a cultural work names the disease, it invokes a chain of signification anchored to painful associations and negative emotions—including illness, death, decay, hatred, injustice, and impurity, among others. Of course, there are different stakes when it comes to explicitly referring to HIV and AIDS in a YA text—especially since young readers today have so much temporal distance from the cultural peak of this ongoing pandemic. Although contemporary readers now inhabit a time in which some negative outcomes and emotions aren't directly associated with AIDS, the historical damage and uncertainty provoked by AIDS continues to remain concealed in our sociocultural psyche. As Gordon has reminded us in the introduction of this book, by assessing how we are "haunted" by this damage, we grapple with the lasting effects of abusive systems that we've supposedly overcome (20).

Even when a literary text implements AIDS in a peripheral or decentralized fashion, a sense of gloom, doom, and destruction accompanies this summoning. It carries a chain of signification inevitably tied to failure, death, and pessimism. In many ways, this historical baggage challenges the overall aims and characteristics of YA literature—a field archetypally imbued with a sense of hope, even when death permeates the text's central themes. The YA novel's embrace of optimism clashes significantly with AIDS literature and its legacies of cultural hurt, mainly since the latter stems from an archive of negative affect that concretizes the sense of sadness and despair intrinsic in the queer imagination. What happens, however, when the optimism and hope often circulated in YA literature meshes with the vulnerability, precariousness, and ambiguity present in many AIDS narratives? What occurs when a YA novel approaches AIDS not only as a form of representation, but also as a framework for organizing and suturing the activist legacies of the past into our current moment? As I show in this chapter, YA fiction centers on a unique positionality that can refute or challenge the expectations that scholars and readers may have of queer and AIDS YA fiction.

I now examine Levithan's *Two Boys Kissing*, a text that exemplifies many of the tensions present through the combination of the seemingly antithetical narratives of hope and despair, past and future. In many ways, this novel embodies what Gabriel Duckels calls a pedagogy of feeling that entails "the deliberate and unambiguous recognition of an intergenerational queer community and intersecting groups of AIDS activists as heroic rather than antisocial or invisible subjects" ("Melodrama" 320). This novel indeed represents people who died of AIDS-related complications as invisible and ghostly, as highlighted in Mason's examination of the text. Using reparative reading strategies, however, I demonstrate how Levithan drags the precarious past of AIDS into the present, and how he exploits the narrative conventions of AIDS fiction to invite readers to bear witness to the hurt caused by AIDS and to acknowledge our connections to this history. Mason's reading compellingly illustrates how Levithan's novel "opens us into the possibility of a network, even if this network often fails to effectively join the past of HIV/AIDS to its present" (*Queer Anxieties* 84). I want to enrich and complicate this understanding by further examining *how* Levithan constructs more than just a network, but an affectively loaded experience narratively and aesthetically connected to a broader legacy of AIDS activism, cultural production, and the imagination. I pay close attention to how the novel uses quilting metaphors and draws from frameworks of hauntology to enmesh queer YA into a broader, more complex understanding of AIDS cultural production and memory. While Mason's examination of the text focuses on the potentialities of the text's anxieties and failures, I instead want to focus my attention on how the text manipulates form, structure, and narrative devices to patch together a history of hurt that directly challenges the so-called "better" world teens now inhabit.

This examination pushes us to understand how AIDS is narrativized in a field primarily targeted toward young readers, and during a time in which AIDS has been relatively normalized due to advances in retroviral medications, the development of PrEP, and the rise of narratives that historize and fossilize AIDS. I consider how the narrative experimentation used in *Two Boys Kissing* facilitates readings that channel the negative emotions and feelings commonly found in earlier queer literature to identify sites of remembrance, reparation, and historically grounded futurism. The narrative mode of *Two Boys Kissing* makes it groundbreaking both as an AIDS narrative and as a YA novel, for its focalization centers the collective consciousness of queer men who died of AIDS during the rise of the disease. The text makes intertextual references to other literary works that thematically center on AIDS, and as I'll discuss later, its narrative structure and form mirror the organization and affective aims of the NAMES AIDS Memorial Quilt. Through a close reading of the narrative and temporal elements of *Two Boys Kissing*, I situate Levithan's text within the broader literary tradition of the "New AIDS Literature," and demonstrate how the novel compels readers to distill contemporary events through the devastations and uncertainties that are ideologically and politically tethered to the AIDS epidemic. Through this approach, Levithan creates a tale that invokes the past to craft a dissonant, fractured, unstable narrative that transforms the pain of the past into a collective, guiding force. *Two Boys Kissing* exploits and reconfigures the negative feelings looming in the archives of queer and AIDS literature, using feelings such as resentment, sadness, hatred, and despair as the very elements that cultivate its hopeful, intergenerational, and future-oriented purview. The text pushes us to meander through the different stories that have been circulated regarding AIDS in an effort to highlight our connection to past struggles, victories, dreams, failures, and desires.

Quilting an AIDS Narrative

I previously alluded to Pearl's conceptualization of new AIDS literature, a group of texts that emerged in the mid-1990s known for their antiuniversalist stance toward identity and their narrative experimentation.

Pearl correlates the rise of New AIDS Literature with the development of (preventative) treatments for HIV, which essentially disrupted the notion of a standardized story of the outcomes of PWAs. A genre of literature once considered straightforward and predictable began to branch out in countless ways. Although previous AIDS narratives almost always ended in death, the literature that emerged after 1995 began to depict alternative endings and narrative possibilities for PWAs. Although Levithan's *Two Boys Kissing* focuses on the experiences of various teenagers coping with the pressures and tribulations of being queer in a contemporary United States context, the novel's structure, narrative mode, and overall themes allow one to neatly situate it within this larger tradition of New AIDS Literature.

Two Boys Kissing exemplifies literary experimentation through its fragmented structure and kaleidoscopic narrative innovations. It binds together diverse queer communities from the past and present to expose their commonalities, differences, heartaches, and aspirations. *Two Boys Kissing* appeared on the 2013 National Book Award Longlist and was also named a 2014 Stonewall Honor Book; however, this YA novel's importance appears first on the book's cover. The novel's title emphasizes the book's cultural and political ambitions, and if the title doesn't garner a response from the reader, the closeup image of two teenage boys locking lips accomplishes this. The novel's cover demonstrates how much has changed in US YA culture regarding the social circumstances of queerness and the representation of nonnormative sexual communities. Decades ago, we could only imagine radical, independent presses publishing books with covers like that of *Two Boys Kissing*. However, Knopf, a prominent and mainstream literary press, distributes this novel. Levithan himself acknowledges that "This isn't a book that [he] could have written ten years ago (*Two Boys Kissing* 199).

Two Boys Kissing narratively centers on Craig Cole and Harry Ramirez, two teenagers (and ex-boyfriends) who attempt to break the world record for the world's longest kiss. When Cole and Harry witness their friend, Tariq, recovering from broken ribs and bruises after experiencing antiqueer violence, they decide to break this record as a way of increasing queer visibility in their hometown—to make queer youth desires both perceptible and palpable. Surrounded by friends and recording equipment that broadcasts a live videostream online, Craig and Harry must keep their lips touching for "at least thirty-two hours, twelve minutes, and ten seconds" at their high school grounds (33). This narrative interlaces with three others: one fixated on Cooper Riggs—a teen who runs away from his home and contemplates suicide after his parents discover his interactions with men in a chatroom; another focused on the relationship between Korean American Neil Kim and his boyfriend Peter; and another focused on a budding relationship between Ryan, a cis teen, and Avery, a trans teen. None of these characters have HIV/AIDS, and the disease remains conceptually and materially absent from the thoughts and dialogue of these characters—which suggests a disjuncture between AIDS and queer youth characteristic of YA AIDS narratives. Despite this disjuncture, AIDS thematically circulates through the novel's narrative voice, its structure, its allusions to AIDS cultural productions, and its exposure of the violence that past queer generations endured as the state marked certain lives, bodies, and practices as expendable.

Through its thematic invocation of AIDS throughout the novel, it embraces elements destabilizing its categorization as realistic or fantastic. Mike Cadden, for instance, highlights the stability and uniformity of YA novel conventions in that they're primarily written in a first-person address that rarely deliberates "multiple perspectives" ("The Irony" 146). Levithan's novel, nonetheless, shatters this expectation by incorporating multiple narrators who *initially* seem to function as a Greek chorus. A few pages into the story, these narrators disclose that they're the collective voices of men who died of AIDS-related complications during the rise of the disease: "We are characters in a Tony Kushner play, or names on a quilt that rarely gets taken out anymore. We are the ghosts of the remaining older generation" (Levithan 3).[1] When the narrators introduce themselves to readers, they make no initial mention of HIV and AIDS. Instead, we must rely on intertextual clues to understand the political and historical filiations of these narrators.

This quasi-realist novel represents contemporary queer teen experiences from the perspectives of men who inhabited an increasingly precarious space due to the unprecedented threat of AIDS. These teens' lives are always focalized through the consciousness of queer men who no longer belong to the realm of the living—men who, because of the social injustices that occurred during the emergence of AIDS, had "such a limited future" (155). Kirk Fuoss points out the imprecision of the problem-realism formula in YA fiction, affirming its embedment "in the assumption that if a topic is earnestly and realistically explored, then the reader will necessarily achieve a more complete understanding of it" (170). By distilling the story of contemporary teens through the consciousness of these narrators, *Two Boys Kissing* avoids falling into the trap of realism by embracing speculative elements, which allows for unconventional methods of achieving a more imaginative and countercultural understanding of contemporary queer youth and their political legacies (see Lothian; Fawaz). The use of ghostly figures also aligns the text with an emotional and political trajectory pursued by contemporary YA novels centered on AIDS, in that they're "shaped by a melancholic politics of memorialization" (Duckels, "From Heterosexualization" 436).

The narrators of *Two Boys Kissing* are at first very ambiguous in disclosing who they are—an ambiguity that I read as a hesitancy for full disclosure. By affirming who they are and by, as Jones would put it, "naming the disease" that killed them, the narrators would instantly summon the negative emotions and connotations associated with the acronym. The narrators introduce themselves by sharing small textual clues with the reader. They reveal, for instance, that they're no longer alive, are watching those who continue to live, and feel resentment and astonishment towards the queer possibilities that the present enables for the living. Through the narrators' divulgence of their historical background, the opening of the novel makes more sense, for readers can comprehend why they feel resentment and astonishment towards today's queer generations. The narrators provide readers with an experimental narrative that connects the past and present, and that also attempts to serve as a spiritual and frequently polemical guide geared towards queer youth inhabiting a rapidly evolving cultural context.

Although the narrators' formal revelation of themselves gives us a clearer sense of the novel's focalization, only people who possess some knowledge of queer literature and culture will recognize this initial disclosure. Readers, for instance, must be capable of detecting and understanding the references to the NAMES AIDS Memorial Quilt and Tony Kushner's *Angels in America*. These intertextual references help us to situate the novel historically and place it in a specific literary tradition. Interestingly, when I taught this text in a course at the University of Notre Dame during my graduate studies, none of my students grasped any of these references. My students only realized that the narrators were PWAs once I thoroughly explained the novel's references to other cultural works centered on AIDS. The allusions to groundbreaking and culturally significant queer works may elude the cognizance of young readers, and this was when I taught the novel years ago. For instance, the allusion to Kushner's *Angels in America* offers us a clue in terms of how this novel should be approached and the sociopolitical work it enacts. Kushner's award-winning play has become one of the foremost literary endeavors to explore the legacies of AIDS in the lives of queer folk during the peak of the crisis.[2] *Angels in America*, however, focuses not on subjects who are dead but rather on subjects who are living, dying, and suffering. Even the dying characters in Kushner's play desperately attempt to avoid the stasis and cessation induced by death through their actions and desires, as best exemplified by one of the play's main characters, Prior Walter, when he exclaims: "I want more life. I can't help myself. I do" (266). Through an intertextual reference to Kushner's *magnum opus*, Levithan's *Two Boys Kissing* not only situates itself amongst a collective of AIDS narratives, but it also assists readers in approaching its narrators as subjects who desire "more life" even though they don't inhabit the realm of the living. Like Pete from Kerr's *Night Kites*, the narrators in *Two Boys Kissing* attempt to rearrange how we understand the world they used to live in—a rearrangement they achieve by deliberately overlapping their histories into the lives of contemporary queer teens.

The novel's narrators exemplify omnipresent attributes in that they can focus on multiple events and people simultaneously; however, they're ultimately not fully omniscient, for they can't anticipate most future-oriented events. Despite their omnipresence, the narrators recognize their spiritual, nearly imperceptible status in the lives of contemporary queer youths. Not only do they lament that the current generation rarely thinks about them anymore, but they also appreciate the rare instances in which a person acknowledges their efforts and afflictions. These moments are expressed in the opening chapters of the novel, where Neil, one of the novel's central characters, visits his boyfriend with some movies in hand and "realizes that part of his good fortune is his place in history" and thinks momentarily of "the ones who came before" (Levithan 2). Here, the narrators approach themselves as a "force" or "abstraction"—implying that they're now remembered not as individuals but as a collective entity unified by their social and political contributions.

Since the narrators function as a homogenous group of speakers that provides commentary for the dramatic action of a work, many, including Levithan himself, have categorized the narrators as a Greek Chorus. While this descriptor explains some of the narrators' traits, it doesn't accurately describe the complexities of their narrative function.[3] The narrators comply with some of our expectations of Greek Choruses, especially when considering the traditional role of this literary trope in Greek tragedy. Helene Foley has pointed out that these choruses are typically known for their passivity and marginality, not only because the members of a Greek Chorus are unable to affect or take part in a work's action but also because "their effective interventions are verbal rather than physical" (14). To some extent, these clichés apply to the narrators of Levithan's work since they can discuss what they observe but can't interact with their surroundings. Their passivity, however, better resembles the traits of the ambiguous Aeschylean chorus, which Foley approaches as a collective whose fate closely attaches to the fate of the protagonist and whose conversation with other actors thus becomes "more involved, searching, and extensive" when compared to the choruses of other Greek tragedies (15). The narrators of Levithan's work are passive in observing and commenting upon the state and condition of contemporary teens. Nevertheless, their active desire to discuss the historical tensions and burdens that haunt current United States contexts challenges their so-called passivity. Although they don't directly partake in the novel's action, they control how the reader interprets it.

The narrators' characterization as a spiritual or ghostly presence with human instincts and desires complicates the expectation of a Greek chorus being separate from the narrative's events. The narrative presence of men who died of AIDS-related complications better fits the parameters of the dead or ghost narrator. Alice Bennett has pointed out how ghost narrators often have access to information "that is unavailable to the living" and how they're commonly used in fiction to expose "some of the unusual, even threatening, knowledge about the minds of the characters which is conventionally held by extradiegetic-heterodiegetic narrators" (117). According to Bennett, ghost narrators are fascinating from a narratological perspective in that they embody an epistemological model situated between the "ignorant human" and the "all-knowing God," thus allowing them to possess and divulge "extended knowledges" (117). This extended knowledge and placement between the human and the divine mobilizes the narrative in *Two Boys Kissing*—it helps the ghost narrators to share information that could only be understood after dying while also allowing them to maintain a sense of humanity that makes them both accessible and trustworthy. A Greek chorus stereotypically consists of entities typically detached culturally and historically from the narrative events. Conversely, ghost narrators used to be human and, therefore, have a greater connection to our history and a more nuanced understanding of human emotions and ideological complexities. For the sake of this discussion, I thus approach them as multivocal ghost narrators that share a historically shaped identity.

The ghost narrators are a personified or concretized abstraction—an invisible force that expresses itself through human characteristics and interactions. They embody a blurred positionality that remains wedged between the realms of the human and the nonhuman, the concrete and the abstract. While all narrators blur this distinction, in that they walk "a line between the presentation of a speaking human being and the awareness that this voice is firmly not a person," ghost narrators often play "on this division spectacularly and often with unsettling effects" (Bennett 118). This play between humanity and nonhumanity, between the abstract and the concrete, reaches its peak during the concluding chapters of the novel, where the narrators attempt to stop one of the characters, Cooper Riggs, from dying by suicide: "We crowd ourselves into a mangled chorus, and in anguish, we hear the nothing that comes from our lips. We try to block him, and he walks right through us" (Levithan 186). The narrators' ghostly status makes them no different from spectators yelling at a screen, attempting to change the events of a prefabricated narrative that they can observe but not interact with. Even though the narrators are aware of their inability to interact with the realm of the characters physically, this doesn't stop them from desperately trying to make a mark on the physical world.

72 The Haunting Presence of AIDS

Two Boys Kissing offers an imagined representation of queer youth based on what the ghosts of these gay men interpret and know based on their observations of contemporary culture. The novel doesn't conceal the fact that it's an ironic narration; it's completely upfront about it. The queer teens depicted in the story have little to no agency in terms of their representation. Although they don't confront the complications or ramifications of AIDS in their everyday lives, the novel's focalization obliges the teens' narratives to be interpreted through, as Pearl would put it, the "devastations and fundamental uncertainties" tied to the AIDS epidemic. The narrators not only share their empirical observations of queer teens, but they're also open and upfront in terms of divulging their past human lives and their painful deaths through AIDS-related complications.

Additionally, the ghost narrators, through their very presence, oblige readers to decode stories about contemporary queer adolescents while at the same time being aware of the historical queer struggles that haunt the present. They offer us a narrative that simultaneously looks forward and backward. This simultaneity induces an effect that theorist Elizabeth Freeman would call temporal drag. Temporal drag can broadly be approached as a performed and embodied anachronism that revives past sociocultural failures. It connects current queer performances to "disavowed political histories" (65)—or histories no longer "helpful" or "relevant" to contemporary communities. A play on the notion of drag performance, temporal drag occurs in moments when one witnesses the queer, uncomfortable "pull of the past on the present" (62) observed via the bodies and practices of living subjects.

For example, we can refer to Alison Bechdel's graphic novel *Fun Home*, where the protagonist reads a lesbian pulp novel from the fifties while riding a subway. Dressed in traditionally masculine attire, she connects her life to the past portrayed in the lesbian pulp novel. She wonders whether she would be able to "pass the three-articles-of-clothing rule" (107) in her current apparel and whether she would've "had the guts to be one of those Eisenhower-era butches" (108).[4] The act of reading the pulp novel dressed in that entire shows how cultural remnanants of this era remain present and intact. In *Two Boys Kissing*, the protagonists' act of protest also presents a case of temporal drag. Their bodies and actions reinvigorate the remnants of a seemingly renounced political history in the present. According to Freeman, dragging the past onto the present reanimates "cultural corpses" that produce discomfort because it reminds one of the past failures that still haunt contemporary society (72). Freeman also rethinks the notion of generation, removing the concept from the family by focusing on generations "linked by political work or even mass entertainment" (64). She also recognizes the ability of technologies and cultural industries to "produce shared subjectivities that go beyond the family" (65).

Two Boys Kissing exemplifies Freeman's notions of temporal drag in a surprisingly apt fashion, in that the ghost narrators are the manifestation of a disembodied cultural corpse that creates the uncomfortable, jarring effect produced by the unification of the past and present. The narrators, using their extended knowledge, remind us of the melancholic history of AIDS in a time when the disease has been relatively normalized and, at times, forgotten. According to Freeman, temporal drag occurs in the contact zone between two or more bodies, which is pertinent to this discussion since Levithan's novel focuses on the contact between living and dead entities. An ardent desire for change and futurity infuses this contact. This desire blurs the boundaries between the past and present, and the living and dead, and it centers on the continuation of a political movement that began with the efforts of the queerly departed.

In addition to being distilled through the perspective of men who died of AIDS, Levithan's formal/structural experimentation makes his novel innovative as an AIDS text in that it deliberately employs a quilting metaphor to discuss the histories of living and dead queer people. This metaphor becomes overt on the novel's first page, as the narrators share vague contextual clues that describe who they are: "We sewed ourselves, a thread's width, into your history" (1). The ghost narrators are aware that they're binding and tethering their own personal and historical narratives to the stories of contemporary adolescents, establishing an inevitable comparison between the social conditions of gender and sexuality in the past and those of the present. Levithan's incorporation of a quilting metaphor into his novel is anything but accidental. The constant allusions to the processes of threading and sewing inevitably refer to an ongoing art installation known as the AIDS Memorial Quilt, created by the NAMES Project Foundation, a memorial for those who have died of AIDS-related complications. From its creation in the late 1980s, the AIDS Memorial Quilt has not only become one of the most significant pieces of community art in the world, but it has also served as a vital material reminder of lives and voices that could have possibly been forgotten from our collective and historical memory (see Figure 3.1). A continuously growing multimodal archive, the quilt's panels are "accompanied by letters, biographies, and photos, all of which speak to the experience of life in the age of AIDS" (NAMES Project Foundation). While this continuous growth bolsters morale in that the lives lost due to AIDS are honored, it also serves as a somber reminder of how the disease continues to affect people today.

The narrative qualities of the Memorial Quilt mirror the narrative qualities of Levithan's *Two Boys Kissing*. Like many other queer texts, the emotionally driven narrative scope of the NAMES Memorial Quilt connects a series of stories, events, and lives to mobilize a broad history of AIDS and the ramifications of this disease in United States culture and history.

Figure 3.1 A Closeup Look of a Quilt Panel Featuring Ryan White and Pedro Zamora (2012 AIDS Quilt DC 13792 – Ryan White and Pedro Zamora, by Ted Eytan, used under CC BY-SA 2.0). Exhibition of the memorial quilt in Washington DC, 2012. Note how the panels of the quilt display different stories, images, symbols, and forms of memorialization, all overloaded with different affective and emotional ranges.

Cleve Jones, the person responsible for conceptualizing and organizing the project, emphasizes the narrative and affective dimensions of the memorial quilt in his reflections on the creative and activist motives for its creation. Jones frames the quilt as an act of storytelling that captures multiple affects and stories about HIV and AIDS. And while it includes celebratory stories, these optimistic narratives are always sewn into other stories focused on grief, homophobia, and the "implacable anger in the blood-splashed quilts blaming President Reagan for ignoring the killing plague" (Jones xvi). The quilt's structure prevents it from being interpreted in a singular way, and strives to highlight various emotions, feelings, and narratives tied to the long history of AIDS.

The narrative and affective power of the quilt intimately connects to how it patches together diverse narratives, and the capacious amount of feelings and emotions it weaves together. Different stories with different emotional frameworks and outcomes merge and overlap. The stories that constitute the quilt share moments of love and hate, loss and triumph, equity and injustice. The stories of subjects who loved each other, have never met, and potentially despised each other are stitched together, creating a tale that exceeds the historical and aesthetic boundaries of the multimodal text. Through this collective of stories and experiences, the quilt became (and continues to be) an endeavor that can accurately be described as larger than life. It's uncanny how the overarching goals of the quilt mesh quite nicely with the goals of many YA texts, particularly Levithan's. While the quilt embodies attributes that allow us to approach it as an archive of negative affect, as made apparent through its portrayal of emotions such as hatred, disgust, and regret, it's also designed to share stories of triumph and optimism. Like many YA texts, the quilt presents stories of accomplishment and survival—and given its continuous growth and expansion, the quilt also embraces a sense of boundlessness and infinity that simultaneously invokes (dis)comfort and hope.

Two Boys Kissing appeals to a sensibility that resonates immensely with the goals of the AIDS Memorial Quilt. The content and structure of Levithan's novel replicate the process of navigating through and decoding this art installation. Brian L. Ott, Eric Aoki, and Greg Dickinson approach the AIDS Memorial Quilt as a "protean, populist, mobile, material, multivocal, spatial, and fragmentary" art form (102). They approach the quilt as a postmodern (anti)form "text(ile) that is simultaneously fragmented and unified, communal and individual" that "invites a critical performance that is equally fragmented and unified, communal and individual" (108). As an aesthetic work, *Two Boys Kissing* embraces many traits that Ott, Aoki, and Dickinson attribute to the quilt. Through these similarities, one can understand why Levithan's *Two Boys Kissing* fits neatly within an archive of AIDS literature, even though none of its main characters are coping with the disease. The quilt embodies various postmodern elements, reflected in the content and form of *Two Boys Kissing*, especially in terms of multivocality, community, and fragmentation.

To start, the novel combines different temporal and narrative modes and focuses on the experiences of different queer characters from various historical periods. Although the novel's narrative focuses on an attempt to break the world record for the longest kiss, the novel simultaneously invests attention in exploring the queer history of AIDS, homophobia, queer affect, gay teen suicide, and the closet, among other ideas. The text's thematic richness and plurality of narratives also increase its capacity to be read or approached in different ways. Furthermore, the novel references other texts targeted at diverse audiences and readerships. For instance, Avery makes the following statement when discussing the ability to blend in: "There are just too many perks to being a wallflower"—an apparent reference to Stephen Chbosky's celebrated YA novel (151). The narrative also references adult-oriented texts that escape the cognizance of your everyday teen, such as Kushner's *Angels in America* and the works of Walt Whitman and James Baldwin. The novel's simple yet poetic prose, in conjunction with its intertextual references to works with different readerships, lures readers of all ages to engage with and connect to its narratives, like how the quilt pushes audiences to immerse themselves in multiple stories and representations. Regarding aspects of community and individuality in the quilt mirrored in Levithan's narrative, *Two Boys Kissing* oscillates between a focus on groups and individuals within said groups. Although the narrators, for instance, witness the novel's events collectively, they also focus on the thoughts and feelings of individuals participating in this collective. While the book attempts to represent the universal emotions and experiences that unite queer subjects as a community, it also takes care to describe the particularities and nuances of individual experiences. The novel's characters and the narrators also represent a range of sexual, gender, racial, and political identities and ideologies—putting into question the cohesiveness of the represented communities.

Lastly, fragmentation is one of the most notable traits of the AIDS memorial quilt and *Two Boys Kissing*. Paragraphs on the same page can focus on entirely different narrative strands; one paragraph may discuss two characters meeting for the first time, whereas the next one may focus on the narrators' musings on relationships. At times, the paragraphs and the sections of the novel embody a patch-like quality, where pieces and fragments of disconnected narrative are sewn together to offer a broader story of the state of contemporary queer youth. The novel's lack of chapters, parts, and section headings enforces a unified approach to the text despite the consistent and sporadic shift of tones, perspectives, characters, and events. Furthermore, the ghost narrators constantly stress how they're simultaneously connected to and disconnected from the realm of the living, adding to the novel's sense of fragmentation.[5] The novel's implementation of narrative conventions used by the AIDS Memorial Quilt shed light on why Levithan thematically invokes AIDS to overlap a narrative focused on the past with a narrative focused on futurity. The novel's combination of community and individuality and its self-conscious oscillation between fragmentation and unification not only assist us in placing *Two Boys Kissing* within a tradition of New AIDS Literature, but they also assist us in further understanding how these postmodern elements aid Levithan in the construction of a reparative and generative AIDS-centered novel. By bringing in the harsh realities that people with AIDS had to endure during the peak of the disease in the 1980s and 1990s, readers of *Two Boys Kissing* can better appreciate the social possibilities and potentialities that the current queer generation revels in. In what other ways do the novel's narrators negotiate the coexistence of paradoxical desires and forces? How does the novel, similarly to the AIDS Memorial Quilt, enable the possibility of commonality and individuality, fragmentation, and cohesiveness through the narrative inclusion of the cultural baggage associated with AIDS?

Making More Than Dust

The narrators in *Two Boys Kissing* are overtly aware of their ghostly status, as reflected in their discussions of how they simultaneously belong and don't belong to the contemporary world. Despite this awareness, they try to overcome the parameters that define them as a spiritual force. Despite being an imperceptible, ghostly presence, they constantly try to be *felt* in a place and time where they barely inhabit the cognizance of living subjects, a struggle that the ghost narrators are familiar with. They had to fight to be heard when they were alive. They highlight their struggles to get attention from the broader medical and scientific communities, and their lack of access to financial resources: "We put our lives in other people's hands, and for the most part, they looked at us blankly and said, *What lives? What hands?*" (Levithan 132, emphasis in original).[6] The ghost narrators struggle with invisibility. They're witnesses who can't affect or change what they observe. The aesthetic rendering of these ghost narrators conveys the idea that subjects who died of AIDS are still fighting to be heard and, even more importantly, not forgotten. The implementation of ghost narrators, especially during the normalization of HIV/AIDS in contemporary society, serves as a stark reminder that the work that they commenced during their lives remains unfinished and that more must be done to mend the damage caused by silence, ignorance, and fear. Even more so, the novel's narrative style pushes readers to assess the degree to which we, as readers and as living subjects, have engaged in this campaign of silence and indifference.

The ghost narrators' desire to be heard while alive (and even after they died) mirrors Harry and Cole's willingness to broadcast their kiss in their attempt to break the world record. "*Silence equals death*, we'd say. And underneath that would be the assumption—the fear—that death equaled silence" (10). AIDS narratives, as evidenced by the narrators' ideas, are tethered to death. Notably, the ghost narrators don't remain silent despite their ghostly status. *Two Boys Kissing* exemplifies how death doesn't necessarily lead to reticence within the fictive domains of the imagination. Even though they're an abstract force, and even though they're meant to assume the role of observers behind a screen, the novel's ghost narrators constantly attempt to contravene the physical and narrative limitations imposed upon them—particularly the limits of death itself, which are transgressed through their role as the narrators and focalizers of the novel. A YA novel materializes the overloaded emotions connected to AIDS, emotions that continue to haunt us in unforeseen ways.

In many senses, fiction possesses the potential to imbue death with life. Bennett argues that ghostly narrators "not only suggest that the end is not really the end, and can be infinitely extended in fiction, they are also constantly aware of their own fictiveness—and this is only heightened by their play with genre fictions" (116). Given the deathly elements present in AIDS narratives, the ghost narrators of *Two Boys Kissing* are designed to play with the genre of New AIDS Literature and invert the very limitations they experienced as people who died of AIDS-related complications. This fictiveness is *overt* given that the narrators introduce themselves not as people, but as fictive elements—they're characters from plays, names on a quilt, a collective yet dissonant force of hope and anguish. Even after their death, these narrators continue to proliferate messages attached to the "backward" histories that haunt us—that compel us to continue living in service of an unforeseen future. These voices struggle to surpass a physical and cultural limitation thrust upon them. True, the teens in the novel don't hear the narrators' voices directly—as succinctly pointed out by Mason's work. However, some characters in the novel do *feel* the presence of these ghosts. They *feel* and *know* pain that is akin to that suffered by the narrators. They're often "struck by a feeling" (Levithan 2) that can't be named or explained, but that affectively weaves them into broader stories, histories, and legacies.

I don't think *Two Boys Kissing* was designed simply to memorialize the queerly departed—the lives lost due to ignorance and state-imposed violence. It's a text designed to provoke, overwhelm, and *affect*. I see where Mason comes from when claiming that this YA novel sidelines "the lived realities of young queers" living with HIV and AIDS and promotes narrative trajectories imbued with privilege (*Queer Anxieties* 85). But in remaining suspicious of the novel's attempts at bridging together dissonant narratives, we potentially undermine how the novel uses feeling, affect, hurt, and pain to create an archive of emotion. By giving PWAs a voice after death, Levithan's novel invites us to feel discordant emotions, outcomes, and possibilities tethered to queer experiences then and now. The book uses the potentialities of a ghostly voice to imagine the narrators not as victims, but as an enduring force impervious even to limitations of death itself. While the novel indeed shields its younger characters from the direct and enduring effects of the AIDS crisis, their stories and outcomes are quilted into histories of joy, pain, impossibility, and anticipation. We're invited to meander through the novel's patchwork and think about the ways in which those unnamed affects and feelings sew us together (and at times, fail to do so).

The narrators' dissatisfaction with their role as ghost narrators becomes even more prominent when considering their cohesiveness as a collective entity. As seen in the passage in which the narrators attempt to stop Cooper Riggs from jumping off a bridge, they "crowd [themselves] into a mangled chorus" (186). The fact that they crowd themselves indicates that they weren't originally swarming together, which implies that these souls only sometimes approach the novel's events as a cohesive group. With this lack of cohesiveness in mind, the tensions and paradoxes often found in the narrators' statements begin to make more sense. While this chorus can initially be approached as unstable and contradictory, it becomes clear that the tension and contradiction perceived in the narrators' words can be attributed to the dissent and disagreement amongst the souls narrating the text.

We're initially given the impression that the novel's narrators are a homogenized group of voices. Breaking conventions and expectations of a joint narrative voice, the ghost narrators are composed of individualized voices with differing opinions, attitudes, and ideological outlooks. This multiplicity of voices emerges when the narrators disagree about whether they like how Ryan and Avery dye their hair in uncommon hues such as pink and blue: "We are rarely unanimous about anything. Some of us loved. Some of us couldn't. Some of us were loved. Some of us weren't" (8). The narrators oscillate between referring to themselves as a collective and a divided group. This fragmentation assists the readers in decoding the various sentiments that individuals may hold toward the possibilities and promises of contemporary queerness. Even more so, it reminds readers that these possibilities could only come to fruition through collectivity and coalition despite these different attitudes and ideological outlooks.

Despite these moments of divergence, the novel depicts the ghost narrators as entities that constantly find themselves uniting as one, especially when confronting the many ways that teens face danger due to the heteronormative damage that continues to hurt today's queer communities. The narrators' oscillation between individualism and collectivity is made possible by implementing a characteristic technique of ghostly narration. Drawing from the work of Brian Richardson, Bennett points out how ghost narrators often disrupt the boundaries of individual personhood through the implementation of a first-person plural narrative mode, which suggests "the blending and bleeding together of consciousness" and the ghost narrators' "capacity to blend, read and merge minds" (126). Bennett points out that this technique of bleeding together consciousnesses:

> throws into question the idea of the narrator as 'someone' who tells a story: after the death of the narrator, the idea of this position as a function of the text as well as a person begins to be more easily thinkable. The dead therefore occupy a space between God and man, but also between persons and non-persons, because they erase any possibility of a façade of natural narration.
>
> (126)

It's precisely through this deliberately unnatural narration that the political function of the narrators becomes more tangible. They provide a voice to the voiceless and promote a generative mode of thinking that transcends temporal barriers. The narrators promote an intergenerational generative narrative that aspires to be future-oriented but aware of historical hurt and struggles.

Although *Two Boys Kissing* can straightforwardly be interpreted either as a coming of age text or as a manifesto for queer teens, interpretations of this YA novel transform drastically when approaching it as a contemporary AIDS text. However, Levithan's narrative mode may be perceived as contrived or forced to some readers precisely because it, in Bennett's words, eschews "a façade of natural narration." Why does the novel need to be narrated and focalized through the perspective of the ghosts of men who died of AIDS-related complications? Levithan's novel uses a literary special effect to frame its narrative by addressing the reader through the second person and by using fictive powers to resurrect the ghosts of people who died of AIDS. This method of constructing an AIDS narrative—rare in both literature written for adults and teens—provides readers with the opportunity to assess the role of HIV/AIDS in a time in which many no longer consider the disease a death sentence. While the narrative mode of *Two Boys Kissing* may seem forced and didactic, the text deliberately and self-consciously reads as unsynchronized through its measured dragging of the past into the present. Just like the AIDS Memorial Quilt, the novel's narrative techniques assist us in weaving together different lives, temporal modes, histories, generations, and emotions. The artificiality of the novel's temporality and narrative style sets the text apart and demands critical attention and deconstruction on behalf of the reader. The novel's ghost narrators coerce readers to think through and reconsider historical events that contemporary adolescents may not know—and thus, even if we approach the text as unrealistic or artificial, it embodies this unrealism and artificiality with a political and historical purpose. Furthermore, the literary techniques employed in *Two Boys Kissing* pressure the pessimistic and deathly teleology typically found in AIDS literature while also connecting the text to the broader feelings and structures of the queer imagination.

Although AIDS informs the novel's form and narrative style—the disease seems strangely disengaged from the text's central plots and main characters, as Mason has succinctly pointed out in their exploration of Levithan's novel (*Queer Anxieties* 71). The presence of AIDS in *Two Boys Kissing* can be approached as spiritual or ghostly in that it haunts the entire narrative. The ethereal presence of AIDS in this novel is troubling, given the genuine complications that HIV/AIDS has in the lives of contemporary people. However, rather than engaging in the suspicious practice of pointing out how Levithan's novel problematically presents AIDS as a nonissue within the context of contemporary American society, I show how this structuring of AIDS allows readers to explore feelings and affects that are increasingly foreclosed due to the impulse of "It Gets Better" narratives. Is it possible for *Two Boys Kissing* to truly channel and transform the negative feelings attached to AIDS literature to facilitate emotionally complex and profound explorations of the imagination?

Although the ghost narrators recognize their inability to completely eradicate the wrongdoings of heteronormativity and homophobia—a daunting task, to say the least— they argue that by focusing on them, we witness the systems that have led them to be trapped in their limbo-like state. These ghosts are forced to continue witnessing the damage of normativity until society finds a way to undo these offenses. As the narrators proclaim when Cooper Riggs—one of the novel's main characters—prepares to end his life by jumping off a bridge: "Why must we die over and over again?" (Levithan 189). First and foremost, note that the ghosts don't see Cooper as entirely different from them, for they include him in their use of "we." Cooper is different from them, but nonetheless part of them—akin to them as Gubar might put it. The souls, despite their oscillation between collectivity and individuality, unite as one as they question and reflect upon the increased attention given to the rate of queer teen suicides that have occurred throughout the last decade.[7] The ghost narrators make a tight, albeit ineffective, "net of [their] bodies" to prevent Cooper from jumping (189). Here, the narrators overlook their differences and become a singular, interwoven entity attempting to foil the system and prevent it from doing further damage. Coalition becomes the priority. This fusion between the members of the chorus can be seen as a vital moment of queer kinship and desire, for we witness the narrators—as Halberstam would put it—working "hand in hand to open up new and different ways of being concerning time, truth, being, living, and dying" (*The Queer Art* 55). These ghost narrators, spiritual remnants of the wrongdoings of heteronormativity and homophobia, take advantage of their liminal ethereal positionality to attempt to ensure a future for queer teens, even if such a goal is impossible or unrealistic. They show how our present continues to be haunted.

Two Boys Kissing compresses time in a fashion that challenges trajectories of development and progress. Narratively speaking, Levithan arranges his novel as a countdown; Cole and Harry must kiss for a minimum of thirty-two hours, twelve minutes, and ten seconds to break the previous record for most extended kiss. While the novel's events develop linearly and straightforwardly, the backward counting of time to reach a designated zero offers a counternarrative that comes into tension with the narrative of progress. The narrators themselves exert pressure over these narratives through their invocation of the historical injuries induced by AIDS into the realm of the present. This notion of historical injury is indispensable when recalling that the ghost narrators describe themselves as a spiritual *burden* that the current generation of queer youth carries with them. In attempting to provide a link between the painful past of the narrators and an optimistic, "painless," invincibility-driven future, Levithan's work essentially forces the reader to witness a past that may very well be on the cusp of forgetfulness, especially when taking into consideration that the novel constantly references the imagined queer teens who rarely remember their queer political ancestry.

The confrontation between a damaged past and subjects who do not recognize this damage summons a series of questions posed by Love, which I explore at length in this volume's introduction. Love critiques the privileging of progressive and emancipatory narratives in queer literature and politics precisely because they leave little room for understanding the connection that exists between a wounded queer past and a damaged queer present. Despite Levithan's progressive narrative, the ghost narrators constantly bring up what Love calls "backward feelings." The narrators, for instance, discuss the pain and loneliness that they endured when dying in hospital rooms. They also discuss the impossibilities they faced in expressing their desires openly and publicly. The temporal disruption that characterizes the story in conjunction with the backward feelings resuscitated through the novel's narrators enhances the notion of the text as one that simultaneously facilitates deconstructive and reparative readings.

Two Boys Kissing complicates the distinction between a narrative of progress and backwardness. Levithan's novel can be approached as progressive since the unfolding of narrative events revolves around whether Harry and Cole will break the record. All the narratives in the novel are centered on a linear progression from pain to relief, anguish to joy, failure to success. Despite the characters' obstacles, they overcome them, and their fates deviate from terrible possibilities and outcomes. Someone saves Cooper Riggs before he manages to jump off a bridge; Avery comes out as trans to Ryan, and they both sail off on a rowboat into an uncertain but optimistic future; Neil and Peter, although unclear as to whether their relationship will stand the test of time, bask into the love and understanding they share in the present.

While the fate of the characters emanates hope, optimism, and progress, these positive associations are constantly pressured and problematized through the shadowy presence of the narrators, who continuously add gravitas to the spiritual and historical burdens that queer youth carry. The narrators' engrossed concentration on the past and the main characters' fixation on the future influence us to approach the narrative in a multitemporal fashion, an inevitable result of temporal drag. By dragging the past into the present, we're invited to partake in the potentialities of futurity while developing an awareness of the people and events that allowed this future to come to fruition in the first place. Even though the novel's main characters all witness potentially optimistic endings, the book still concludes with a lack of total closure since the souls of men who died of AIDS continue to haunt the present, and since the text never actually represents Cole and Harry breaking the record. It refuses to focus on this small victory and, instead, focuses on a broader project. Thus, the story ends with a call to the reader, indicating that the ghost narrators still can't rest, given that much damage remains undone.

The call to continue this political movement becomes direct and concrete at the end of the novel when the narrators implore readers to "Make more than dust" (Levithan 196), which I reference in the title of this section.[8] Through this statement, they implore us to live in service of an open and enabling future for forthcoming queer generations. An act of selflessness, the impulse to make more than dust connects to a broader disposition to think and act generatively. On the one hand, the novel can be approached, along the lines of Love's views, as a call to look and feel backward to fully understand the pain and agony that queer subjects continue to feel today despite drastic changes in the perception and representation of sexual identity and gender. On the other hand, the ghost narrators concede that "If you play your cards right, the next generation will have so much more than you did" (195). The reference to card-playing inevitably brings up images of gambling—and this is precisely what the ghost narrators want us to do: to invest our energies in a future that has yet to arrive. Drawing from the work of Walter Benjamin, Miriam Bratu Hansen points out how the act of gambling requires contact between physical beings and fate—it requires openness on behalf of the individual to attune the body in a way that allows one to "seize the current of fate" and use chance as a way of visualizing a future that departs from current conditions (6–7). The ghost narrators thus urge readers to embody this sense of openness to work beyond the present and the self to visualize alternative, more compassionate, and more communal ways of being and existing in the world. As an imagined community, they attempt to inspire connections between the queer and the living, the present and the future.

Mending With Patches

As readers, we have a particularly queer relationship with the ghost narrators portrayed in *Two Boys Kissing*. The lingering presence of the ghost narrators—a presence from the past that continues to haunt us today—can be approached as a "hiccup in sequential time" (Freeman 3) that enables a connection between individuals, both real and imaginary, that in no way resembles a normative relationship. The past serves as an outlet for sensing and feeling a sense of futurity not readily available in the present. The narrators of *Two Boys Kissing* not only drag a past of hurt into the present, but they also tap into the unvoiced pain that they felt as subjects dying of

AIDS and force us to witness their suffering. Through this channeling, we as readers have the potential to internalize the visions that these ghosts share; through this very act of sharing, the ghost narrators are ultimately able to transcend the limitations of death and exist once again, at least on the page or screen, or in our minds. By reading the narrators' words, we give them a sense of legitimacy that was denied to them during their lives, and even more so, we give them a (albeit limited and fictive) future.

The text artistically represents the souls who died of AIDS as an invincible, unconquerable, unassailable force that refuses to be forgotten even though people can't always perceive it. The ghost narrators continue to haunt despite the pain and agony of doing so. Like the invincibility and hope associated with ideologies and stereotypes of adolescence, the invincibility of the narrators may be perceived as slightly self-centered and overly demanding of attention—artificial, if you want to call it that. But sometimes, artificiality, fiction, and the imagination can show us alternatives for undoing the cultural and historical damage of heteronormativity and homophobia. This demand for attention pushes the narrators, the novel's characters, and us as readers to trust in the potential of coalition and of histories of hurt to spark repair in a disconnected and fragmented world. Despite the presence of disconnection, fragmentation, and separation, the message of these narrators emanates clarity and urgency: never stop connecting, never stop repairing, the work must continue.

Through temporal drag, thwarting the limitations of ghostly narration, and combining archives of negative and optimistic affect, Levithan's novel represents a revolutionary, transhistorical, and emotionally overloaded narrative that invites readers to juxtapose the devastations of AIDS with the ongoing formation of a contemporary, politically conscientious, queer community. Although the burdens and harms of heteronormativity engender the narrators' ghostly status, these narrators refuse to accept the fictional and narrative limitations that define them. Even though they recognize the futility of interacting with the physical world, this limitation does not stop them from working and thinking collectively. The novel emphasizes the differences that exist between the ghost narrators and the queer youth they watch over. I agree with Mason that this novel indeed creates a temporal split that casts AIDS as a historical issue that bears little effect on living teens. I also agree that the failure of connection between the ghosts and the living teens helps to partially drive the narrative's critique regarding the forgotten histories of HIV and AIDS. However, I also think there's something to be said about the affective and emotional threads that the narrators weave between their stories and the issues that queer teens experience today. They show how histories that we deem dead are still very much alive. They show how the queer ghosts of the past are still quite akin to us. They materialize the potential of fiction to patch these ghostly narratives onto the gaps in our own stories. The ghost narrators work hand in hand to challenge the narrative and physical restraints imposed on them. Rather than basking in the silence imposed on them during their lives, the ghost narrators overcome the narrative convention that defines them. They're a somewhat-Greek chorus that has something to say. A chorus that refuses to stay in the margins and becomes *the* dominant voice in a narrative. Levithan's novel reanimates these ghosts. We witness them. Through fiction, the novel gives them the means to speak to us and affect us.

Unlike the ghost narrators, the imagined queer teens in the novel *are* perceptible. They *are* visible. Moreover, they emotionally and physically affect the people around them. Craig and Harry respond to the sentiments expressed by their queer legacies and work hand in hand, lip on lip, to repair the damage imparted by normativity and release the ghost narrators from their limbo. Their ongoing kiss represents the novel's most remarkable instance of temporal drag, for this staged and recorded act of queer intimacy "reanimates the corpses" of past acts of queer resistance and activism. This instance collapses the distinction between the narrators and the novel's characters. By streaming the kiss live through the internet, Craig and Harry, like the narrators, develop a sense of omnipresence in that they are present in more than one place. Like the ghost narrators, the two boys abandon their individuality and "become a blur" (46), cognizant of the fact that there's "something bigger than the two of them just outside the kiss" (47). Like their queer ancestors, Craig and Harry recognize that their actions won't necessarily change things, but they know that the spirit and *feeling* invoked by their kiss "will live on in everyone here, everyone who sees. That spirit will change things" (194). Through the kiss, a thread weaves its way through different times. Different generations become more akin to one another. It reanimates cultural corpses, and in doing so, different queer generations are connected *not* through familial filiation but rather through feeling and through political convictions. Although it may seem that the novel portrays AIDS as an issue disassociated from the lives of contemporary queer teens, the narrative parallels between the narrators and the queer teens demonstrate how the historical damage instantiated by AIDS haunts and lives through us all.

Through its implementation of temporal drag, the novel serves as a call to recognize the past to ultimately "Make more than dust" (196). We witness contemporary damage tethered to the past, and are moved to work collectively in repairing this cultural, emotional, and psychic hurt. The narrators' call for reparation uncannily echoes *Night Kites*, the first YA novel to include a character with AIDS. Like *Night Kites*' Pete, who expresses his desire to rearrange his world through the process of writing, *Two Boys Kissing* shows us how the written word reassembles and patches together elements in service of an ongoing fight. The novel grants a voice to a group of frequently ignored and silenced people. Although Levithan's novel fits neatly within traditions of AIDS literature through its narrative form and its portrayal of negative affect—its narrative refuses to wholeheartedly embrace the negativity and doom present in the broader archive of queer AIDS literature. The costs of living queerly are front and center in Levithan's novel, but these costs don't necessarily require further death, sadness, illness, suicide, or agony to be paid. *Two Boys Kissing* carves paths to futurity not by ignoring a painful past but by making this past tangible and perceivable—by reinvigorating a history on the verge of forgetfulness and making this history palpable to the sensations. The novel takes the invisible and makes it visible, takes the abstract and makes it felt. The narrators of *Two Boys Kissing* implore us to live in service of an open and enabling future for forthcoming queer generations, and we might just be compelled to think carefully about what this means and whether this is possible.

Although the novel was written over a decade ago, I continue to be delighted, disturbed, confused, and moved with how this text generates meaning, and what it could go on to mean during a time in which HIV and AIDS problematically continue to be normalized . I first explored the notion of intergenerational connection in this novel over a decade ago, a conversation that Mason was able to brilliantly connect to a larger discussion regarding the broader anxieties of YA criticism. But here, I've tried to connect Levithan's text to a broader representative and aesthetic legacy, one that tries to channel diverging feelings and experiences that can't be reduced to a singular story, viewpoint, or emotion. While AIDS doesn't have a concrete presence in the world of teens, its structures, feelings, and histories are sutured throughout the entire text.

The legacies of PWAs thus inspire connections amongst not only the queer but the living. Through these connections, fictional subjects surpass the narrative limitations imposed on them and develop alternative pathways to futurity. Older and newer generations, through these linkages, obtain sustenance in a culture that refuses to sustain them (Sedgwick, *Touching Feeling* 151). The novel's construction of a queer community via narrative innovations, quilting metaphors, and implementation of temporal drag stress the importance of not only looking back but feeling backward. I don't think it's entirely generative to compartmentalize the ghosts' stories and the micronarratives focused on contemporary queer and trans youth. Just like the AIDS memorial quilt, the novel invites us to wander around the narrative, patching together different stories overloaded with different emotions, possibilities, paradoxes, and outcomes. A quilt can never tell a complete story—it only contains scraps of what used to be much larger pieces of fabric and materials. But this story—this narrative quilt—was never meant to be complete, as we never actually see the final outcome of the two eponymous boys and their act of protest. The NAMES

AIDS memorial quilt is designed to never be completed as well. *Two Boys Kissing* stands as a culturally significant model for how the social devastations and uncertainties instigated by AIDS can be transmuted into compelling, thought-provoking YA literature. It's through this very power that we can generate alternative ways of not only representing AIDS in YA, but of connecting YA to broader histories of pain, hurt, suffering, and healing.[9]

Notes

1. David Levithan first implemented this unique narrative mode in his short story "A Word from the Nearly Distant Past,"—which he later expanded into the novel that became *Two Boys Kissing*.
2. In his discussion on gay and lesbian American theater, Douglas W. Gordy points out that this play not only demonstrated the ability of queer theater to "transcend its limitations as a ghettoized genre," but he also argues that no other individual gay play has had the impact of Kushner's masterpiece (185).
3. On his personal website, David Levithan explains that *Two Boys Kissing* is "narrated by a Greek Chorus of the generation of gay men lost to AIDS" ("My Books...").
4. New York implemented the three-articles-of-clothing law during the mid-1900s. Under this law, women could avoid arrest for dressing in a masculine fashion if they wore at least three "feminine" articles.
5. In his discussion on "Postmodernism and Fiction," Barry Lewis approaches fragmentation as one of the most common narrative elements in first—and second-wave postmodern texts. Fragmentation refers to the disruption of linear narrative and chronology in favor of a presentation of "slabs of event and circumstance" (173).
6. These questions resonate significantly with those posited by Judith Butler in her lecture "Performativity, Precarity, and Sexual Politics." In this lecture, Butler points out how the rise of the AIDS epidemic led queer theorists to develop central questions that have haunted both real queer lives and the queer imagination: "how does one live with the notion that one's love is not considered love, and one's loss is not considered loss? How does one live an unrecognizable life?" (xiii). The question of livability became central to much of Butler's later work. For more information, please see Butler's *Undoing Gender* (2004) and *Precarious Life: The Powers of Mourning and Violence* (2006).
7. In the novel's afterword, Levithan discusses how *Two Boys Kissing* was partially written as an aesthetic response to the issue of gay teen suicide, a problem that has received significant media attention in the twenty-tens. Levithan's narrative focusing on Cooper Riggs was written as a response to cases such as Tyler Clementi's unwarranted and tragic death. For a more detailed account of Clementi's story and the well-documented trial that ensued, please read Ian Parker's "The Story of a Suicide" (2012).
8. This statement echoes one found in Gore Vidal's *The City and the Pillar*, one of the first post-war American novels to overtly discuss homosexuality in a somewhat positive and honest fashion: "Of course his dust would be absorbed in other living things and to that degree at least he would exist again, though it was plain enough that the specific combination which was he would never exist again." Vidal's novel was not only one of the first American texts to depict two men engaging in sexual acts, but it is also approached by Michael Bronski as

"the postwar homosexual novel that garnered the most notoriety, and criticism, for its explicit homosexual theme" (343).
9 This chapter is loosely adapted from my essay "Queer Consciousness/Community in David Levithan's *Two Boys Kissing*: 'One the Other Never Leaving,'" published in *Gender(ed) Identities: Critical Rereadings of Gender in Children's and Young Adult Literature* (Routledge 2016).

4 On Mortality and Permalife

In a poignant moment in Anna-Marie McLemore's trans YA novel *When the Moon Was Ours* (2016), Aracely, the protagonist's older sister, reveals that she transitioned in gender and age before the novel's events. While trying to save her sister, Miel, from drowning in a river as a teenager, the water wraps around her body and returns her "back as the girl he's always wished he could grow into. Not a girl. A woman, finished and grown" (McLemore 102). While Aracely is uncertain as to why the river transformed her body in such radical ways, she acknowledges how the water "felt her sorrow" and thus "aged her heart" (102). Rather than depicting a moment in which a trans teen dies in an attempt to salvage her family, *When the Moon Was Ours* instead invokes the possibilities of the fantastic to imbue Aracely with life and to bestow upon her the existence that was denied to her by her culture and upbringing. Trans life is not cut short; time and space bend and twist Aracely's flesh and spirit to better channel the emotions, feelings, and desires that "match her bitter heart" (McLemore 102). Negative emotions and pain fuel, rather than hinder, this transformation. The text identifies avenues beyond the parameters of the real and the ordinary to explore feelings tethered to queer and trans life. It uses language to refashion a potential moment of death into a beginning, a possibility, and an alternative.

Of course, Aracely's transformation, magically induced by the river's waters, is impossible given the limitations of our material world. In the study of trans youth literature, there are deep-rooted concerns regarding the role of the fantastic and the nonhuman in mobilizing trans themes, issues, and practices. These apprehensions can be traced to historical representative tendencies that represented trans life as monstrous or otherworldly (see Henderson). In "Trans People Aren't Mythical Creatures," Laura M. Jimenez critiques a children's picture book due to its use of mermaid imagery: "It comes from a place of privilege that would rather a mermaid trope carry the message and ignore the very real issues at work." Parrish Turner, a sensitivity reader who specializes in trans youth

DOI: 10.4324/9781003038627-4

This chapter has been made available under a CC-BY-NC-ND license.

literature, has further highlighted how the process of transitioning is commonly represented as an animal desiring to be another creature—reifying discourses that strengthen essentialist approaches to gender identity and showing how the nonhuman and speculative are at tension with some of the representative politics of youth literature (Turner). The critical mood of these approaches doesn't emerge out of a vacuum. In her exploration of the figure of the Dark Other in youth literature, Ebony Elizabeth Thomas points out how "for many, the struggle for liberation in the world that we know is epic enough without imagining a completely different world, with different rules and different outcomes" (24). The significant issue here is that the fantastic, the magical, the animal, and the nonhuman are sometimes used to mask the realities of trans lives and practices, making their implementation seem optimistically cruel (see my discussion of Berlant in Chapter 2). Trans practices, lives, and experiences commonly appear in youth texts only if they assume the guise of the marginal, the nonhuman, or the Other—increasing worries regarding their use and place in the literature. These practices of representation are in no way exclusive to trans youth literatures. Edith Campbell, for instance, has highlighted the historical analogies established between ape and simian imagery and Black communities, which led to hundreds of years of people using this correlation to perpetuate racist and white supremacist thinking. Campbell provocatively interrogates the continued presence of anthropomorphized monkeys and the excessive use of simian imagery in children's literature, and how these images frequently reinforce the view of Black children "as unruly, angry or as a threat," consequently promoting the discipline and regulation of Black youth and their bodies (Campbell).

The fantastic and the nonhuman are malleable—they can be molded and shaped to comply with different political outlooks, ideologies, and narratives. Sometimes, the imagination congeals, and creates impressions that affect our bodies and that don't fade with the passage of time. The figure of the monkey and the use of simian imagery could summon a broader history of cultural damage, racial violence, and hurt when used. However, the text's context matters. Consider, for instance, Gene Luen Yang's graphic novel *American Born Chinese* (2006), which draws from 16th-Century Ming Dynasty imagery, practices, and narratives to mobilize a speculative exploration of identity and the pressures of assimilation in Chinese American contexts. The text heavily references a deity known as Sun Wukong, or the Monkey King, and anthropomorphized monkeys and simian imagery are found peppered throughout the text. Here, the figure of the monkey connects to different historical and sociocultural realities that aren't connected to the racist implementation of simian imagery in US historical contexts. This is precisely why context, historicization, and intersectional thinking is vital in not only creating youth literature, but in critiquing it as well.

These discourses are further complicated by critical work that highlights the connection between fantasy, marginalized identities and bodies, and the politics imbricated in the speculative. In her examinations of hopescapes in children's literature, S.R. Toliver highlights how representations of Black girls are often rooted in realism, thus limiting how these girls are and *could be* imagined in youth cultural productions. Toliver is critical of texts that attempt to represent Black girlhood through normative lenses that simply wedge Black girl experiences into realist narrative structures, and holds authors, critics, readers, teachers, publishers, and editors accountable for how the Black imagination has been limited and "stuck in a box perfectly outlined to specific proportions designated by" institutional, capitalist, and normative forces (19). Toliver pushes us to resist the lure of realism and presentism, and to instead consider the affective and political importance of "texts that move beyond 'what is' and 'what has been' to allow for texts that highlight 'what if' or 'what can be'" (19), especially when it comes to representations of marginalized lives and bodies. The political potentialities of the fantastic and the speculative can also be present in how we critically frame and interpret texts—and the lenses we bring in. This can be seen, for instance, in work that draws from queer and trans theory to examine mermaid imagery in classic children's fairy tales, and to highlight how these stories provide blueprints for trans being and becoming (see Spencer; Hurley); or in Sara Austin's research, which has highlighted how the motifs of monstrosity and the nonhuman have politically been used in youth literature to "include bodies and identity positions that have previously been left out" by the dominant culture (155). Just because a text departs from the rules, expectations, and logics of our world doesn't mean that we can't engage with a text thoughtfully, imaginatively, or politically.

Implemented creatively—and with a mind toward history and context—the fantastic can mobilize important and healing discussions on queer and trans life, not to mention that it can offer unprecedented ways of "engaging with the same core issues that can be found both in realist texts and the known world for many transgender teens" (Corbett, "There's More" 149). As E.E. Thomas further argues, the normativity and supposed universality attributed to the fantastic demands further scrutiny of how it's implemented in YA—especially in how the logic of the fantastic marks subjects as others through elements of spectacle and binary thinking (24–25). While there's indeed a fatigue that comes with trying to envision new worlds while living in one that's so broken, there's also so much potential and pleasure to be found in this process of foreseeing and imagining. In "articulating and enacting what previously might have been unimaginable, a movement offers a scene and future possibilities that surprise, entice, exhilarate, and electrify" (Fawaz 29). Let's think more expansively about the use of the fantastic in *When the Moon Was Ours* by further contextualizing the book within the tradition of magical realism, and by examining how the speculative is used to contest the deathly dimensions attached to trans life.

Anna-Marie McLemore, a nonbinary Latine author, draws from both queer and Latine storytelling and narrative conventions to mobilize a story focused on exploring how bodies, both young and old, are regulated by normative forces and practices. Its implementation of fantastic imagery—including glass pumpkins growing in fields, painful roses sprouting out of Miel's wrists, Brujeria, and references to the Latine-centered folk legends such as La Llorona—stands in contrast to its realist backdrop and situates the text within the tradition of the speculative. At its time of publication, *When the Moon Was Ours* was one of the few YA texts to depict trans life through the conventions of the fantastic, conventions that were in tension with those adopted in the "mostly realist first wave of trans YA fiction" (see Sandercock, Chapter 4). More specifically, *When the Moon Was Ours* meshes with magical realism's narrative and political expectations, drawing from Indigenous and pre-colonial knowledge and combining realist and fantastic storytelling conventions. The genre has significantly impacted literary production globally, leading critics to claim that it has "modified realism to such an extent that it is no longer what it was" (Faris 116). Although it started off as a countercultural form of storytelling, the merger between the real and the fantastic is now used by authors with different and sometimes opposing political inclinations and sensibilities (Faris 116). In surprising ways, however, queer YA can channel the critical ethos of this literary tradition and tap into the genre's countercultural bent.

Through the combination of realist and speculative elements, magical realist YA novels invite readers to "question and destabilize the values and assumptions of the dominant, i.e., adult, society" (Latham 60), thus showing how YA magical realism is aligned with queer frameworks in its effort to destabilize hierarchies of power. This makes YA magical realism particularly ironic, as it often focuses on critiquing the powers that generate YA literature. But this irony presents a unique opportunity to explore the dialectic relationship between pain and healing and between reality and the imagination. McLemore's nuanced destabilization of the boundaries between the fantastic and the "real"—especially as they are connected to trans youth representation—mobilize significant counternarratives regarding trans youth in YA culture and beyond. Christine N. Stamper and Mary Catherine Miller highlight this critical tendency in their examination of the novel and claim that magical realism, "often characterized by fluidity, intangibility, and the abstract," provides the means to examine and explore "gender and sexuality, which are similarly fluid and intangible" (172). Aracely's transformation, to some extent, also highlights the constructed character of categories of age and development, thus inviting audiences to think of how trans youth and trans adulthood are akin to each other, as Gubar might phrase it. By inhabiting a body that transitions in gender *and* age, characters such as Aracely highlight and interrogate what Gabrielle Owen calls "the performative functions of categories of age," categories that obstruct the recognition of youth as beings with complex lives that "are as various in personality, feelings, and needs as adults" (20). The magic in this novel is not meant to obscure the realities of our world but instead, focus our attention on them.

Nonetheless, we can already anticipate suspicion creeping in when focusing on the fantastic elements that saturate Aracely's transformation in the novel. We don't inhabit a world where water can transform our bodies to reflect our inner feelings and desires or help us transgress the limitations imposed by constructed identity categories. Here, there might even be a tendency to invoke how the use of the speculative overshadows the genuine issues that trans youth and adults face today—especially since Aracely's transformation is tied to discourses of death. Here, we must first acknowledge that both academic and popular discourses tend to overemphasize trans death to validate the existence and legitimacy of trans folk, a tendency that only attributes value to trans life by instrumentalizing loss: "it is in their death that poor and sex working trans people of color are invited back in; it is in death that they suddenly come to matter" (Snorton and Haritaworn 74). From this perspective, McLemore's narrative representation of Aracely through the conventions of magical realism contests these necropolitics in vital ways. By refusing to let Aracely die as she tries to save her younger sister—and by converting what should've been a moment of death into a moment of bodily transformation—*When the Moon Was Ours* presents us with a character imbued with life and whose meaning extends beyond the deathly act of jumping into a river. We must also recall that YA novels often reinscribe the notion that queerness "is fundamentally incompatible with adulthood" (Browne 16), which makes Aracely's transition into womanhood and adulthood mold breaking within the context of trans YA representation.

McLemore is self-aware about the politics of death in trans representation, as made clear not only in their representation of Aracely's transition but also by further channeling magical realism's ability to exploit the seams between the queer imagination and real-world concerns regarding trans livability and survival. McLemore's YA novel directly addresses the suspicions that could be raised regarding Aracely's transformation by contrasting it with the trans trajectory of Samir—Miel's love interest, the novel's other protagonist, and a teen who is connected to non-Western gender practices. Unlike Aracely, Samir is a character grounded in realism. The book emphasizes how the magical doesn't assist him in transforming or altering his body, and he relies on practices such as chest binding to be more comfortable with how he presents himself to the world. Samir is also bacha posh—a term that loosely translates to "dressed as a boy" in Dari Persian—which refers to a cultural practice that takes place in countries such as Afghanistan and Pakistan where girls are socially, culturally, and politically raised as boys to "either enable mobility or overcome the lack of a boy child in the household" (Corboz et al. 597). This practice is meant to be ephemeral, however, in that once "girls raised as boys reach puberty, they are usually 'converted' back into girls," which presents a dilemma since they come to understand the affordances of freedom and mobility "only to have this freedom restricted when being required to re-adopt a feminine identity" and sometimes prepare for marriage soon after (Corboz et al. 587). Unnati Jain has highlighted how the figure of the bacha posh exposes the inconsistencies present in how gender is framed in some Middle Eastern contexts, for these people "experience greater freedom and opportunities" by temporarily inhabiting this role, all while reinforcing traditional views towards femininity and domesticity (Jain 144). While the bacha posh cultural practice is usually imposed on young girls to uphold patriarchal ideologies and practices, Samir, who is partially of Pakistani descent, willingly embodies the role of the bacha posh to expand the contours of his gender identity while not renouncing his history or his cultural attachments. A narrative of restriction and oppression is reconfigured into one of potentiality.

This willing attachment to what is often deemed a normative gender practice in Pakistani and Afghan culture rewrites the story and flips the script. Rather than being projected as an identity that is ephemeral and violently imposed on the body, Samir instead approaches the bacha posh practice reparatively and uses it as a way to sustain him emotionally and physically in a world that doesn't provide the language or frameworks to understand his experiences. For instance, when Samir's grandmother first informed him about the bacha posh practice, "he felt a clawing envy as strong as if he knew these girls by name" (McLemore 36). After his grandmother's death, he assumes the identity of a bacha posh, understanding how this way of living is meant to "expire" once he comes of age—and much of the novel focuses on the agony that he feels as this anticipated embodiment of womanhood approaches. While there have been real-world documented cases of bacha posh refuting the expectation to become a woman during puberty and "enjoy mobility and opportunities for their entire life" (Jain 141–142), Samir is unaware of how people who have partaken in the practice have refuted the developmental and narrative trajectories imposed upon them. Despite its ephemerality and root in patriarchal ideologies, Samir views the bacha posh practice as one that allows him to further explore and negotiate his place in the world without having to label his thoughts or feelings according to Western identity labels and practices. This practice gives him the space and time to explore his body and emotions, even though everyone around him pushes him to align with binary modes of gender identity.

Aracely's alignment with magical, fantastic forms of representation is constantly pressured by Samir's inability to tap into this magic himself—presenting us with a case in which a speculative imagining of trans life clashes with a representation grounded on real-world concerns and practices. The novel constantly shows how Samir has to negotiate his identity—and how he goes through hurt and pain that Aracely didn't experience due to the fantastic nature of her transformation. During a moment of crisis in the novel, Samir stands in front of a river and prepares to jump in, hoping that "it would do to him what it had done to Aracely," and if not, that the river "would have enough mercy to just take him under and turn him into the water" (McLemore 131). It's here that both the deathly resonances and necropolitics attached to trans life come into play, not to mention that this narrative event harkens back to the crisis of queer and trans teen suicide that I explored with more depth in Chapter 1. Samir jumps into the water and starts to drown, all while desperately hoping for the transformation the water bestows to Aracely. This transformation never occurs. Samir's body remains the same, and he doesn't drown because Miel rescues him before he loses consciousness.

This failure to transform through the river's magic is at the heart of this novel's central critique. Through this event, the novel inserts itself into discourse regarding the potentialities and limitations of the fantastic in youth literature, as mobilized through the figures of Samir and Aracely. While Aracely facilitates the exploration of discourses that facilitate an enchanting representation of trans life imbued with magic and possibility, this imagining is always foiled by Samir's inability to access the possibilities of the fantastic. Even more so, the contrast between these two characters allows readers to encounter different models and representations of gender variance. Here, the mixture between the fantastic and the real is precisely the point and emphasizes the critical bent of magical realism. Through the merger of realist and fantastic discourses, the novel pushes us to witness the realities that haunt trans life without limiting the representation of these characters to these realities. This narrative merger simultaneously highlights the material disadvantages that trans youth may face today, while not diminishing the political, aesthetic, and imaginative potentialities of the fantastic and speculative.

This political and countercultural bent to the representative politics of queer YA can perhaps best be seen in the novel's ending. Here, Samir leaves behind the cultural practice of bacha posh and goes on to embody gender practices that defy normative narratives present in trans YA, where fulfillment is only achieved once the body is fully transformed. As Samir approaches Miel for an intimate encounter, he shows up in her room with no chest binder on, letting Miel see "more of the shape of him than he'd ever let her see" (McLemore 266). Through this moment of intimacy, through this removal of the chest binder, Samir realizes that "there was a story told not just in the contours of his chest and what he had or did not have pressing against the seam of his jeans" (McLemore 266). At this moment, Samir defies categories of language. In a sense, this ending harkens back to Jules Gill-Peterson's observation that trans children have identified "livable ways to grow up as trans children without needing" concrete and definitive categories and without aligning themselves to the normative medical discourses present in Western contexts (92–93). It shows a negotiation of being and becoming that simultaneously looks back and forward and that refutes the normative, neoliberal pathways often celebrated in queer YA criticism. The narrative draws parallels between histories of hurt and future imaginings; it makes trans youth and adults akin to one another and uses the imagination to expand, rather than limit, understandings of what it means to be trans. Even Aracely's transformation, which is speculative and magical in nature, connects to pain and hurt in some way: "Maybe I got all of me all at once, but I lost everything else. Don't you dare think there's any water in the world that makes that easy" (McLemore 155). After all, Aracely became an adult woman but lost time and experience in the process—a whole part of her life was entirely skipped through the water's transformation of her body.

When the Moon Was Ours draws from both realist and speculative traditions to shape a trans narrative that celebrates the joys of the imagination without diminishing the historical role of pain and hurt in nonnormative forms of storytelling. It positions itself in the spaces between reality and the imagination to show how inextricable they are from each other. They both signal different ways of feeling about—and dreaming about— our bodies, our place in the world, and the lengths we must go to seek fulfillment. As can be seen through Samir's attempt to jump into the river in search of either transformation or death, *When the Moon Was Ours* attaches itself to discourses on queer teen suicide and trans necropolitics but manipulates the possibilities of genre and aesthetics to imagine different outcomes and pathways for trans life in YA. It does so not by fulfilling the deathly narrative pathway attached to trans and queer representation but by not allowing the narrative to ever come to fruition. The deathly narrative doesn't culminate in death. These trans characters, even when opting to embrace death because of normative pressures, don't succumb to these powers and are offered opportunities to live on their own terms.

When the Moon Was Ours, in many ways, builds upon and transforms how death is handled in trans YA and challenges the expectations of queer-centered grief novels in that it looks both within and *beyond* mortality to "find opportunities for community and self-understanding" that help us to survive in the world (Browne 18). Life becomes bearable and survivable even within the context of death itself.

In the study of queerness and video games, *permalife* is a notion used to describe rules and mechanics in which video games allow players to bypass the logic of death normatively elevated in video game culture. In *Video Games Have Always Been Queer*, Bo Ruberg approaches permalife as a game logic where "players are forced to go living on indefinitely—even, or perhaps especially, in the face of death" (160). This concept was developed in contrast to the notion of *permadeath* celebrated in normative game cultures, in which a character that dies in the fictive world of the game can no longer participate in the game's narrative. Simply put, if the character dies in the digital world, the character also experiences a digital death that prevents players from engaging with them. Suppose you were playing a round of *Super Mario Bros.*, and you fell into a pit in the game. If this game were designed with permadeath mechanics, once you fall into the pit, you would no longer be able to play as Mario and instead would have to use another character entirely or start the whole game over again. Ruberg critiques how life and death are handled in neoliberal representations of queer life and calls attention to "the oppressions of hegemonic culture at the precarious line between life and death, always struggling forward, compelled to go on by narratives of progress" (Ruberg 171). Narratives of progress always dictate an order in which milestones should be accomplished, and even more so, they elevate certain narratives at the expense of history, hurt, and pain. They glorify traditional models and pathways towards success—pathways often in disservice to minoritarian subjects. Permalife highlights a queer and hopeful vision of the future through the processes of "micro-world building" (Ruberg 169), constructing fictional worlds that do not reject deathly discourses but rather transform them.

Although the concept of permalife arises mainly from video game studies, I nonetheless find it helpful in examining the politics of life and death in queer YA productions, especially in terms of how they navigate the relationship between hope and despair and between reality and the imagination. In a sense, McLemore's novel metaphorically bestows a sense of permalife to its trans characters, in that they are allowed to continue living, growing, being, and becoming, *especially* "in the face of death" (Ruberg 160). Through the power of language and aesthetic representation, McLemore usurps narratives of death present in trans and YA contexts to challenge the deathly trajectories present in these stories, presenting us with cases in which trans characters can, in a sense, "live indefinitely"

(Ruberg 160). In doing so, McLemore's novel honors queer YA's foundations of negativity while also carving out space for hope, for anticipation, for envisioning a world different from the here and now. Samir and Miel "would both become what they could not yet imagine, and that they would still be what they once were" (McLemore 270). Products of both a past that has occurred and a future that has yet to arise, the novel's attachment to permalife allows us to acknowledge how fiction can look beyond the parameters of the real to reimagine different prospects for futurism, living, and imagining.

I'm interested in further expanding this discourse on permalife and applying it more expansively to the study of queer youth culture. Part of what makes this concept so pertinent for this discussion is the concept's fixation on notions of hope *and* despair, how it integrates the notions of livability centralized in this project, and further expands on the possibilities of the fantastic in addressing, channeling, honoring, and transforming the role of death in queer narratives. To accomplish this, I'll return to the video game roots of the concept of permalife and examine how its logics operate in Supergiant's 2020 independent game *Hades*—a narratively heavy action video game where queerness is integral to the game's plot and structure. I intend to not only further flesh out the concept of permalife by examining this game, but to also signal how video games can contribute to our understanding of queer YA culture and its emotional politics. I then return to YA literature once again through an examination of Patrick Ness' YA novel, *More Than This*, which concentrates on deathly themes similar to those raised in *When the Moon Was Ours* and focuses specifically on the topic of queer teen suicide through a speculative lens. Through this exploration, I hope to further mobilize conversations on the role of mortality in queer YA in light of the normative critical tendencies that haunt queer YA culture.

"Life and Death, One and the Same"

There are apparent differences between video games and novels, especially regarding their rules, conventions, methods of disseminating knowledge, and interaction. But here, I'm less interested in parsing out further differences between the two and instead, more interested in thinking about the narrative and affective connections that they share in handling death in queer and trans cultural productions. In addition to focusing on queerness as a method of normative disruption and reconfiguration, I'm interested in the worldbuilding capabilities of queerness and its ability to create alternative ways of dwelling, living, and desiring, and how it accomplishes this by centering, rather than sidelining, the ties between queerness and death. *Hades* is a text that I want to bring in to further flesh out how permalife operates within video games spaces as both an embrace and refusal of queer necropolitics. Similar to *When the Moon Was* Ours, Hades reconfigures the deathly narratives imposed on the queer subject by tapping into the queer potentialities of the fantastic. In *Hades*, no matter how often you fail to accomplish your objective and how much bodily destruction the protagonist experiences—he simply can't die.

In this roguelike video game, you control the character Zagreus, the immortal, queer, and polyamorous son of Hades, the Greek god of the underworld. Roguelike broadly describes a subgenre of video games "known for procedurally generated levels… items bearing randomly assigned properties, and irreversible death" (Craddock 1–2). Your primary objective in the game is to fight through different levels of Hades' domain to escape to the surface and contact Zagreus' mother, Persephone, who resides in an ethereal space between the Underworld and Mount Olympus. With the aid of powers and abilities granted by the gods of Olympus, you help Zagreus in his efforts to hack and slash his way through the underworld and forge relationships with various denizens that reside within the Palace of Hades and the underworld. From a narrative perspective, *Hades* is fascinating because the story is incredibly contextual and sensitive to player input and control. For instance, other characters in the fictive world will remind you of moments of failure you encountered in the game. You're given the opportunity to romance a man, a woman, both, or neither within the context of the game's story, and the narrative gives players choices as to what forms of kinship to pursue during play (see Figure 4.1). Characters both celebrate and mock you for your achievements, and the game constantly remarks on how characters in this universe don't need to abide by the laws of desire, attraction, and relationality constructed by humans. Notably, *Hades* is the first video game to receive a Hugo Award, an accolade given yearly to outstanding works in speculative fiction.

Part of what makes *Hades* so compelling from a queer viewpoint is its spatiality and the fact that the underworld is designed as a site of containment that punishes anyone who tries to escape—an ever-changing, ever-shifting prison of sorts.[1] With each round of play in this roguelike game, players assist Zagreus in a literal upward battle to escape the hegemonic confines of his household and literally climb out of the depths of hell to reach the surface. These escape attempts, however, are complicated not only through the sheer difficulty of the game—in which Hades' minions desperately try to overwhelm you, destroy you, and prevent you from escaping—but even more so through the game's spatial mechanics. Whenever the player is destroyed by an enemy and experiences a dreaded "game over," Zagreus returns to his father's home in the furthest depths of the underworld, where he must once again escape the building and begin the ascent toward the outside world.

Figure 4.1 Queerness is explicitly part of *Hades*' narrative structure, and players are free to explore different structures of kinship, romance, and sexuality. Here, we see Zagreus conversing with Aphrodite about his potential escape from the Underworld, and witness how she deviates from normative understandings of sexuality and relationality (*Hades*, original gameplay screen capture).

Further complicating this attempt to escape, the game implements a procedural algorithm that reconfigures the structure of Hades' domain with each escape attempt: rooms constantly shift in shape, size, and order every time the player loses a round, thus resisting player attempts at mastering the layout of the underworld and engaging with the game linearly. As the narrator discloses early in the game, "Composed of such innumerable ever-shifting interlocking chambers, the Underworld of Lord Hades all but guarantees the dead shall there remain until the end of time" (*Hades*). Critic Whitney Pow highlights the ability of video games to reproduce how spaces *feel* like to a queer subject, in that they "centralize experiences and affects that exist at the periphery in mainstream game scholarship: the experience of *inability*, of being unable to move freely, to make choices that matter, of the constant and unavoidable experience of failure" (45). While from a representative standpoint, Zagreus embodies queerness and pansexuality through his desires and kinship practices, it's precisely the feeling of containment and disorientation that highlights the game's queer and affective significance. The game's structure resists the player's desire to memorize, control, and understand it. You're forced to navigate the gameworld of *Hades* with no potential map, pathway, or blueprint—echoing how many queer folks are forced to power through a confusing world that's not designed for us, that prevents us from escape. The spatiality of the video game and of the underworld itself makes such an escape utterly impossible, thus emphasizing the feelings that have historically been attached to queer life and narrativizations.

In some regards, *Hades* is an exercise in futility and impossibility—irrespective of how many times the player attempts to escape the House of Hades and the domain of the underworld, they find themselves reiteratively failing to remain dwelling on the surface. When and if the player eventually reaches the surface after potential hours of gameplay, they find out that Zagreus can't survive in the world of the living due to his godly ties to the space of the underworld. Thus, the game presents us with a space, and more specifically, a home from which there is no respite, meant to imprison and literally contain Zagreus and control both his body and his mobility. *Hades'* framing of Zagreus' home as a site of oppression mirrors how homes are commonly represented in Western queer narratives, framed as spaces that can't accommodate the bodies, feelings, or desires of people that deviate from normative expectations. Gregory Woods has suggested that queer characters, especially in classic coming out narratives, often develop a sense of selfhood and explore their queerness only when departing from the confines of the home, a space that frequently serves as a hub for "parental power and its related instruments of discipline" (346). The game's implementation of spatiality and the normative foundations of the home seem overwhelming and deterministic from both a narrative and gameplay perspective. The domain of Hades is most definitely attached to parental power, seeing as Zagreus' father purposely designs and shifts the underworld to prevent his son's escape and stop him from meeting his estranged mother. In countless ways, we can interrogate the queer ethics and perverse pleasures of engaging in a game in which we assume the positionality of an overtly queer character who is unable to escape from the clutches of his father and home. We're forced to spend our time finding ways to carve out space in an unpredictable and ever-changing environment and failing to do so. As Hades and the "game over" screen repeatedly remind both Zagreus and the player every time they fail to reach the surface, "There is no escape" (*Hades*).

From a suspicious perspective, the queer implications of this entrapment become even more layered when thinking about its stakes vis-à-vis the frameworks of negativity and unhappiness that frequently mark queer experience. After all, what do we make of the fact that gameplay is designed as a Sisyphean struggle in which escape and relief are impossible for a queer subject? What are the implications of a queer character being trapped in a home that refuses to provide him with comforts (queer or otherwise), where he's always under the watchful gaze of his father, and where space itself twists to prevent the mapping of alternative pathways and routes of escape? Zagreus' father reinforces this sense of containment, constantly questioning Zagreus'—and, by extension—the player's motives behind engaging in this endless cycle: "Why? Why do you keep showing up? Despite knowing that the outcome shall be just the same as how it always was?" (*Hades*). From a temporal perspective, notions of cyclicity go hand in hand with notions of sequence and linearity that reinforce the very heteronormative logics that push us to organize our thoughts and actions according to the demands of normativity. As Elizabeth Freeman has compellingly argued, "the idea of time as cyclical stabilizes its forward movement, promising renewal rather than rupture" (6), and in *Hades*, the very cyclicity that structures the game's chronotope prevents the same break from the home that Zagreus craves and needs. However, Zagreus' immortality allows him to think differently about time, teleology, and kinship, for he's not restricted by the same limitations that our bodies and minds face (see Figure 4.2).

Through its spatial and temporal frameworks and atmosphere, *Hades* responds compellingly to the necropolitical dimensions often found within queer narrativizations, especially given the prominence of deathly discourse in queer fiction published throughout the 20th Century. As I explored in earlier chapters of this volume, some of the first representations

Figure 4.2 During a discussion with Thanatos, the god of Death, regarding the nature of their relationship, Zagreus highlights how the underworld operates under different structures, rules, and norms regarding time, highlighting how relationships in this fictive universe are not reliant on the chrononormative logics present in real world, capitalist contexts. Zagreus does not see the need or rush to align his relationship with normative pressures, expectations, and timelines, for he has an infinite amount of time ahead (*Hades*, original gameplay screen capture).

On Mortality and Permalife   103

of queerness approached nonnormative expressions of gender and sexuality as limiting, and critics such as Jenkins and Cart have argued that queer texts, especially those crafted for teen audiences, often characterized queer folk as "lost souls doomed to either premature death or the solitary life of exile at the margins of society" (xii). To make matters even more pressing from a media and literary representation perspective, in the last century, we've seen a drastic rise in the "Bury Your Gays" trope present in texts with queer couples and pairs, in which "one of the lovers must die or otherwise be destroyed by the end of the story" and typically occurs moments after queerness is made overt to an audience (Hulan 17). Through its structure and ludic frameworks, *Hades* seems to replicate the doom-ridden, capitalist cycles of repetition and (re)production that limit the possibilities of queer life (see Halberstam, *The Queer Art*), and it puts the player in a position where death is inextricable from the feelings and experiences projected through the game's narrative and mechanics. We witness and, to some extent, embody a queer character dying repeatedly in his efforts to escape the confines of a repressive regime. We further see how Zagreus' familial and blood ties ultimately keep him tethered to the space of the underworld—which pressures queerness' tendency to look beyond blood ties and genetic bonds when assessing kinship, dwelling, and belonging. Zagreus' blood and lineage keep him attached to a space meant to confine and control his body, reinforcing temporal narratives that enforce ties between blood, genetics, trauma, and discipline (Freeman 46–47). Even when players successfully manage to escape to the surface, Zagreus' blood ultimately betrays him, and he's dragged back to the depths of his father's domain.

Hades' implementation of spatiality may seem potentially antiqueer in its scope. But at the same time, it puts us in a position where we not only consume but deeply interact with a queer life, and in the process, potentially question the forms of containment, oppression, and mortality used to frame queer practices. Ian Bogost reminds us that video games are "models for real and imagined systems" that encourage players to "explore the possibility space of a set of rules" and to consider "how social or cultural systems work in the world—or how they could work, or don't work" (136). In a sense, it's an exercise that pushes us to think broadly about how fictional worlds are built and (de)constructed and how similar strategies are present in real-world queer thought and practices. Mia Consalvo further approaches video game engagement as a moment of liminality where normative beliefs and aspirations can be highlighted and possibly challenged: "As the rules of real life are temporarily lifted, so are social expectations, at least for some players." *Hades*, through play, invites us to interact and shape a queer narrative that makes us aware of the normative logics that we attach to spaces and narratives and, even more important, the relationship that exists between the deathly dimensions of videogames and the handling of mortality in queer YA literature.

Perhaps one of the most essential rules temporarily lifted during gameplay is the finiteness and role of death itself. Like death is framed as a narrative impossibility for Aracely and Samir in *When the Moon Was Ours*, *Hades* approaches death as a narrative and gameplay impossibility. Here, I return once again to Bo Ruberg's concept of permalife, which was developed in response and in hopeful opposition to the hypermasculine concept of "permadeath" present in some contemporary video games. Roguelike games such as *Hades* are notorious for using permadeath to push players to develop expertise at playing the game and to elevate the difficulty and stakes of gameplay. Games situated around the gameplay mechanic of permadeath expect a degree of skill and perfection. If you haven't mastered the game rules and mechanics, the game punishes you and forces the player to engage with the narrative from the beginning. As John Harris puts it, permadeath is a game mechanic designed for the "player to catastrophically fail, losing the game, without recourse to continuing play other than starting over."

Presented as a counternarrative and countermechanic of sorts to the norms of permadeath, Ruberg uses the term permalife to describe games that make it impossible for characters to die, in that "players are forced to go on living indefinitely" (Ruberg 160). Permadeath is not designed to be an enjoyable or "feel good" experience given its fixation on normative gameplay and punishment; and instead, it's a "moving, eudaimonic experience, especially when players are attached to their characters" (McKay et al. 194). Drawing from Judith Butler's work on grief and state violence, Sara Ahmed talks about how dead subjects are still able to leave impressions on the living through memories—impressions that we keep alive and active through our living thoughts and practices. By allowing the memory of the dead to mark us—especially when these memories are tethered to histories of oppression, sadness, and violence—we "keep their impressions alive in the midst of their death" (Ahmed, *Cultural Politics*, 434). *Hades* becomes increasingly compelling in light of narratives of queer memory and grief in that its protagonist can never indeed die. Zagreus' pain is centered not on the fear of death but rather on the fear of containment and the fear of *not knowing*. Players aren't given a chance to grieve the loss induced by death; instead, death frames itself as an opportunity to begin the narrative once again, but this time, with different structures, knowledges, and outcomes on the horizon. Not to mention that this mechanical and narrative rendering of death also challenges the affective dimensions of roguelike games, which typically consist of creating "a tense, unforgiving atmosphere" through the implementation of mechanics of permadeath and narratives of loss (Andiloro 566).

On Mortality and Permalife 105

In previous chapters, I've discussed the importance of queer YA in pushing readers to engage in the act of witness or testimony to better understand the connections between the "bad" past and the "better" present, and to effectively visualize a multiplicity of future possibilities and outcomes. Because of *Hades*' interactive structure as a video game, we're given a chance to not only explore the relationship between narratives of mortality and queer forms of storytelling but, to some extent, *embody* it. With every press of a button or click of a key, we integrate and project our own thoughts and moods into the avatar observed on the screen. Through play, we perform and narrativize Zagreus' queer journey through a queer space framed by an even queerer sense of time. Through this embodiment and performance, we generate "a modality of knowing and recognition among audiences and groups that facilitates modes of belonging, especially minoritarian belonging" (Muñoz, *Cruising Utopia* 99). We're given a chance to participate and make decisions—to generate pathways—that are connected to both queer and negative affective modalities.

These notions of interaction, play, and embodiment have significant ramifications for how we understand *Hades*' implementation of space and queer narrative, and it pushes us to experience—and potentially interrogate—the implications of allowing a queer character to bypass the teleology of death altogether. These issues become even more charged when considering how the video game gamifies the struggle of a character who can never escape a home space that is designed to contain him. On this surface, the literal warmth and light of the sun greet him on the horizon (see Figure 4.3). But this light, this horizon, is ephemeral and always out of reach. In many ways, and despite the game's speculative and fantastic framing, *Hades*' implementation of permalife mechanics, in combination with its unstable and ever-changing spaces, emulate the realities that many queer players and subjects experience, especially since "they have been positioned permanently by the oppressions of hegemonic culture at the precarious line between life and death" (Ruberg 171). Through control of Zagreus' avatar and by reiteratively trying to escape the depths of hell with and through his focalization, players are interpolated between the forces of life and death. They're invited to explore (and perhaps even question) what mobility, progress, and success mean when utopia and freedom are impossible. They're invited to see the glow of the rising sun, the illumination of "another time and place that is simultaneously not yet here but able to be glimpsed in our horizon" (Muñoz, *Cruising Utopia* 183). Along with Zagreus, we move and dwell in service of a future that can never be touched.

Video games always, albeit not consciously, communicate a political and social meaning that extends beyond the game's parameters, a meaning that has the potential to create what Ahmed would call an "impression"

Figure 4.3 If Zagreus manages to escape the underworld, he encounters a sunrise for the first time. Given that Zagreus' body can't survive the outside world, this horizon is perpetually out of reach. He can still see and feel glimpses of it, and he continues trying to reach it (*Hades*, original gameplay screen capture).

on players. Indeed, while the desire for progress completion, mastery, and entertainment might fuel a player's decision to play the game repeatedly despite the presence of any sense of resolution, this reiterative play ultimately imbues a queer character with life that persists and continues marching forward in the face of violence, oppression, and impossibility. It also pushes us to view what failure means within the context of this queer world—primarily when mortality is normatively implemented as a form of punishing the player for performing "poorly." This connects to broader conversations mobilized by critics such as Halberstam, Ruberg, and Mason regarding the queer potentialities of failure in video game play and design and how such failures assist us in "shoring up structures that privilege narrative and sexual teleology" (Mason 85). What makes *Hades* compelling from this viewpoint is not only its capacity to dismantle teleology but, even more so, to challenge broader and normative applications of death and despair in queer narratives. Through reiterative play, we may realize that the goal of *Hades* is not to escape the underworld but rather to connect with other characters and forge relationships with non-playable characters that transcend the limits of space, time, and death. The game becomes less about escape and more about forming connections and coalitions that transcend barriers of identity and even species. The game's greatest pleasures aren't found in the hypermasculine attempt to violently escape from the house of Hades, but rather, in getting to know and develop intimacies with the various underworld denizens. As a matter of fact, the game cheekily states that the social and narrative elements of the game are more difficult than its brutal gameplay elements (see Figure 4.4).

Hades doesn't entirely sever the ties between notions of death and queer narrativizations, but it stops death from becoming a finalizing and totalizing narrative that both marks and forecloses the survival of queer lives within oppressive regimes. I'll admit that the implementation of permalife mechanics in the game could be an attempt to address the notion of loss aversion central in the design of video games, where designers consider ways to ensure that games don't induce a sense of anxiety or disdain through their mechanics and rules (Engelstein 112–113). Dying in a video game doesn't *feel* good, and permalife, in many ways, undercuts this bad feeling, this anxiety. Notwithstanding, *Hades*' content and queer design logics overload this mechanic and inevitably tie back to the necropolitical negotiations that take place in our readings of queer (YA) texts. Art critic Jean-Ulrick Désert has suggested that queer spaces are often generated through "wishful thinking or desires that become solidified: a seduction of the reading space where queerness, at a few brief points and for some fleeting moments, dominates the (heterocentric) norm, the dominant social narrative of the landscape" (21).[2] *Hades* taps into this wishful thinking and offers players an interactive virtual location, a temporary dwelling, where narratives of death are intimately tied to queer storytelling and where queerness eclipses the heteronormative impulse that saturates video game design and culture.

Figure 4.4 Zagreus shares how disclosing his feelings to Thanatos is more difficult than eliminating his father's forces in the Underworld (*Hades*, original gameplay screen capture).

The structure and organization of this video game convey an atmosphere that connects us to broader queer histories and affective legacies. Through play, we're immersed in this atmosphere, "eliciting in us a wholistic complex of emotions, feelings, and embodied sensations," attuning us to the "looking-moving-feeling" in ways that help us recognize genres and a text's connection to other cultural productions (Andiloro 562).

What I find so compelling about *Hades* is precisely its implementation of queerness from a representation *and* design perspective, and how it combines gameplay and adaptive storytelling to create a very queer atmosphere designed to be decoded and *felt*. The game invites readers to reiteratively inhabit a virtual space in which they temporarily become one with a queer character whose story can't be foreclosed by death. Death is subverted and rendered not as a point of failure or a conclusion to Zagreus' story but as a simple roadblock in his never-ending journey to reach the surface, find his mother, and connect with the underworld's denizens. While Zagreus can't escape hell, he's able to forge stronger bonds with other characters in each playthrough, and there are even opportunities for him to mend his troubled relationship with his father. The queer space of *Hades* is absolutely imbued with wishful thinking that is characteristic in the design of queer spaces, but there's something to be said about the joys and pleasures of engaging with a queer character who can't be buried despite perpetually experiencing death. For a fleeting moment, we're given the chance to queerly live, and live, and live again in the face of death—a notion that has significant implications and stakes for a homonormative culture and space that constantly tries to remove death altogether from queer YA culture and criticism.

Once again, we must acknowledge that the queer spaces, mechanics, and relationships present in this game are indeed only possible through the structures, tropes, and narratives present in the speculative and fantastic. Whereas the game stages different ways of approaching life and death in a queer context, players in the real world don't always have the privilege of framing their own queerness through the optics of life, much less permalife. But such a fixation on realism, especially given the constructed nature of narratives of realism and authenticity, short-circuits attempts to interrogate the promises of the speculative and to identify how and why it pushes us to feel beyond the parameters of the here and now. As video game critic Adrienne Shaw has argued, realism can be tyrannical in that

> it forces game makers and critics alike to focus too much on questions of accuracy rather than emancipatory possibility [...] If we can only imagine new ways of viewing what has been, we never get a chance to imagine what might be.

(21)

Hades pushes us to ask, "what if," and in that process of questioning, turns wishful thinking into a queer space that can be inhabited momentarily—a digital, virtual space in which livability, not death, becomes the defining element that drives the game's queerness. What makes games such as *Hades* different from most youth texts is the game's interactive quality and ability to channel player choice and input to facilitate underexplored ways of dwelling and feeling.

More Than a Character

I've focused significant attention on how video games push us to embody experiences and feelings of mortality in queer YA culture, but I don't want to normatively argue that video games are more effective in how they narrativize and frame queerness due to their interactive qualities. While the theoretical applications of permalife are useful in examining how mortality is structured and gamified in video game culture, similar logics can be traced in how queer experiences are structured in prose fiction. At the beginning of this discussion, I demonstrated how McLemore's *When the Moon Was Ours* breathes life into its trans characters when they approximate death—challenging the deathly dimensions that haunt trans representation in YA culture and beyond. Trans characters can't face death in this narrative even when they aspire to do so. I want to close this chapter by examining a YA novel that harkens to the logic of permalife through its narrative structure, organization, and reparative aims.

Many of the texts explored in this book deliberately challenge the normative trajectories of growth, development, and fulfillment that we've come to expect from YA narratives. Levithan's *Two Boys Kissing*, which I discussed in a previous chapter, begins with death instead of ending with it, as seen through its narrative framing using the voices and collective thoughts of people who died of AIDS-related complications during the peak of the epidemic. *More Happy Than Not* shows the past rupturing in the present, and how the past is sometimes concealed to enable normative pathways toward happiness. Past and present merge in queer and unexpected ways. *Mosquita y Mari* shows us an anti-coming of age trajectory that twists and turns and never reaches fulfillment—ending in ambiguity and refuting the uplift expected by normative audiences. Here, we can notice how many of these texts share commonalities in how they represent time, and how they disrupt normative and linear narratives of growth and desire.

Jodie Taylor, for instance, points out that heteronormative temporality functions "under the assumption that a life course is (or should respectably be) conducted in a linear, sequential progression—that is, birth, childhood, adolescence, early adulthood, marriage, reproduction, child-rearing, retirement, old age, death and kinship inheritance" (894).

Historically, queer individuals have been excluded from this linear pathway, whether due to the inability of queer couples to biologically reproduce or due to their exclusion from social institutions such as marriage and adoption. Unsurprisingly, literary works that contain disruptive queer content often implement narrative structures that are purposely non-linear and that challenge the expectations of heteronormative sequential progression. Although *When the Moon Was Ours* is a YA novel and *Hades* is an action role-playing narrative video game, both offer a speculative take on the cycle of life and death that dismantles the deathly teleologies and normative understandings of time often overloaded onto YA narratives. While death and despair are very much the framing devices implemented in these texts—they don't shy away from mortality whatsoever—both apply a queer attitude towards dwelling and existing that allows them to carve a sense of queer futurism in seemingly futureless spaces. Aracely and Sam find different pathways to becoming that disobey the laws, expectations, and realities imposed on their bodies. Zagreus manages to create networks of connection and feeling in the *underworld*, of all places.

Of all the texts explored in this volume, Patrick Ness' *More Than This* takes perhaps the most drastic approach towards inverting the teleology of queer narratives in that the novel begins with its main character—a gay teen who goes by the name of Seth Wearing—drowning himself in the violent, cold waters of a Washington State beach. The first sentence of the novel's prologue opens with the line "Here is the boy, drowning" (Ness 1), and Seth's death is then described in visceral and excruciating detail. As he jumps into water, a wave crashes his body against the wall and fractures his skull and spinal chord, "an injury from which there is no return, no recovery. No chance. He dies" (Ness 3). The clinical description of Seth's death resembles the distant, objective, and precise character of a coroner's report, with the exception being that his death is described in present rather than past tense. But more than being clinical, the introduction to Ness' novel obliterates all hope that Seth will survive the ocean's grasp. This pessimistic opening becomes even more distressing when considering that Seth regrets his decision soon after he immerses his body into the water. The "gasping horror of knowing" that he's undoubtedly going to die causes Seth to panic and attempt to resist the waves (2). He tries to survive. The novel opens with Seth's death and reverses the trajectory of development commonly found in YA fiction. Rather than introducing us to a boy preparing to cross the threshold into adulthood, the narrative presents us with a boy who never fully engages with this developmental process—whose story literally begins at the moment of his death.

Ness' *More Than This*, like David Levithan's *Two Boys Kissing*, is unmistakably a literary reaction to the rise of queer teen suicides that saturated the news and media during the early 2010s. However, the way these two novels approach this issue is radically dissimilar. Whereas Levithan shares a story in which a character is saved just as he's about to jump to his death, Ness' character has no means of salvation. After reading the prologue of this novel, one might expect to encounter a retelling of the events that led Seth to die by suicide, but this is far from the case. Immediately after dying, Seth wakes up in a perverse version of his childhood home in England—the one place that immediately reminds him of the pain that he and his parents endured before moving to the United States. Although Seth recognizes the architecture and furniture present in his childhood home, he notices sweeping differences in terms of the place he knew as a child and its current condition: thick, ashen dust covers nearly every nook and cranny of the house and its surrounding premises, and everything seems abandoned and mistreated—as if nobody has inhabited the house or the neighborhood for decades. Rusty water comes out of the kitchen sink; he hears no creatures or animals outside, and strangely enough, he wakes up with a strange webbing covering nearly every part of his body. Seth immediately believes that he now inhabits "A hell built exactly for him" as a punishment for dying by suicide (20). The parallels between this moment in the novel and the concept of permadeath are uncanny. Even though Seth deliberately tries to embrace death—and even though he outright dies—Seth is compelled and forced to continue moving on.

More Than This exudes ambiguity. The narrative initially fools readers into believing Seth's interpretation of his post-death space as a personal hell. As the novel develops, however, we receive conflicting knowledge that makes it difficult to understand and *know* the novel's setting. For instance, Seth still feels hungry in this post-death world, so he often eats tin-canned food that has passed its expiration date. He also drinks the murky brown water that comes out of the kitchen sink of his dilapidated childhood home. Seth questions why he would have the means to satiate his thirst and hunger in hell, leading him to question whether his current setting is truly a punishment in the afterlife. In this world, Seth feels exhaustion, and he sleeps as he used to back in his pre-death life. Every time he sleeps, he has vivid dreams in which he relives crucial moments from his past life. He relives these moments again and again. Death does not stop the cycle.

By deviating from the typical orientation of linear, developmental narratives and by writing a novel that begins with death, Ness opens unexpected pathways towards queer repair that shed light on the role of closure in speculative YA literature with queer characters and themes. Earlier, I alluded to the trope of "Bury Your Gays," which involves the death of a queer character (who is often paired with another person), typically after audiences have developed an emotional or parasocial attachment to said character. By starting the narrative with the character's death, this trope is somewhat inverted and contested. Death is not a punchline, a culmination, it's not a "gotcha!" for feeling a connection with a queer character. It becomes a moment of (dis)orientation. In *Queer Phenomenology*, Sarah Ahmed suggests that the notion of orientation exposes how normative pressures push people to pursue some life pathways over others. Our life trajectories are oriented by the pathways we see and observe, and we're often pushed to imagine futurity "in terms of reaching certain points along a life course" (21). If a "good life" entails imagining a future contingent on reaching milestones or normative events along a life course, Seth's suicide in the novel's introduction constitutes a point of deviation, or better said, an unwillingness to partake in "such gestures of return." Rather than working as a point of narrative closure, his suicide becomes a point of narrative aperture. As he dwells in the post-death world, Seth reflects actively on how he failed to make these gestures of return—highlighting how he constantly disappointed his family, and how he failed to follow the straight and normative pathways carved before him.

One of the most critical vivid dreams in *More Than This* takes place almost a quarter of the way into the novel, in which Seth lies naked in bed next to Gudmund—Seth's best friend and love interest during pre-death days. This scene is the first time in the narrative that Seth's queerness is disclosed to readers, and the depiction of queer sexuality is unusually physical, intimate, and overt for a YA queer novel. While in bed, Gudmund pulls out his phone and takes a picture of him and Seth together, an image which later circulates among their friends, family, and peers. This latter event becomes one of the catalysts for the events that push Seth to consider suicide as a solution to his pain. This scene has two pivotal narrative consequences: firstly, it is at this moment that we connect Seth's suicide to his queerness, especially since the narrative initially provides no motive for Seth drowning himself in the novel's opening. Secondly, this vivid dream prompts Seth to reflect upon the role of Gudmund in his life, a reflection that is telling in terms of Seth's views towards relationships:

> The *ache* of it... the ache of missing something that was his own. His own private, secret thing that belonged to no one else, that was no part of the world of his parents or his brother or even his friends.
>
> (Ness 105)

The language of exclusivity and possession saturates Seth's reflection. His intense desire to possess another person exclusively, monogamously, is imbued with language of objectification, a sense compounded by Seth's description of his boyfriend as a "thing of his own."

In the post-death world, Seth's existence consists of surviving the harsh conditions of a lifeless, ash-covered London while attempting to cope with the pain of the memories that flood his mind every time he sleeps. The memories are painful. Seth can't escape the hurt of these dreams even when attempting to. He continues to be disturbed by visions every night, including the final conversation he had with Gudmund before he was transferred to another school: "You're everything I've got, Gudmund [...] You're it. I don't have anything else." He responds to Seth by stating he "can't be anyone's everything" (150). Unable to bear the weight of the memories that continue to haunt his dreams and even less capable of bearing the intense solitude that he feels in the so-called afterlife, Seth runs away from his childhood home, preparing to die by suicide once again in the new, ash-covered world. Here, the narrative begins to break down and fragment, and temporality collapses violently.

    The descriptions of Seth running towards his second death are interspersed with an almost *exact* reiteration of the novel's introduction—the pages that describe Seth dying for the first time. Seth's first death is now narrated in past rather than present tense, and the retelling of the first suicide is interjected with moments that reflect Seth's current fears and regrets. The text alternates between snippets of Seth's first suicide and his race towards the side of a hill. The narrative creates parallels between Seth's intolerable overflow of solitude as he runs towards the cliff and the feeling of drowning in the sea, thrashed by the ocean's waves. Seth's first death is retold almost in its entirety, but just as the narrative is about to retell the moment Seth cracks his skull and dies, he notices a black van driving in the distance. Overwhelmed with the possibility of other people inhabiting what he perceives to be the afterlife, Seth runs toward the vehicle as he yells at the driver, only to be pulled away (Ness 163). While the interlacing past and present narratives initially lead us to believe that Seth will die once again, the presence of other bodies in the post-death environment interrupts both the interlacing process and Seth's second suicide attempt. Again, note how logics of permalife operate similarly in this narrative. Every time Seth encounters death, or comes close to it, the narrative finds ways of prolonging his life and pushing him to continue moving forward.

    The implementation of permalife serves as the novel's self-conscious and metafictional attempt to undo the damage caused through its initial depiction of Seth's death, for the introduction of other characters into the narrative stalls the cyclical and reiterative suicide account from going full circle. While readers might anticipate a deathly outcome given Seth's history, the novel uses this to highlight how futures can turn out differently—how they don't need to assume the same shape as the past and present Seth knows. The fact that the successful suicide is repeated almost word-for-word, except for the actual paragraph in which Seth dies, can be read as a reparative undoing of Seth's death, nearly as if Ness himself were attempting to rewrite or reorganize the events in his novel. Seth doesn't die once again, and he continues to live. Perhaps he never died at all. After Seth's interrupted second suicide attempt, both the content and genre of the novel shift dramatically as if the interruption of the second suicide narrative caused a reorientation of the original story being told. The first parts of the novel lead readers to believe that *More Than This* is an almost theological and philosophical exploration of the afterlife, in which a queer teen is forced to relieve viscerally emotional and painful memories each time he attempts to rest. However, after Seth is pulled away from the black van, the novel becomes dystopic and post-apocalyptic.

Seth has been pulled away from the black van by two people: Regine, a Black girl close to Seth's age who speaks with a British accent, and Tomasz (Tommy), a young and precocious Eastern European teenager who is later revealed to be a Polish refugee. This meeting brings together three different people who, for one reason or another, are marked as nonnormative through their performances, orientations, bodies, and alignments with futurism. Seth, for reasons mentioned above, is marked as queer through his sexual desires. Regine's Blackness undoubtedly marks her as Other. Tomasz is marked as an Other through his status as a refugee. It's also worth noting that as a refugee, not only is Tomasz's future uncertain, stalled, or negated, but he also inhabits an undefined space—in that he died after leaving Poland but before immigrating to the United Kingdom. Tomasz represents both the liminality of youth and the uncertainty that futurity poses on different bodies—a futureless and nationless character who challenges the expectations of innocence thrust upon children.

Seth, Regine, and Tomasz all become refugees in the post-death world. Seth questions the presence of other humans in his so-called personal hell. Regine, the person who has been in the post-death world for the most extended amount of time, reveals that the place they're now found in is actually the "real" world, whereas the world in which Seth died is a virtual simulation that people permanently joined about eight years before current events: "Everyone left the real world behind [...] and moved to one that was entirely online. Some completely immersive version that didn't look like being online at all" (Ness 211). To avoid an unexplained environmental catastrophe (which partially explains the presence of ash all over the land), humans willingly inserted their bodies in protective, casket-like structures that nourish their bodies and muscles as their minds remain connected to a virtual world. The influence of *The Matrix* film series in this novel is evident, and the book is self-aware of these allusions. Seth's response to Regine's revelation supports this notion: "That kind of crap only happens in movies. You'd always be able to tell the difference. Real life is real life" (211).[3] When Seth questions how they escaped the online world and why he didn't die, Regine divulges that all three of them died by hitting a specific spot in their head, which led to a "malfunction right at the point of connection that overloads the system and instead of killing us, disconnects us" (219). This spot is the same exact point where Seth crushed his skull while drowning in the sea in Washington State.

The novel complicates the reader's ability to fully trust in this dystopian narrative. Seth understands that the presence of a digital alternate reality explains many things about the "real" world, but he also admits that this explanation is full of gaps. Further complicating Seth's ability to trust in the "real" post-apocalyptic world are the inexplicable coincidences that he encounters regularly. Loose ends tie a little too nicely, Seth is always rescued from danger at the last possible second, and objects sometimes materialize when he thinks about them. His distrust in the real begins to peak when he encounters Regine and Tomasz, who rescue him right before he is about to die by suicide once again: "Something's still not right about this. These two just *happened* to be there when he was running toward the hill" (183, emphasis in original). Here, we have a queer teen character questioning the function of narrative and, even more so, questioning what Frank Kermode refers to as a novel's "lie" or "reduction of the world." Kermode argues that as soon as the story

> speaks, begins to be a novel, it imposes causality and concordance, development, character, a past which matters and a future within certain broad limits determined by the project of the author rather than that of the characters. They have their choices, but the novel has its end. (140)

Here, Seth becomes aware of the potential "lie" that he is experiencing, and he begins to question how much choice he has in the larger narrative of his life.

Because Seth can identify patterns of "causality and concordance," he begins to believe that what he's experiencing is simply a "story that he's telling himself" (Ness 250)–fully establishing the novel's metafictional status. The novel's metafictional aspects are highlighted earlier when Seth encounters a book he read as a child. While re-reading this novel, he reflects on the nature of books and how these objects can contain a reality within their pages: "A book… *It's a world all on its own, too.* He looks at the cover again. [...] *A world made of words,* Seth thinks, *where you live for a while*" (135, emphasis in original). Although Ness uses italics to mark thoughts that are substantiated in Seth's mind, these italicized phrases inevitably highlight vital phrases and ideas: a) Seth is a protagonist who literally lives in a world made of words; b) Through reading *More Than This*, we as readers "inhabit" a world made of words; and c) Seth is aware that he's a character in a story. Readers are actively pushed to question whether the events occurring in the novel are truly happening, or whether the entire text should be approached as a metafictional discussion of queer literature and narratives of death.

Seth ventures through the ash-covered plains with Regine and Tomasz as they all attempt to escape the clutches of the Driver—the entity driving a van that tries to reinsert the characters in the digital world so that their deaths can be fulfilled and finalized. When a person is reinserted into the virtual realm, they proceed to die as they originally meant to in the "real" world. While escaping the Driver and attempting to survive the conditions of the post-apocalyptic space, the three teens must look beyond their surface and bodily differences and engage in practices of coalition in order to survive the damaged world they now dwell in. Regine and Tomasz also challenge Seth in important ways, pushing him to interrogate the hierarchies and binaries he imposes on others.

Seth constantly and explicitly approaches Regine and Tomasz as potential fictional characters that simply exist to mobilize the plot of his story. This, of course, is a meta-comment on the nature of secondary characters in a novel and how they exist to aid in a protagonist's development. In *One vs. the Many*, Alex Woloch argues that "the discrete representation of any specific individual is intertwined with the narrative's continual apportioning of attention to different characters who jostle for a limited space within the same fictive universe" (13). Furthermore, Woloch discusses how the vigor and realism of protagonists as characters depend on their positioning against minor characters, with the author often deciding to represent secondary characters using only a "few features or a small segment of the personality to the neglect of much that would make the figure a full human" (43). Ness counteracts the reductive tendencies of the secondary character by providing Regine and Tomasz with complex personalities and backstories, and even more so, by having the secondary characters *challenge their very existence* as secondary characters in Seth's narrative. As Regine points out when confronting Seth's self-centered tendencies:

> The way you think, you have the right to know everything. That it's all about you. I mean, even thinking me and Tommy are here to help you somehow. How self-centered is that? You ever think maybe you're here to help *us*?
>
> (Ness 329)

Here, a "secondary" character from a work of literature pushes the novel's protagonist to come to terms with the binaries and hierarchies often implemented through representation, and by viewing people through their function rather than their personhood. Regine's attempt to challenge Seth's self-centeredness is not only her attempt to gain more agency within the limited space of the fictive universe, but it is also her attempt to push Seth to think more generatively—to be more attuned to how realities affect others besides the self.

It also pushes Seth to think about the narratives that we frame our lives around, and the sequences that stories follow in the pursuit of happiness. In her examination of narrative and sexuality, Judith Roof highlights the normative and performative contours that come along with narrative representation:

> Narrative's apparent rendition of life experience, then, is already an ideological version of (re)production produced by the figurative cooperation of a naturalized capitalism and heterosexuality. Narrative's dynamic enacts ideology and narrative's constant production proliferates that ideology continually and naturally, as if it were simply a fact of life and sense itself.
>
> (xvii)

Seth's views himself as a protagonist and his companions as secondary characters, inserting himself into the heart of the narrative. By having Regine and Tomasz challenge their status, they oppose the hierarchies and ideologies that narrativizations produce. By starting the novel in death and ending in ambiguity, the novel destabilizes the normative trajectories of life experience and capitalist success espoused by YA culture. As the conclusion of the novel draws near, Seth reveals that he died soon after he realized his boyfriend, Gudmund, was also sleeping with his friend, Monica—who was also the person responsible for circulating the photo of Seth and Gudmund together in bed. Seth acknowledges that his reaction to the situation was "extreme" (426), but it was primarily due to his inability to understand how anyone can assume the task of being "anybody's everything" (423). While discussing these notions with Regine and Tomasz, Seth approaches Gudmund's desires and actions in a less self-centered fashion. Does Gudmund's adherence to non-monogamy undo or diminish the love and affection he felt towards Seth? Does Seth have to die because his relationship wasn't successful, at least according to normative understandings?

Gudmund's non-monogamy didn't fit within the narrative parameters of the virtual world, where heteronormativity and patriarchy offer nothing but a linear, sequential progression that must be followed to assure a "good life." Since these events didn't comply with this expected sequence, and monogamy wasn't a possibility, Seth couldn't visualize the "good life" that hung in front of him like a carrot on a stick. He therefore views himself as lacking, as not enough. Since he was unable to view alternative pathways due to the contexts he was immersed in, he tries to remove himself from the pathway entirely. However, the logic of permalife grants Seth the opportunity to start the path anew, but this time with different knowledges, a less self-centered attitude toward others, and friends that join him in coalition despite their sociocultural and intersectional divergences.

Seth now dwells in an ambiguous, uncertain space where the rules and values of the pre-apocalyptic world no longer hold true. He has found a community constituted by people who were considered nonnormative or subpar for various reasons, but who possess the ability to make him think differently about himself and his place in the world: "*surprising* people, with unexpected, unimaginable stories of their own. People who looked at the world in a completely different way and by doing so, *made* it different" (471–472, emphasis in original). Seth rejects the norms and expectations upheld by his nuclear family plugged into the virtual world and forms his own queer kinships in the real dystopian world—a family linked not through blood or genes, but rather, through political and affective convictions. But Seth, ultimately, decides not to remain in this world. With the queer knowledge that he's obtained by inhabiting a post-apocalyptic world and by immersing himself in the lives of those who surround him, Seth decides to plug himself back into the virtual world to see if he can repair it and undo the hurt caused to himself, and the pain he caused to others.

More Than This forgoes a concrete ending in favor of ambiguity and uncertainty, similar to other texts explored in this book such as *Mosquita y Mari* and the 2015 version of *More Happy Than Not*. We never find out if Seth is experiencing the "real," whether he's living in a narrative that his mind created to cope with his suicide, or whether he's simply a literary character lost in a sequence of random events. We never find out if he succeeds in his effort to return to the virtual world, or whether he was able to address the hurt and cultural damage that led to his death in the first place. But even though he's uncertain of what will happen, "he knows he can live with it" (472). This ending forgoes the certainty expected and celebrated in queer YA culture in an attempt to frame queerness as an ongoing process. When Regine, Tomasz, and Seth first discuss the possibility that they're inhabiting a fictional story, Regine reflects on the nature of narrative and how it ultimately exists for affective purposes: "People see stories everywhere [...] We take random events, and we put them together in a pattern so we can comfort ourselves with a story, no matter how much it obviously isn't true" (217). But does the truth of the events affect the impact that they can ultimately have? Does their fictionality undo their effects and affects? *More Than This* is precisely about *not* being able to know and how, by not knowing, we can carve alternative pathways to comfort ourselves, orient ourselves, and find our place. While logics of permalife are indeed disconnected from the ways in which mortality operates in the real world, it nonetheless highlights the potential of fiction, fantasy, and the imagination to challenge the very elements of mortality and survival tethered to queer stories—while at the same time not obliterating or undoing this connection entirely.

No Escape?

Given the rise of critical conversations regarding the place of death, violence, and mortality in queer YA narratives, the texts I've examined in this chapter pose further challenges against the normative impulse to filter out violence, death, and despair as tied to queer experiences. Despite their differences in genre, medium, and structure, *When the Moon Was Ours*, *Hades*, and *More Than This* exploit the fantastic potentialities of fiction to transform the tense relationship between queerness and mortality. Death isn't removed from these texts. However, all of them transform and reconfigure death, uncoupling it from the linear pathways, orientations, and teleologies commonly celebrated in YA culture. They conjoin narratives of hope and despair, life and death, beginning and end, creating fictional worlds in which mortality can't completely control the narratives and orientations of queer characters.

We don't have access to the mechanics of permalife in the real world. Death and violence are very real elements in the lives of so many queer and marginalized folk, and the ties between the two have created expected and anticipated pathways for how queer lives are represented and structured in our imaginations. Permalife can't undo the violence and deathly connotations that haunt queerness, but it can provide us with opportunities to interrogate what lives count as livable, what narrative paths we follow, and how the fantastic can be summoned as both a source of relief and as a challenge to the dominant culture. It pushes us to further examine the dialectic relationship that exists between life and mortality in queer YA cultural productions and to think carefully about how our own world is built and structured. What opportunities for futurism do we anticipate when witnessing queer and trans lives that can't die within a fictive universe? What are the broader implications of imbuing queer characters with a sense of life and continuity that can never be stripped away? What happens when queer YA doesn't shy away from discourses of mortality, but instead, finds ways to reconfigure them, deconstruct them, and explore how they move and affect us?

In *Hades*, every time the player dies and loses a round, a cutscene is shown of Zagreus dragged into the air as blood bursts out of him, and he then sinks into a bloody currents of the River of Styx. After Zagreus dies after several playthroughs and countless hours of gameplay, the cutscene slightly changes. Zagreus is still dropped into a pool of blood, but before returning to the underworld, he sticks his hand out of the pool and gestures a peace sign to the player (see Figure 4.5). There's something

Figure 4.5 Zagreus' hand emerges from a pool of blood and gestures a peace sign to the player when dying later in the game (*Hades*, original gameplay screen capture).

deeply—perhaps morbidly—satisfying about seeing a queer character being so blasé in the face of death. Death no longer defines Zagreus' experiences, and no longer imposes a true sense of finality to his never-ending quest to reach the surface. And while this invincibility doesn't mirror reality for any of us mere mortals, there's something to be said about the feelings we embody through playing his journey. A queer character's story isn't stalled by the narrative forces of mortality. He celebrates and rejoices knowing that death can't stop him—it instead drives him to continue dashing and slashing his way through the hurt and oppression of the underworld, compelled by the lure and promise of an unreachable glow on the horizon.

Compared to *Hades*, YA novels such as *When the Moon Was Ours* and *More Than This* are more static in how they (de)narrativize the links between mortality and queerness, and don't offer the same opportunities that video games can in terms of interaction and embodiment. However, all of these texts are akin to each other in their use of the narrative and speculative devices to breathe life into queer and trans mortality narratives. They approach mortality not as a punishment for queer characters, but as a call to rethink, reassess, restart, and continue on. Death is a call and opportunity for transformation, a call to feel not good about, but—and I use this word lightly—*better* in the face of death. As Ahmed reminds us, "for those whose lives have been torn apart by violence, or those for whom the tiredness of repetition in everyday life becomes too much to bear, feeling better does and should matter" (*Cultural Politics* 201). These texts, despite their differences in medium, invite us to partake in dreams where waters transform rather than drown, where teens venture hand-in-hand to survive the ash-laden lands of homonormativity, and where queers arise from the blood with more knowledge to dwell through the structures and narratives that contain our bodies and desires.

Notes

1. The development of queer kinship and identity through containment and constraint was a prominent notion present in the development of queer communities in the 1970s and 1980s. As Richard Dyer discusses in his now classic discussion on camp, constraint pushes queer people to develop complex relationships with our surroundings, finding different strategies to dwell in a world shaped by heteronormativity: "We find it easy to appear to fit in, we are good at picking up the rules, conventions, forms and appearances of different social circles. And why? Because we've had to be good at it, we've had to be good at disguise, at appearing to be one of the crow, the same as everyone else. Because we had to hide what we really felt (gayness) for so much of the time, we had to master the façade of whatever social set-up we found ourselves in—we couldn't afford to stand out in any way, for it might give the game away about our gayness" (114).
2. In *Sexual Politics, Sexual Communities*, John D'Emilio explores the connections between queerness and spaces such as bars. He argues these spaces facilitated the formation of a community "around a shared sexual orientation," a cooperative existence that "would have important implications in the future for the shape of gay politics and gay identity throughout the nation" (195). We must be wary, however, in donning a romanticized perspective when thinking through the sense of community enabled by such spaces, and how they thrived through practices of exclusion.
3. Given the parallels between *More Than This* and *The Matrix* trilogy, the character of Regine can be read as an allusion to the Oracle character in *The Matrix Reloaded*, especially in terms of her ability to know and understand the structure and function of the post-apocalyptic world. She is the oldest person in the trio and has spent the most time in the ash-covered land.

5 Catastrophic Comforts

Time has been a constantly resurfacing issue in this discussion of the reparative impulse of queer YA literature. Many of the texts I've discussed stress the importance of using the past as a conduit to activate and reinvigorate more generative ways of existing in the world. However, the YA literature and media discussed in this chapter are primarily concerned with looking forward and envisioning futures and conclusions that steer far away from what normative narratives consider happy. In his discussion on epilogues in children's and YA fiction, Mike Cadden points out how these forms of narrative closure often sacrifice literary merit in that they are written to provide younger audiences with a sense of ease that favors emotional dimensions over literary innovation or experimentation. He argues that epilogues are "a risky re-immersion for the purpose of reassurance. It's aesthetically clumsy but clearly believed to be effective for being affective" ("All is Well" 345). Epilogues prioritize comfort over narrative logic. However, it's worth thinking more carefully about how the epilogue's affective dimensions are ideologically framed and how they enable (or hinder) the queer potentialities of a text. While epilogues are designed to make readers feel a sense of comfort and wellbeing, many times, their emotional dimensions are contingent on the perpetuation of heteronormative and antiqueer ideologies that foreclose queer thinking and possibility.

My relationship with the Harry Potter series, for instance, started to collapse way before J.K. Rowling's alignment with transphobic discourses and practices came to light.[1] I remember reading the last line of the now infamous epilogue of *Harry Potter and the Deathly Hallows*, and recall feeling an intense pit of disappointment in my stomach. After all of the sadness, trauma, and heartbreak that these characters endure, the happiness and comfort reinforced by the epilogue felt too little, too late. "All was well" (759). What assures this sense of wellness? This sense of happiness? Normative comforts and aspirations such as heterosexual coupledom, marriage, reproduction, and child-rearing. The now grown-up wizards are steeped in the promises of heterosexual bliss, and the cycle

DOI: 10.4324/9781003038627-5

This chapter has been made available under a CC-BY-NC-ND license.

Catastrophic Comforts 123

of futurity remains secure with a fresh crew of magical children on their way to experience a life of wonder that only Hogwarts could provide. My disappointment in this epilogue extends beyond the heteronormative implications it espouses. The epilogue involves a burial of hurt. There may be small traces of trauma in the form of a scar, but echoes of pain are absent from this marking. Epilogues are narrative devices that typically don't heal pain, but rather, mask it. They're attempts at repairing the forms of violence present in the narrative for the sake of making the reader feel good. The epilogue, in many ways, embodies cruel optimism.

In the second chapter of this volume, I examined how Adam Silvera's later inclusion of an epilogue in *More Happy Than Not* (2015/2000) situated a radically queer text within the normative parameters of success and happiness expected from YA texts. In many ways, the epilogue acts as a "straightening device" (Ahmed, *The Promise of Happiness*), reorienting characters towards dominant understandings of achievement and fulfillment. Can YA speculative works employ the emotional perks of the epilogue without succumbing to the impulse to provide clarity? Can epilogues provide a sense of comfort that resists reinforcing adult-oriented, normative views of what counts as happy, appropriate, or healthy? Can readers find respite and solace in closures commonly viewed as pessimistic or undesirable? To address these questions, we must turn our attention to speculative YA works that are driven by bleakness and despair—works that present readers with queer dreams and normative nightmares. (Post) apocalyptic texts with queer themes and sensibilities are the ideal works for this discussion. This literature aligns with a queer sensibility that rejects many of the norms and ideologies that are elevated in real-world contexts. These texts envision futures that highlight the failures of past lives and communities and often serve as critiques of naïve optimistic and hopeful thinking. Dystopia, after all, is utopia's unruly twin sister.

The apocalyptic genre's proclivity towards negative affect, pessimism, and cynicism often clashes with the narrative closures typically found in YA texts—closures that convey a sense of "possibility and resilience" (Coats 326). Here, we encounter an issue in that many YA dystopian and post-apocalyptic texts offer promises of hope that are optimistically cruel, in that protagonists often yearn for the very things that hurt them—and at times, embrace the very practices and ideas they initially resisted. A scrutiny of Suzanne Collins' *The Hunger Games* series will illustrate many of the issues that are at stake in this discussion. Although this series has no characters that explicitly identify as queer, it still espouses nonnormative inclinations in that its protagonist expresses fluidity in terms of her gender performance and shuns the demands of reproductive futurism. Furthermore, and particularly in the first two books of the series, Katniss expresses an aromantic sensibility, in that she "indicates a low interest in romantic contact" and doesn't organize her life "according to a hierarchy that prioritizes sexual and romantic couples" (Przybylo 5). The novel's epilogue, however, forecloses this potentiality in troubling ways. A scrutiny of *The Hunger Games* series, focusing primarily on the final chapters and epilogue of Collins' *Mockingjay*, will shed light on problems present in (hetero)normative narrative closures. Afterward, I examine Andrew Smith's *Grasshopper Jungle*, and show how it provides us with an alternative, twisted version of an epilogue that refuses to offer readers a sense of comfort through normative or traditional means.

Worse Games to Play

Toward the culmination of Collins' *Hunger Games* trilogy, protagonist Katniss Everdeen witnesses the slow recovery of a destroyed District Twelve after overthrowing the dictatorship known as the Capitol. As Katniss observes hundreds of people returning to the district and lush vegetation returning to its charred meadows, she considers the importance of optimism in moments of despair: "What I need is the dandelion in the spring. The bright yellow that means rebirth instead of destruction. The promise that life can go on, no matter how bad our losses. That it can be good again" (*Mockingjay* 388). Although the tyrannical rule of dictatorship known as the Capitol has been dismantled—at least for the moment—nightmares haunt Katniss and she relives the atrocities of this dystopian government. In her nightmares, she reiteratively confronts the ghosts of people whose lives were lost during the Mockingjay revolution. She unsurprisingly reveals that Peeta, District 12's other victor, fulfills the promise of life and goodness in moments of despair. Hope lurks in every corner of the ideological frameworks of *The Hunger Games*, and the narrative overtly informs readers how the fictional world of Panem—a post-apocalyptic version of the United States—operates under the logic of cruel optimism.

The film adaptation of the first novel emphasizes the devious role of optimism—how it's cast as something people yearn for, but that nonetheless maintains the status quo. In a revealing moment in the first film, Cornelius Snow, the President of Panem, and Seneca Crane, the game designer of the seventy-fourth Hunger Games, discuss the role of hope in controlling the Capitol and its districts. Snow suggests that the dynamic between fear and hope possesses the potential to simultaneously liberate or control society:

President Snow: Seneca, why do you think we have a winner?
Seneca Crane: What do you mean?
President Snow: I mean, why do we have a winner? I mean, if we just wanted to intimidate the districts, why not round up twenty-four of them at random and execute them all at once? Be a lot faster.

Seneca: [...]
President Snow: Hope.
Seneca Crane: Hope?
President Snow: Hope. It is the only thing stronger than fear. A little hope is effective. A lot of hope is dangerous. A spark is fine, as long as it's contained. (*The Hunger Games*, 2012)

President Snow exposes how optimistic thinking can have cruel implications. While explaining the dangers of hope to Seneca, Snow prunes a white rose—stripping it of its thorns and removing its leaves (see Figure 5.1). Discourses of hope echo in the scene as Snow removes the rose's mechanism for defending itself—his hands prune and trim the rose to fit a uniform aesthetic: tame, subdued, controlled.

The society portrayed throughout the *Hunger Games* series came to fruition through warfare. The class distinction that was upheld between citizens of the Capitol and inhabitants of the impoverished districts gained credibility and power through acts of systemic violence. The role that optimism plays in perpetuating forms of violence that aren't overtly tangible or perceivable sheds light on its potential to be both helpful and dangerous. While a discourse centered on hope haunts the entire *Hunger Games* trilogy, I want to redirect our attention to Katniss' development throughout the series, and the series' eventual reinforcement of normative dynamics of gender and sexuality that quash the antinormative sensibility present in the novels and their film adaptations.

After impulsively assassinating President Coin—the mastermind behind the Mockingjay revolution—as a way of preventing the perpetuation of the ritualistic televised combat known as The Hunger Games, Katniss remains

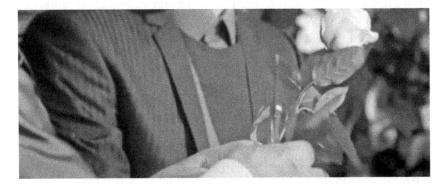

Figure 5.1 President Snow frames hope as both a generative and destructive force all while audiences are shown a close-up shot of his hands stripping a white rose of its leaves and thorns (*The Hunger Games* 2012).

locked in solitary confinement during her trial. Here, Katniss abstains from eating and contemplates suicide, all while reflecting upon the violence and despair maintained by quotidian human life. Throughout the series, Katniss has always presented herself as odd or different in that she embodies ideals and practices that mark her as "unfeminine" and queer, in that she negates the impulses of reproductive futurism and expresses no desire to be in a relationship with another person. As a matter of fact, before reading the final novel in the series, I approached Katniss as a character completely disinterested in sex and romance, a character that lived against the normative expectations and pressures of sexusociety (see Przybylo).

Various times throughout *The Hunger Games* series, Katniss discusses the futility of prospects such as romance and sexuality in her life, and even more so, she repudiates the social demand to marry, have children, or even love. As Peeta grows upset over Katniss' inability to articulate her wants or desires towards the end of the first novel, she makes her detachment from normative aspirations clear:

> it's no good loving me because I'm never going to get married anyway, and he'd just end up hating me later instead of sooner. That if I do have feelings for him, it doesn't matter because I'll never be able to afford the kind of love that leads to a family, to children. And how can he? How can he after what we've just been through?
> (Collins, *The Hunger Games* 373)

Katniss uses the word "afford," a term loaded with monetary and economic implications, which implies that she has neither the material nor affective resources needed to form a family. Furthermore, her use of the terms family and children, rooted in normative notions of what connectivity, legacy, and kinship constitute, also negates the strength and validity of the bonds that she has established (and, at times, lost) during her time in the Hunger Game Arenas—such as her close relationship with Rue—therefore reinforcing dynamics of oppression and white supremacy saturated throughout the text (see Ebony Elizabeth Thomas 42–45).[2] In this passage, Katniss also connects notions of love directly to the creation of a biological family unit. Regardless of the motives behind her statement, Katniss deliberately tries to distance herself from desiring or working toward heteronormative milestones.

By stating that she can't afford the affective and material costs of love, family, and children, Katniss situates herself at odds with the societal demands of reproductive futurism, motherhood, and heteronormativity. She views herself as a futureless being, a perspective that dramatically crystallizes towards the end of *Mockingjay*, as she proclaims her disconnect with femininity and, even more so, with her humanity. While locked alone in isolation, Katniss disavows her allegiance and connection to the "monsters" known as humans, claiming that there's something fundamentally "wrong with a creature that sacrifices its children's lives to settle its differences" (*Mockingjay* 377). Throughout the series' three-book run, Katniss has served as a symbol of the resistance—fighting and advocating for the liberation of people living in subpar and inhumane conditions in Panem's various districts. But after realizing that the very members of the resistance, and even the resistance's leader, desire to perpetuate Panem's ritualistic sacrifice and have the children of the Capitol's citizens compete in a televised deathmatch, Katniss questions whether humanity deserves to continue living on. She questions the value of living for, fighting for, or dying for the preservation of human society and culture when it's so hellbent on self-destruction.

Katniss' musings on the folly of humankind and the potential benefits of its collapse are the pinnacle of her sinthomosexual inclinations. The sinthomosexual—a concept developed by Lee Edelman in *No Future*—denotes people who reject social norms and who resist the tendency to work towards futurity and sociality. They move "beyond compulsory compassion, beyond the future and the snare of images keeping us always in its thrall" by repudiating "*all* social action, *all* responsibility for a better tomorrow or for the perfection of social forms" (101, emphasis in original). Katniss' musings on the collapse of humanity and their replacement with a more compassionate species echo sinthomosexual sentiments in that she abandons a utopic envisioning of the future in favor of a more fatalistic, antisocial purview. Through these musings, Katniss envisions how the eradication of humans would lead to a state of heteronormative dormancy, and it would lead to the undermining of political, cultural, and social orders that lead to stasis, normativity, oppression, and violence. There's an ironic sense of hope that she finds in this vision of despair.

While *Mockingjay*'s epilogue attempts to offset the overall sense of hopelessness present in past books, it remains a bittersweet closure to the series for various reasons. Katniss and Peeta now have a daughter and a younger son. Panem seems to be in a state of peace, and the survivors of the Mockingjay revolution strive to honor the lives that were lost during the reign of the Capitol. The epilogue becomes increasingly tense from a queer perspective, however, when Katniss shares her feelings towards her children and her decision to have them in the first place:

> It took five, ten, fifteen years for me to agree. But Peeta wanted them so badly. When I first felt her stirring inside of me, I was consumed with a terror that felt as old as life itself. Only the joy of holding her in my arms could tame it. Carrying him was a little easier, but not much.
> (Collins, *Mockingjay* 389)

Katniss, who adamantly refutes the impulse to have children throughout the entire series, chooses to have them mainly because her partner yearned for offspring and a biological legacy. In a sense, both Peeta and Katniss cement the ideology of children as torch-wielders for hope and futurity, a dynamic akin to the one we see in the epilogue of *Harry Potter and the Deathly Hallows*.

Katniss refutes the possibility of children because she doesn't want to be responsible for bringing a human being into a damaged world that will continue to break. On the one hand, Katniss' eventual decision to have children could be approached as a marker indicating that the conditions of the human world have changed to the extent that she now views it as a livable place. On the other hand, Katniss' decision to have children, especially when considering that she had them mostly because "Peeta wanted them so badly," can be approached as symptomatic of patriarchal and ideological vestiges that have stubbornly secured themselves to the world that Katniss and her family inhabit. She lives in a renewed society in which the desires of her partner—a man—are still prioritized over her own fears and apprehensions, and where both monogamy and children are portrayed as necessary components for hope, pleasure, and futurity.

The second part of *Mockingjay*'s film adaptation increases the strength of this reading significantly, for its epilogue problematically makes various adjustments to the novel's narrative that increase the draw and prevalence of heteronormativity and reproductive futurism. For instance, the epilogue shows Peeta playing with the older child over the renewed meadows of District 12. Katniss, who dons a cheery, yellow flowery dress, watches the two people playing from a distance as she cradles her younger child—now represented as an infant and not a toddler—in her arms. In the film, Katniss utters portions of the novel's epilogue verbatim, but rather than delivering these words to an indeterminate listener, we see her say these words directly to the infant. The film's epilogue not only emphasizes a dichotomy between active masculinity and passive femininity but also reinforces Katniss' role as a mother and feminine woman while simultaneously elevating the infant as a symbol of hope and the future (see Edelman 12–13). The words of the epilogue are projected onto the image of an infant, imbuing the film with a sense of heteronormativity that surpasses that present in the novel's bittersweet conclusion. The scene's nondiegetic music and bright, vibrant colors—which can be described as both cheery and uplifting—buffer the possibility of noticing the negative emotional dimensions present in the novel's epilogue (see Figure 5.2).

While Katniss' decision to have children can be seen as an effort on her behalf to live a more collective and less "self-centered" existence, I can't help but speculate whether it would be possible for Katniss to achieve any semblance of comfort and happiness without the presence of children or a male partner in her life. Katniss's story complies with a teleological

Catastrophic Comforts 129

Figure 5.2 Katniss watches Peeta and her older child playing in the meadow as she cradles an infant (*The Hunger Games: Mockingjay Part 2*).

metanarrative that aims toward normative narrative closure through heteronormative aspirations:

> biological reproduction—and, by extension, heterosexual marriage—is connected to the seasons, the weather, to bodily realities of life and death; it is the template for narrating time and change, for depicting the rhythm of our selves and bodies as we move toward death.
> (McCrea 13)

After experiencing so much hurt and precarity, and after expressing aromantic sensibilities, Katniss still finds herself aligning with this template, replicating (hetero)normative narrative trajectories. Katniss' embrace of romance and biological reproduction seems necessary and inevitable in providing the closure we encounter in *Mockingjay*. She adheres to chrononormative temporal ideologies and normative narrative templates by engaging in heteronormative coupledom and becoming a mother—an act that further establishes a wedge between the self-centered and "queer" teen Katniss represented throughout the series and the "feminine" and nurturing adult Katniss represented in *Mockingjay*'s epilogue.[3] Given the ties between biological reproduction and closure, I'm not surprised that Collins—similar to Rowling in the epilogue to the *Harry Potter* series—uses children to attempt to counteract the suffering that the protagonist goes through. As Sara Ahmed has argued, "The absence of children is one signifier of the absence of somebody to whom I can defer my hope, for whom I can justify my present suffering. Children, in other words, bear the weight of this fantasy" (*The Promise of Happiness* 184). In the epilogue, Katniss now has people who justify and potentially ameliorate her suffering. While children often serve as a fantasy to explain the pain of living, this justification reinforces to the very ideologies and practices that led to this suffering in the first place. How cruel indeed.

Even after complying with a normative template of biological reproduction, the novel ends on a somber note, in which Katniss confesses that some days it's difficult for her to conciliate her past and present:

> it feels impossible to take pleasure in anything because I'm afraid it could be taken away. That's when I make a list in my head of every act of goodness I've seen someone do. It's like a game. Repetitive. Even a little tedious after more than twenty years. But there are much worse games to play.
>
> (Collins, *Mockingjay* 390)

In analyzing this epilogue, Mike Cadden highlights its bittersweet nature and questions the authenticity of Katniss' forced and constructed happiness. Cadden observes that the epilogue portrays the reality of living with trauma. At first glance, it may seem impossible for Katniss to find happiness given her mental and physical state at the end of the book. The epilogue presents a compelling case for how she resorts to finding happiness as best as she can (Cadden 354). How much comfort and optimism can we find in this closure, especially given its normative structure and content? Perhaps the epilogue offers comfort from a normative, individualistic perspective in that Katniss can potentially find pleasure despite her dire past, but matters become more complicated when thinking about happiness and its normative aspiration to comfort.

For Katniss to cope with her present and ultimately feel pleasure in it, she constantly looks back and plays a game in which she exhaustively lists acts that assure her of the "goodness" of life. This game that Katniss plays over a two-decade span serves as a manifestation of what Love calls backward feelings, for it signals "the ruined state of the social world," it demonstrates the continuities that exist between a damaged past and a still damaged present, and even more so, it highlights the shortcomings of progress-driven narratives (27). *Mockingjay*'s epilogue effectively catalogs the backward feelings that permeate Katniss' purview, illustrating how the resonances of the Capitol's violence continue to trouble her present. In the words of Berlant, the game that Katniss plays becomes "shaped by [a] crisis in which people find themselves developing skills for adjusting to newly proliferating pressures to scramble for modes of living on" (8). Perhaps the human spirit has endured the Capitol's rule. Nevertheless, the endurance of this human spirit also entails the survival of ideologies, codes, beliefs, and practices that will continue to cause an overall sense of strife and inadequacy for the Other. Collins' *Hunger Games* series spotlights the normative baggage that often comes with epilogues, and its attempts to artificially provide readers with a sense of closure. Its epilogue not only concludes the series in an ideologically troubling way, but it also distances the associations between queer modalities and positive affect. This conclusion, like that of *Harry Potter*, demonstrates that queer experience and thought have little to no space within the mainstream epilogue's aspiration to comfort.

Countless critics have hailed *The Hunger Games* series for inverting and, to some extent, destabilizing binary approaches to gender in literature written for younger readers. Collins does much to ensure readers can detect a reversal of traditionally feminine and masculine traits in her main characters. In her assessment of gender and queerness in the series, Jennifer Mitchell argues that "Katniss's ability to negotiate, try on, and experiment with various gender roles is a testament to the lack of stable substance underneath them" (129). In other words, Katniss' ability to perform multiple gender roles highlights both the performativity and constructed nature of these performances. Although none of these roles involve romance with other women or sexual desire towards the same gender, their fluidity, interchangeability, and connection to gender performativity make this experimentation embody a queer ethos. Furthermore, Katniss' lack of interest in children, marriage, romance, or relationships aligns her with an asexual and aromantic potentiality that's undeniable and explicitly articulated throughout the series. Leah Phillips, for instance, highlights how Katniss pressures the gendered connotations attached to her body through the eschewal of heteronormative imagery, as seen when she "burns away the wedding dress she would have worn to marry Peeta" (18). If Katniss' mobility between gender performances exemplifies the character's queerness and the sociocultural construction of gender categories, the trilogy's epilogue and the destabilization of the Capitol's power essentially coerce this potential queerness to vanish. The ability of the "girl on fire" to navigate various identities essentially cools down and extinguishes. A survivor, a wife, and a mother, the Katniss depicted in the trilogy's epilogue now resorts to the static and reiterative processes of list-making, child-rearing, and remembrance.

I'm not arguing that marriage and motherhood constantly undermine queerness or are negative aspirations, but I can't help but view the nefarious normative tendencies at place here, especially given Katniss' explicit rejections of romance and sexuality. Katniss' compliance with patriarchal and normative expectations and her assertion that her children instill a sense of hope and optimism in her life inevitably invoke the very ideologies and tensions that broke the world to begin with. To some extent, the fact that the Capitol televised a deathmatch with child and adolescent participants can be seen as a partial rejection of the image of the child and reproductive futurism (see Edelman). However, since the ritual of televised combat amongst children and teens was created to instill a sense of powerlessness amongst the residents of Panem, the values and ideologies imposed upon younger people are thus reinforced. After all, it would not be much of a punishment if the population were to sacrifice something with no ethical, material, or ideological value.

In her theorization of childhood and adulthood in YA science fiction, Kay Sambell points out that speculative YA texts commonly represent the future "as a terrifying nightmare that child readers must strive to avoid at all costs" (247). To what extent is *Mockingjay*'s epilogue the nightmare we should avoid? Along these lines, Elaine Ostry points out that the YA science fiction genre usually depicts oversimplified debates that make "an ideological point about the fixed quality of human nature and values," especially regarding representations of biotechnology and the posthuman (243). YA dystopian and post-apocalyptic fiction, even when void of overt discussions on posthumanism, archetypally centers on this ideological fixation in that the human spirit commonly prevails even after social, biological, technological, and social breakdown. And by "human spirit," I'm referring of course to normative, dominant forces. Despite changes that the body, culture, or environment undergo—humanity and its associated ideological baggage always triumph. They always persist.

The unassailability of the human spirit and its ideological baggage reverberates in Collins' trilogy. Katniss overthrows the Capitol and prevents President Coin from reestablishing Panem's murderous ritual. Even though Katniss and her team of revolutionaries catalyzed the Capitol's breakdown, they know that the threat of war and discord always remains on the horizon. As Plutarch Heavensbee—the former Head Gamemaker of the seventy-fifth Hunger Games and subsequent leader of the Mockingjay rebellion—indicates when Katniss questions whether more war awaits in the future: "collective thinking is usually short-lived. We're fickle, stupid beings with poor memories and a great gift for self-destruction" (*Mockingjay* 379). The solutions offered in the novel's conclusion and the positive emotions tied to these solutions are, therefore, constructed as provisional and temporary.

I'm interested in pressuring the values commonly found in (post)apocalyptic YA adult literature by further interrogating the uses and values of the epilogue. I pressure this ideological fixation by considering narrative structures and closures of YA texts that refute the happiness and optimism tied to normative ways of existing in the world—literature that favors alternate models of relationality, futurity, "human" values, and teleology. To accomplish this, I want to move our attention to a text that focuses explicitly on the experiences of queer, nonnormative characters living through cultural, social, and environmental breakdown. Smith's 2014 novel *Grasshopper Jungle* represents an imagined world that pushes us to question whether "essential" human values can or should be preserved. It takes the sinthomosexual sentiments present in the *Hunger Games* series and exploits them to no end. This novel presents the world's end and society's collapse as an unavoidable nightmare: human populations dwindle exponentially and the remaining humans now live in a constant state of precarity—knowing that their remaining days on Earth are numbered. The future portrayed in this text seems bleak and antithetical to the positive feelings that YA cultural productions generally espouse. In a way, *Grasshopper Jungle* disrupts and complicates understandings of YA culture as a happiness enterprise fixative on normative understandings of comfort, hope, and optimism.

Sambell interrogates YA's ability to be upfront about the gloomy truths "of the forces against which [they caution], while simultaneously guiding the reader towards hope, often viewed as essential for young readers" (251). Despite their pessimism and melancholy "truths," I argue that (post)apocalyptic YA novels with overt queer themes and characters pave the way for deviant narratives to thrive, stories in which societal and structural collapse allows teens to perceive and embody nonnormative and generative forms of kinship, love, and being. A handful of novels achieve this by approaching the affective goals of the epilogue and turning them on their head: instead of providing readers with traditional "happy endings," positive outcomes, and what Cadden refers to as the adult's desire to comfort, these queer narratives provide closures that frustrate the reader and challenge adult and normative conceptions of what optimism and happiness entail. These texts often thwart the heteronormative issues circulated in novels such as *Mockingjay*, in that they provide readers with conclusions that instill hope by dismantling the normative values and aspirations attached to the concepts of happiness and comfort.

Exploring the Jungle

Over the past decade, Smith has become one of the most prominent and controversial authors to explore alternate forms of sexuality in his works. He commonly implements narrative and aesthetic elements that loosely situate his work within the realm of the strange and the "New Weird." Jeff VanderMeer defines the New Weird as "secondary-world fiction that subverts the romanticized ideas about place found in traditional fantasy, largely by choosing realistic, complex real-world models as the jumping off point for creation of settings that may combine elements of both science fiction and fantasy." He notes that New Weird fiction tends to make use of "surreal or transgressive horror for its tone, style, and effects" and in terms of form, many authors of this genre make "use of postmodern techniques that do not undermine the surface reality of the text" (xvi). *Grasshopper Jungle* implements self-conscious and self-reflexive narratives that constantly undermine and bring into question the plausibility of the novel's events. Consider, for instance, the disclaimer at the story's beginning, stating, "Ealing Iowa is a fictional town. None of the characters and places in this book actually exist. Any similarities between events and characters to actual history only occur in the true portions of this book, which aren't that many." Given the novel's compliance with many of the features of the New Weird, the events in Smith's book have a *surface reality*—while they can indeed be approached allegorically, my reading assumes that *Grasshopper Jungle* depicts a world in which actual giant praying mantises become the new apex predators of planet Earth.

In addition to focusing on fantastical elements such as the presence of giant killer praying mantises, *Grasshopper Jungle* also plays with real-world fears that embrace multiple definitions of queerness, such as "weird," "astonishing," "radical," and "out of place." Such connotations can be observed through events such as the development of genetically modified "unstoppable corn" with deadly castrating side effects, hemophilic blue bioluminescent mold that causes mutation, and hidden underground nuclear silos. This YA novel centers on protagonist Austin Szerba's efforts to document history during and after the end of the world—an end that was triggered by an antiqueer act. The novel's portrayal of charged topics such as sexual assault, cannibalism, mass murder, drug addiction, and testicular dissolution imbues the narrative with a sense of horror that tests the generic and emotional parameters of YA literature. By far one of the novels that most embrace the austere disposition of contemporary dystopian literature, *Grasshopper Jungle* depicts a brutal and violent apocalypse that can't be avoided or reversed.

Despite the novel's embrace of despair and pessimism, its inventive representation of queerness and its surprising narrative closure prevents it from fully succumbing to complete negativity and nihilism. The novel's epilogue presents readers with a postapocalyptic society in which some troublesome gender ideologies remain fixed and in place. However, as Muñoz has argued, "We may never touch queerness, but we can feel it as the warm illumination of a horizon imbued with potentiality" (Cruising Utopia 1). *Grasshopper Jungle* doesn't present us with a story where we've touched queerness, but by envisioning the end of the world, the novel brings our reach closer to it, allowing us to feel the promise of its warmth. Its epilogue overflows with tensions, disparities, and ambiguities. It offers readers a sense of narrative and affective closure that deviates immensely from the one depicted in Collins' *Mockingjay* and Rowling's *Harry Potter* series. It exploits and reconfigures the affective function of the epilogue in efforts to challenge common understandings of hope, happiness, and collectivity.

Derritt Mason has explored this novel with depth and nuance—highlighting how the gaps and omissions present in the text harken back to broader anxieties connected to adult power and control (*Queer Anxieties* 103–104). While Mason's analysis succinctly demonstrates how queerness only exists in the periphery of the text, I'm less interested in tracing the anxieties behind the impulsive history that Austin creates, and more interested in examining the composition of the history itself. I examine how the novel highlights the use and value of creative practices in challenging and transforming "existing epistemologies and the possibility to create new, more liberating ones" (S.A. Rodríguez 11). I approach the cultural work that the novel's epilogue mobilizes within the broader context of YA narrative and through the use of queer narrative and ecological lenses.

I especially want to focus more attention on how *Grasshopper Jungle*'s epilogue offers readers a queer chronotope[4] that challenges conventional aspirations toward happiness and success elevated in queer YA criticism and culture. I personally find the novel's epilogue morbidly comforting. However, this sense of comfort is not contingent on traditional or normative understandings of this feeling. Smith's epilogue presents a case in which positive affect and outcomes are not reliant on monogamous relationships, conventional modes of child-rearing, or approaching children as torchwielders for futurism. Or even the continuation of humans as a species, for that matter. I don't view my reading as entirely oppositional to Mason's—I view it more as a continuation of the conversation in light of discourses of narrative, repair, and the affective burdens of history explored in this volume. As Mason put it succinctly, "you can't get everything in a book chapter" (*Queer Anxieties* 104). There's plenty left to be said. And we still have to discuss and examine the bison, don't we? After all, "the bison is the important member of the team" (Smith 305).

Unlike Collins' series, *Grasshopper Jungle* has an explicitly queer narrative that radiates through the protagonist's sexual practices and desires. Austin has been in a relationship with his girlfriend, Shann, for a couple of years, but while in this relationship, he realizes that he loves and desires his best friend, Robby Brees. Austin's perception of his sexuality becomes increasingly complex as the novel develops. He discloses that although he's dated Shann for years, he still hasn't had sex with her because being alone with her makes him feel "timid and restrained" (Smith 30). He unsurprisingly blames his sexual shyness and restraint on the fear that he might be queer. Austin's hesitation to acknowledge his potential queerness stems from the fact that he inhabits a rural space away from the queer comforts of urban space. For instance, after he kisses Robby for the first time, Austin tells him that "If you ever want to get shot in Ealing [Iowa], do *that* in someone's yard at night" (47), thus alluding to the perceived threat of physical violence that exists towards queer people in the United States, especially in rural spaces.

Austin's associations between the fictional rural town of Ealing and homophobic violence aren't entirely unwarranted. Austin and Robby's queerness achieves representation through a spatial organizing logic that, as pointed out by Julie Abraham, presents "antigay violence as a product of rural locations" (275), although she acknowledges that this association doesn't always hold true. This association between violence and rural spaces frames the tensions and terrors portrayed in *Grasshopper Jungle*'s narrative. Although, to some extent, it does depict rural areas as lackluster spaces with a notable absence of a vibrant queer community, the narrative's setting helps to disrupt metronormative notions that prioritize urban spaces over rural spaces in terms of their ability to accommodate queer people and establish a sense of community between them. As Scott Herring would phrase it, *Grasshopper Jungle* makes use of "rural stylistics" in order "to fashion critiques against lesbian and gay metropolitan norms," and against most norms, for that matter (6). Through its representation of rural space, the novel already begins to distance itself from the (homo) normative narratives typically found in queer YA novels, which take place mainly in urban and suburban spaces. This, in turn, allows Smith to challenge and reconfigure common perceptions and narrative representations of queerness and sexuality in YA literature.

The dangers of being queer in Smith's fictive world become concrete right from the novel's introduction, where Austin and Robby encounter antiqueer harassment and violence while skateboarding. Here, a bully named Grant Wallace and his gang of homophobic accomplices brutally attack Austin and Robby at a lot known as the eponymous Grasshopper Jungle. After the boys are left alone, Austin notices a stream of blood dripping out of Robby's nose. Robby survives the attack, and he uses the blood dripping from his nose to spell the incomplete phrase "GRANT WALLACE MURDERED ME" on the asphalt, an act which Austin characterizes as "artistic" (Smith 17). However, his spelling of this phrase remains incomplete because his nose does not expel enough blood to finish his masterpiece—thus resulting in the words "GRANT WA" (17). Robby uses the product of a homophobic encounter to create an aesthetic statement against the person who attacked him because of his sexuality. This product of pain becomes one of the catalysts that trigger the end of the world. Here, the novel takes a turn for the bizarre, as Grant Wallace and friends steal a jar with a pulsating, bioluminescent cauliflower-shaped mass labeled *MI Plague Strain 412E*, hidden in a nearby thrift shop. They carelessly drop the bioluminescent mass over Robby's masterpiece.

Unbeknownst to these first epidemic victims, the MI Plague Strain 412E has hemophilic properties, which activate when encountering blood or blood-adjacent substances.

To understand the apocalypse portrayed in Smith's novel, one must understand the convoluted history of the MI Plague Strain 412E—a weird history, to say the least. According to the novel's lore, during the 1960s in Ealing, Iowa, scientists spliced grasshopper semen with corn pollen to produce an insect-resistant vegetable called *Infinita Frumenta* or "Unstoppable Corn." Scientists soon discovered that this vegetable, despite its resistance to pests, had adverse effects when consumed—the most notable of which was "testicular dissolution" in men (233). The U.S. Department of Defense was interested in this corn and created McKeon Industries (MI). This company employed nearly 3,000 scientists to develop two projects: one invested in weaponizing the emasculating corn and the other in creating genetically modified super-soldiers. Scientists soon discovered that decaying Unstoppable Corn produces a photoluminescent mold known as *412E*, which turns into a ferocious pathogen when combined with human blood. This pathogen leads to the incubation of Unstoppable Soldiers: any human that encounters the blood-soaked mold becomes a host for a creature that rips the human into two once it matures. The creature resembles a giant praying mantis "with jagged bear-trap mandibles and folded claw-arms prickled with mountain ranges of knife-blade, triangular teeth" (261). The emergence of these insect soldiers marks the beginning of the apocalypse, for they reproduce at an alarmingly high rate and insatiably consume human flesh. Although the insects do not exhibit a command structure like human armies, they were created and marketed as *"Bulletproof, tireless machines of conquest"* by McKeon Industries (285). How's that for a summary of the novel's lore?

The horrors of biotechnology and the products of homophobic violence serve as the necessary ingredients for the creation of Unstoppable Soldiers. Notably, "Unstoppable Soldiers" is always capitalized in the novel. Given that the novel can be read as an allegory that exposes the horrors of capitalism in the United States, it's no coincidence that the Unstoppable Soldiers can also be abbreviated into the acronym "U.S." The 412E specimen was created through a capitalist enterprise focused on the biotechnological production of mass-produced corn and military weaponry. The capitalist logics of biotechnology are a heteronormative enterprise, for as Halberstam would argue, all capitalist ideologies mark queer people as subjects that fail "to embody the connections between production and reproduction," which consequently casts the queer "as inauthentic and unreal" (*The Queer Art* 95). Austin's exhausting compulsion to describe the Unstoppable Soldiers as creatures that are only interested in, and capable of, eating and mating reinforces the capitalist logic of the narrative:

"Bugs do two things. They eat and they fuck" (135), "bugs only want two things" (192), an Unstoppable Soldier "was doing the two things bugs like to do" (203), and so on, and so on.

The constant reiteration of the Unstoppable Soldiers' reproductive and dietary drives resembles what Halberstam calls "the grim, mechanical, industrial cycles of production and consumption" standard in capitalist enterprises (*The Queer Art* 29). The spread of the 412 Plague Strain assists in making sociocultural tensions visible—a reification often seen in outbreak narratives. As Priscilla Wald argues in *Contagious*, diseases and outbreaks make visible the nature of

> exchanges that are often concealed; communicable disease offers records of desire, of violence, of sexual commerce, all which are especially apparent in sexually transmitted diseases. The outbreak narrative incorporates those records as it fashions the story of disease emergence. (38)

The outbreak of the 412 Plague Strain thus renders visible the records of violence, production, and reproduction embedded and often disregarded in contemporary society. We're all too familiar with these dynamics today, especially after seeing how the COVID-19 pandemic materialized and visibilized injustices and inequalities across the globe.

Given our awareness of *Grasshopper Jungle*'s implementation of the outbreak narrative, we must confront the fact that the plague that leads to the end of the world is triggered by the blood of a gay teenager. Inevitably, the associations that exist between blood, gay men, and disease trigger parallels between the fictional plague strain in the novel and HIV/AIDS—opening the potential for *Grasshopper Jungle* to be read not only as an outbreak narrative but also as an allegory for AIDS (Mason, *Queer Anxieties* 95). As I have suggested in Chapter 3 of this book, AIDS narratives often epitomize the negative feelings commonly associated with queer narratives. Thus, the apocalyptic event in this novel could potentially embody all the connotations and emotional baggage typically associated with the AIDS epidemic. Although the blood of any human being can activate the 412 E Plague Strain, the blood of a *gay teen* triggers the events that lead to the proliferation of Unstoppable Soldiers. Given the associations that exist between gay men, AIDS, and the fictional 412 E virus, it can be argued that queerness leads to the destabilization of the world and the destruction of millions, if not billions, of lives.

The novel, however, escapes these tense interpretations in two ways. Firstly, while Robby's blood activates the contagion, he doesn't carry the 412 E Plague Strain. Therefore, he avoids becoming a Patient Zero for the plague strain, and this lack of embodiment prevents Robby's demonization and stops the Plague Strain from being humanized (Wald 234).[5] Additionally, *Grasshopper Jungle* narratively renders Robby's blood as the catalyst and salvation for the praying mantis infestation that threatens Earth. At various points throughout the novel, characters realize that the Unstoppable Soldiers flee at the sight of Robby and avoid going near him. After perusing multiple documents and media found in the McKeon Industries headquarters, Austin and Robby determine that the blood that activated the 412 E Plague Strain could also kill the Unstoppable Soldiers. Austin and Robby weaponize Robby's blood by injecting it into paintballs, using this as their primary defense against the insect menace.

Although the novel provides little explanation for why Robby's blood kills the Unstoppable Soldiers, this turn in the narrative alleviates some of the potential issues suggested by reading the story as an AIDS text. The blood of a gay teen does trigger the disease that leads to the end of the world, but his very blood has the potential to undo some of the damage caused by the plague—making Robby's blood a plot device that possesses both destructive and reparative potential. The narrative takes the source of the novel's pessimism, destruction, and bleakness and portrays it as a potential source of hope and optimism. Furthermore, if we're to approach the 412 E Plague Strain as a reification of capitalist modes of thinking and production, we don't have to read Robby's blood as the catalyst for the apocalypse, but rather, yet another facet of human culture absorbed and appropriated by capitalist modes.

The ties between sexuality and the praying mantises in the novel are complex. Praying mantises, female ones specifically, are stereotypically known for biting off their mates' heads and eating them after engaging in sexual intercourse. The mantises in Smith's novel also put into practice this penchant for decapitation and consumption, as we see in an instance in an interaction between Eileen Pope, the queen mantis, and Devin Stoddard, one of Grant Wallace's companions who was converted into an Unstoppable Soldier: "Devin Stoddard continued pumping semen into Eileen Pope even after she had eaten his entire head" (Smith 203). Through its depiction of an insect invasion, *Grasshopper Jungle* draws elements from B-horror, science fiction, and fantasy horror film, literature, and television—another characteristic commonly observed in the New Weird and second-wave postmodern literature, in that low and high cultural productions, motifs, and imagery are deliberately mixed. Especially in television, the praying mantis has been a figure used to represent male teenage anxiety or apprehension towards sex, gender, and sexuality. Consider, for instance, the fourth episode of *Buffy the Vampire Slayer* entitled "Teacher's Pet," where the creature-of-the-week is a giant praying mantis disguised as a seductive substitute teacher. This teacher imprisons teenage boys in her lair and tries to mate with them before Buffy saves the day. Similarly, in an episode of *The X-Files* entitled "War of the Coprophages," Agent Fox Mulder shares a childhood story in which he confused a leaf with a praying mantis, leading him to scream because he came face to face with "some before unknown monster that had no right existing on the same planet [that he] inhabited." Mulder's partner, Agent Dana Scully, speculates whether Mulder's scream was "girlie" or not, thus revealing the gender anxieties that surfaced during his encounter with the praying mantis.

The novel challenges this heterosexual and reproductive imagery, in that the mantises are shown to partake in contingent homosexuality when a female mate is not present—as seen in the interaction between Roger Baird and Tyler Jacobson: "Roger Baird was not very happy after being disturbed from his rest by another male Unstoppable Soldier that was in the act of copulating with him. Tyler Jacobson was confused" (Smith 300). Tyler Jacobson decapitates Roger Baird's head while mating with him, thus complicating the typical sexual dynamic performed by praying mantises. This queering of the imagery used in science fiction and horror illustrates how the horrors of normativity and capitalism affect the lives of those directly and indirectly engaging in these enterprises. Nobody's head is safe when these systems are in place.

Bison, Bisexuality, and the Follies of Historical Representation

Now that we're aware of the lore and queer dynamics present in the novel, we must ask: how does *Grasshopper Jungle* provide a sense of resolution to the seemingly unrelenting forces of antiqueerness and capitalism as represented through the giant praying mantises? Furthermore, how does the novel deal with its two central tensions: the insurmountable threat of the Unstoppable Soldiers and Austin's inner turmoil concerning his sexuality? To provide a simple answer, the novel avoids resolution almost entirely. Despite Robby's blood being the key to human salvation, a single human body doesn't contain enough blood to eliminate the rapidly increasing praying mantis population. However, they create enough blood-infused paintballs to protect themselves from immediate harm. The Unstoppable Soldiers continue to eat and mate until they replace humanity as the apex predators of the world, thus demonstrating how the endless and repetitive cycle of production and reproduction finally leads to the world's undoing. The novel's capitalist, heteronormative, biotechnological narratives not only emphasize the displaced disposition of queerness within the confines of this fictional world, but also amplify the discussion and importance of sexuality within the narrative parameters of (post)apocalyptic YA literature.

Unlike Katniss Everdeen, Austin and Robby aren't victorious in overthrowing the looming threat of the oppression and violence they battle against. This notion goes against a central expectation of YA literature in that these books are expected to comfort readers and provide them with a hopeful, emotionally nourishing outlook. Cadden argues that an adult's desire to comfort a younger reader can directly correlate to the temporal distance between the end of a novel and its epilogue (355). For instance, the epilogue of Collins' *Mockingjay* takes place many decades after the events discussed in the novel's ending. The epilogue of *Harry Potter and the Deathly Hallows* takes place nineteen years after the defeat of Voldemort. What can be said about the epilogue of *Grasshopper Jungle*, which takes place only five years after the novel's conclusion? To fully understand how the story culminates in the epilogue, we must first unpack how it approaches the triangular tension in Austin, Robby, and Shann's relationship. Furthermore, we must also discuss the role of history, art, ecology, and temporality in helping Austin embrace nonnormative thinking modes. As discussed before, McCrea argues that biological reproduction often becomes a model for narrativizing time and change. What's distinctive about *Grasshopper Jungle*'s epilogue is how it precludes normative notions of time by demonstrating the fictiveness of temporality, and by showing how time no longer controls human bodies. It provides a twist on normative bodily and ontological rhythms. This alteration facilitates the stalling of full narrative closure without resorting to the narrative notion of arrested development often connected to queer lives and queer discourse, and even more so, by reconfiguring the expectations of futurity that are usually imposed upon children and teens.

The looming threat of the end of the world pushes Austin to spend an increasing amount of time with both Robby and his girlfriend, Shann—forcing him to obsessively think through his love for two people with different gender identities, and the impossibility of loving more than one person at the same time given his current social and cultural circumstances. In a moment of contemplation, Austin recalls how he and Robby were "beaten up for being queers by those four assholes in the alley at Grasshopper Jungle" (Smith 160) and how he and his best friend faced violence simply because their desires and mutual intimacy aren't aligned with normative ideologies or expectations. Austin's remembrance of this violent incident leads him to fully articulate the confusion that he's felt throughout most of the novel:

> I was ripping my own heart in half, ghettoizing it like Warsaw during the Second World War—*this area for Shann; the other area for queer kids only*—and wondering how it was possible to be sexually attracted and in love with my best friend, a boy, *and* my other best friend, a girl.
> (Smith 162)

Austin's use of words such as "half" and "ghettoizing" demonstrates how his current cultural conditions lead to both binary and hierarchical thinking.[6] In other words, Austin buys into the socially constructed divide between homosexuality and heterosexuality, and by alluding to terms such as ghettoization, he clearly sees one form of sexual identity as more valuable and desirable than the other. He not only has difficulties understanding why he loves people of different genders, but even more so, he has trouble understanding how a person can genuinely love two people simultaneously. Austin attempts to deviate from both heteronormative and homonormative ways of thinking, and in the process, interrogates the tyranny of practices such as monogamy and compulsive heterosexuality.

Austin places the blame for his sexual confusion not overtly on heteronormative pressures but rather on historical representation, which in his view, complicates notions of free will and creates the binaries and hierarchies that create such immense angst in his life. In a pivotal scene in the novel, Austin reflects on the representations of hunters and bison that early human cultures drew on the walls of caves, claiming that "once the historians put the thing on the wall, it was almost as though every bison for all eternity became doomed to face the hunter's interminable slaughter" (305). Here, he deliberates how historical and artistic representations concretize and stabilize certain attitudes regarding how humans interact with one another and the world around them. The representation of humans as hunters and the bison as the hunted on cavern walls perpetuates hegemonic ideologies that reinforce the hierarchy between humans and nonhumans, and ultimately lead to the creation of rules that regulate what humans can or should do (see Figure 5.3).

Austin's disdain of the normative ideologies reflected and reinforced by historical representation reaches its peak when he claims, "*We made this stupid rule and this stupid rule. Boys are not allowed to love each other. Then we painted a bison on the wall*" (320, emphasis in original). Here, Austin starts to develop the antinormative and antiuniversalist stances implicit in queer modes of thinking. In this moment, we're invited to consider the effects of textual, linguistic, and aesthetic representations in solidifying an oppressive perspective or practice, making something seem natural, like "the state of second nature, no longer an [unfamiliar] or obtrusive activity but a recognizable and reassuring rhythm of thought" (Felski 21). At this moment, *Grasshopper Jungle*'s metanarrative exudes a degree of self-awareness in that we witness a textual representation pushing us to think beyond the limits and parameters instantiated through the acts of textual, artistic, and linguistic records—as we saw with the implementation of metafictional devices in Patrick Ness' YA novel *More Than This* in the previous chapter.

Figure 5.3 "The Shaft," *Lascaux III* by Ministère de la Culture/Centre National de la Préhistoire/Norbert Aujoulat, used under CC BY-NC-ND 4.0. This image is an exact replica of the Lascaux cave paintings located in southwestern France created approximately 17,000 years ago. Known as "The Shaft Scene," this cave painting represents a bison wounded by a human-made weapon, and we can clearly observe the bison's entrails protruding out of its body.

Artistic and historical representation and the blurring of the lines between the human and nonhuman are the elements that help Austin internalize and resolve some of the tensions he experiences throughout the story. While thinking about the bison painted on cave walls, Austin considers interpreting the artistic creations not through a human perspective but rather through the perspective of the animal: "I have been devoting too much thought to the guys who painted the bison on the wall of the cave, and too little attention to the bison itself. I mean, *the bison is the important member of the team*, isn't he?" (305, emphasis mine). By prioritizing the bison's importance over the human hunters' position, Austin subverts the traditional human-animal hierarchy that has been prevalent in countless human cultures for literally thousands of years. Austin's statement regarding the bison's positionality becomes critical in understanding the affective goals of the novel's epilogue. Let's bring a queer ecological purview into the conversation.

In "Queer Ecology," Timothy Morton argues that a perspective that considers both queer and ecological theories "might regard beings as people even when they aren't people" (279), and it should ultimately strive to illustrate how "interconnectedness is not organic" (279). In other words, Morton argues that relationships, affinities, and desires between two beings are *always* socially and culturally constructed, and that queer ecology works not only to highlight this sense of artificiality but also to decentralize the hierarchies and binaries used to approach our environment. Queer ecology also aims to show that desires, affiliations, and identifications can and should be expressed toward the nonhuman, thus emphasizing the queerness of this critical exercise. After all, a desire or sense of affiliation expressed towards a nonhuman remains outside of the scope of heteronormative ideologies. Because ecology and queer theory share similar antihierarchical aims, Morton goes as far as to claim that "fully and properly, ecology is queer theory and queer theory is ecology: queer ecology" (281).

A queer ecological approach helps us better grasp the significance of Austin's contemplation on bison precisely because this reflection pushes him to come to terms with the constructed nature of all relationships—not just the relationship between humans and animals but also the relationship between himself and other humans. Austin develops a suspicion towards the ideologies cemented through historical and artistic representation and begins to see himself as an element within the *mesh*, which Morton approaches as a conceptual web that connects everything that exists in our world, a "nontotalizable, open-ended concatenation of interrelations that blur and confound boundaries at practically any level: between species, between the living and the nonliving, between organism and environment" (*The Ecological Thought* 275–276). Austin's contemplation pushes him to better visualize this sense of interconnectedness, in that he not only subverts the constructed human-animal dyad but also gives serious thought as to what the bison think and *feel*, which mobilizes the potentialities of queer ecological thinking. Along the lines of ideas discussed by Laura McMahon and Michael Lawrence, *Grasshopper Jungle* plays around with textual and visual representation to foster a sense of disorientation that allows the "planes of human and animal being" to coexist, producing an image that deflects rather than reflects the human and suggests "a commingling of human and nonhuman realms" (7). Through this conceptual commingling, Austin understands the harmful effects that binary and hierarchical modes of thinking enforce upon him and all living creatures.

How can bison escape the wall on which they are drawn? Does artistic representation enforce bison to perpetually embody the positionality of the hunted? Is Austin, as a character, ultimately as limited as the bison are in terms of what his body, his sexuality, his desires, and his gender performance can or can't mean? Answers to these questions are found in the novel's epilogue. As discussed above, Austin and friends don't prevent the

Unstoppable Soldiers from infesting the world. The praying mantises continue eating and mating, thus driving Austin, Robby, Shann, and a handful of their family members and friends to seek shelter in an underground silo known as Eden, the site where McKeon scientists conducted some of their experiments until the scientists either fled or were murdered by the first army of Unstoppable Soldiers developed during the 1960s. After this failure, the novel's epilogue fast-forwards about five years. The remaining population, who now refer to themselves as "New Humans," live in this abandoned silo: a place destined to fail and collapse because, according to Austin, Eden's breakdown "is going to happen eventually" (Smith 385). The threat of Eden breaking down adds a sense of gloom and despair to the New Humans' everyday lives, implying that the remnants of humanity have their days numbered.

New Humans soon discover that the Unstoppable Soldiers leave Iowa every winter for warmer weather, thus offering Austin and Robby the opportunity to venture out into the open world to gather food, supplies, and cigarettes. Austin and Robby call these risky endeavors "Cigarette Runs" (383). Although Eden has more than enough supplies to sustain a small community of people for a couple of years, the two young men go on these runs to spend some time alone with each other. They never encounter other human beings on the Earth's surface. Furthermore, they don't view the absence of other humans as a pessimistic development, for the two teens ultimately desire this absence of human life when venturing through the outside world: "I do not believe that Robby and I *wanted* to find anyone else, but we never said that aloud. We did not need to say such things" (384, emphasis in original). Austin and Robby's feelings toward each other and their desire to be alone don't have to be verbally articulated to be understood. As Mason argues, their desire remains within the periphery of the text. In this moment, we observe queer affect escaping the trappings of linguistic representation through moments of silence—a moment of intense feeling and emotion that transcends language and the written word.

Although the silo offers New Humans shelter and protection, Austin points out that regulations regarding gender and sexuality are often imposed by older adults, such as Shann's mother, who make "rules about things like when boys and girls can take showers" in Eden (382). Austin points out that he and Robby "do not follow [her] rules very well" (386), thus exemplifying how the novel's young adult characters resist embodying and reifying the validity of moot sociocultural rules and ideologies in Eden. Despite the collapse of the old world, however, some odd and knotty gender-related dynamics remain at play in the domain of the New Universe. For instance, Robby and Austin are the only two characters that venture out of Eden, whereas women always remain in the silo—therefore reinforcing associations between women and indoor domesticity and men and outdoor freedom. Although other men also stay in the silo, the novel still depicts a notion of queer exceptionality in that nonnormative people are free to venture through the outside world, whereas those who don't identify as queer are restricted in terms of what they can or can't do.

The novel's epilogue reinforces many normative gender ideologies. First and foremost, the epilogue falls into the trappings of gender essentialism because Austin presents his need to leave the silo and explore the outside world as a "natural" male instinct: "There is something inside all boys that drives us to go away again and again and again" (385) and "all boys build roads that crisscross and carry us away" (387). The novel's narrative could've easily avoided this conundrum by having Shann join Austin and Robby during their escapes into the outside world. Alas, Shann and many other secondary characters remain peripheral in the narrative and peripheral to the freedoms of the outside world. This issue can be traced back to an even more considerable gender-related concern in Andrew Smith's oeuvre, in that he commonly represents teenage boys as exciting and complex characters. At the same time, his representation of women, for the most part, can be approached as one-dimensional and, at times, downright misogynistic. For instance, even though the novel implies that Shann, Robby, and Austin are potentially engaged in a queer, potentially polyamorous relationship, Shann remains sidelined in this narrative, and we have little insight as to what her desires, motives, or feelings are.

On the one hand, part of this has to do with the fact that Austin acts as the narrator and focalizer of the text, and thus, his consciousness has complete control over how we approach the events represented in the novel. Austin is selfish, self-centered, and believes in male exceptionality. Are we surprised that Shann is repeatedly sidelined in the text? On the other hand, this issue can be traced back to Smith's problems regarding the representation of women in his books. In an interview published by *Vice* magazine, Smith was asked why his works do not cater to women and why his novels lack female representation, to which Smith replied: "I consider myself to be completely ignorant of all things woman and female" (Ryan). As can be expected, this interview created a lot of backlash for Smith, and he was accused of perpetuating harmful and stereotypical tropes that frame women as foreign, unknowable creatures.

I'll be upfront: the novel's epilogue has many issues regarding matters of gender and sexuality, and in a sense, this culmination seems to perpetuate many of the frameworks and topics present in *Mockingjay*'s two-decade leap into the future. However, I argue that a lot of the queer potentiality present in *Grasshopper Jungle*'s epilogue could be better understood and appreciated by implementing a queer ecocritical lens and understanding the politics of temporality, futurity, and emotion that it ultimately mobilizes.

By reading the novel's epilogue with these elements in mind, the story still manages to, in the words of Muñoz, reach out to queerness. When we pay close attention to the relationships that develop in the postapocalyptic universe of the New Humans, *Grasshopper Jungle* does bring us closer to a queerer, albeit still challenging, future. The way that kinship and affinity are represented in Eden bear little resemblance to heteronormative linkages that were established before the apocalypse, and they're a far cry from the ones seen in the epilogue of Collins' *Mockingjay*—where Katniss buys into the pressures imposed by Peeta and abandons her potential queerness and aromanticism in favor of monogamy and motherhood.

Grasshopper Jungle exudes queerness through the relationship between Austin, Shann, and Robby, and even more so by thwarting the role of children in the YA epilogue. In a moment of lust before the novel's conclusion, Shann becomes pregnant after sleeping with Austin at a bowling alley, opening the possibility that this sexual encounter and the pressures of fatherhood will assure Austin's adherence to heterosexuality and resolve the novel's central love triangle. Nonetheless, after five years living in Eden, Austin reveals,

> I continue to be torn between my love for Shann Collins and Robby Brees. But I no longer care to ask the question, *What am I going to do?* Sometimes it is perfectly acceptable to decide not to decide, to remain confused and wide-eyed about the next thing that will pop up in the road you build.
>
> (383, emphasis in original)

Austin's unwillingness to choose between his love for Shann and Robby is reproduced in the spaces he inhabits, in that he refuses to share a dwelling space with either person (383). True, Austin's decision may be even more evidence that proves his selfishness and his inability to make decisions. However, it can also be interpreted as an attempt to dismantle the heteronormative ideologies that were in place before the reign of the Unstoppable Soldiers.

Not only does Austin avoid falling into the pitfall of monogamy in the novel's epilogue, but this section of the novel also implies that Austin is the primary caretaker of his child when present at the silo—as evidenced by the fact that he shares a room with his son, and not with the people who he shares a sexual or romantic partnership with. The epilogue also implies that Austin's son, Arek, grows in an environment in which he loves people who are not his parents with the same degree of intensity and emotion: "Robby gets out of the car and trudges across the snow to say a last good-bye to Arek. Like his father, Arek also loves Robby Brees very much" (388). Robby has a paternal relationship with Arek, Shann, and Austin's son, and when Austin and Robby leave for one of their outside ventures, Shann kisses Austin and Robby on the lips.

New Humans not only live during a time when one could love a person of the same gender, but they can also love more than one person simultaneously. Monogamy or heterosexuality aren't viewed as compulsory, women aren't expected to be the primary caregivers of their children, and different forms of kinship and connectivity are constructed. Even though biological reproduction provides a template for closing this novel, we must recall that Arek lives and dwells in a *futureless* society. Eden will break down, New Humans will be unable to produce weapons using Robby's blood once he passes away (unless he has biological children of his own who inherit the ability to repel the giant praying mantises), and the Unstoppable Soldiers show no signs of halting their habits of consumption and propagation.

Here, we must recall Lee Edelman's concept of reproductive futurism, which he approaches as a phenomenon that elevates the cultural centrality of heteronormativity and the Child by centering "the reproductive mandate inherent in the logic of futurism itself" (117). As discussed by Edelman and Ahmed, babies and children assure a sense of futurity, redemption, and justification of one's suffering. However, all these notions are pressured in *Grasshopper Jungle*, given that the New Human society remains futureless and on the brink of destruction. Thus, the novel's epilogue offers an instance in which children can't perpetuate the politically conservative tendency to assure futurity and continue the status quo. There's no guarantee that further biological reproduction can counteract the effects of this apocalypse.

This lack of futurity in the world of the New Humans destabilizes narrative temporality in ways that allow *Grasshopper Jungle* to escape the teleological and biological template commonly found in heterocentric narratives. In many ways, time itself collapses narratively and literally in Smith's novel, as seen through a joke that Robby performs during his Cigarette Runs, in which he brings Shann a Rolex wristwatch each time he returns. Austin comments that he has "a difficult time imagining anything as useless in Eden" as these watches (Smith 387). In the postapocalyptic world of *Grasshopper Jungle*, chrononormativity, as Elizabeth Freeman would put it, along with all its heteronormative and productive connotations, has been disrupted and queered. This temporal disruption not only provides a sense of ambiguity to the passing of events, but it also blurs normative temporal measurements such as beginnings and endings while counteracting the horror instilled by the capitalist and heteronormative enterprises found within the outside domain of the Unstoppable Soldiers. Freeman alludes to Judith Butler's notions on recurrences and repetitions, and more specifically, how "rhythms of gendered performance" congeal gender "into timeless truths of being" (4). Within the confines of the emerging post-apocalyptic world of *Grasshopper Jungle*, neither time or the pressures of capitalist being can effectively regulate New Humans' bodies or practices, thus allowing the space for the rhythms of gendered performance and sexuality to switch tempos, skip beats, or stall entirely.

Unusually for a YA novel, *Grasshopper Jungle* offers a radical solution to its love triangle and its central tensions in that it provides no resolution.[7] Rather than deciding between the two people that he loves, and rather than deciding to categorize himself as either straight or gay, Austin forgoes choosing entirely. His avoidance of monogamy and his choice to love *both* Robby and Shann are queer potentialities that become realities through the collapse of human culture and society. Robby and Shann's relationship with each other also aspires to queerness in many ways. They both love Austin, but they love each other as well. The destruction of human society and its capitalist and temporal baggage allows these young adults to devise their own terms for kinship and connectivity. The two characters that achieve mobility in the outside, insect-ruled universe are those who were considered queer before the end of the world. In a somewhat surprising inversion, the domestic sphere becomes the public sphere—the sphere where people interact and come into contact, whereas the realm of the praying mantises becomes the private sphere for the New Humans. No longer confined to bedrooms, rooftops, or other restricted spaces, Austin and Robby's queer relationship now flourishes in the private yet open world created by cultural, biological, and technological collapse.

The possibility of this queer openness becomes tangible as Austin and Robby contemplate flying a "two-man ultralight aircraft" despite never having piloted an aircraft before: "We will fly over Grasshopper Jungle in our own airplane, and Robby will sing Rolling Stones songs and I will smoke cigarettes and spit on the planet called Earth" (386). Fred Erisman points out that early 20th-Century boys' books invoked aviation as a "shaping force in society" (294). Airplanes and aviation were implemented in narratives to denote a changing world where notions of distance and space were challenged and disrupted (293). The aircraft not only provided humanity with unprecedented mobility, but it also allowed people to overcome both physical and ideological barriers. Erisman points out that aviation narratives "consistently project a sense of a progressive future" and "held out the golden dream of a better world to come" (299). These linkages between the portrayal of aviation and notions of progress and futurity are particularly fascinating and ironic in *Grasshopper Jungle* precisely because the airplane becomes a symbol of a past that rarely resonates with the post-apocalyptic future.

The image of Austin and Robby desiring to fly over Grasshopper Jungle conveys that these young men can overcome physical and ideological limitations. It conveys a sense of freedom and distance from the rules of the past world. The planet called Earth, where humanity rests on the brink of extinction, will become a distant, minute, and inconsequential element for the two queer boys in the air—a fact emphasized through Austin's desire to "spit on the planet." Just as Austin presents indifference, perhaps even disdain, towards planet Earth, the Earth shows complete and utter indifference towards New Humans. Here, the airplane doesn't represent a golden dream and a progressive future; instead, it shows us a bird's eye view of a careless planet that will continue to exist regardless of whether people inhabit it. The aircraft becomes a symbol of futurity rooted in the past, a remnant of an ideological and technological history that no longer has a firm hold on the present.

Grasshopper Jungle presents readers with an undoubtedly queer and unstable epilogue, especially compared to the ones of other dystopian and post-apocalyptic YA novels. In terms of temporality, queerness, and narrative, it fosters ambiguity and uncertainty rather than providing readers with a sense of resolution and epistemological grounding. Perhaps this has to do with, as Cadden would argue, the distance between the end and the epilogue: given that so little time has passed between the ending and the epilogue, maybe we're witnessing a case in which the epilogue opens, rather than forecloses, avenues of inquiry and being. Do these temporal and narrative innovations preclude *Grasshopper Jungle*'s epilogue from inducing the comfort traditionally conveyed through such closures in YA speculative literature? Given the discussion above, my answer would have to be a resounding "no," but only under the condition that we deviate from normative assumptions of what happiness and comfort entail. *Grasshopper Jungle* illuminates the fluidity, cruelty, and possibility of happiness. By challenging the notion that happiness is merely a result of cause and effect, the novel disrupts the correlation between heteronormativity and happiness and instead presents an alternative framework in which queer modalities are closely linked to it.

A lot of sadness and despair can be found in *Grasshopper Jungle*'s epilogue. The epilogue elevates male-centered and misogynist ideologies. Humans will cease to exist. Even though queer relationships are more of a possibility in this postapocalyptic world, various normative practices are still in effect in the sociocultural realm of the New Humans. Male experiences and freedoms are prioritized in this text, whereas women are relegated to the background. However, perhaps we should consider the novel's advice and stop viewing this epilogue through a human-centric perspective and instead adopt the positionality of the nonhuman when approaching these outcomes. *Grasshopper Jungle*'s epilogue poses a messy and convoluted thought experiment of sorts in that it pushes us to witness the horrors, hurt, and pain caused by humanity, capitalism, consumption, and greed—and it further pushes us to deliberate sinthomosexual sentiments like those that Katniss Everdeen expressed while awaiting her trial. Would the world be better off if we destroyed one another and allowed another more deserving species to thrive? Does it benefit anyone to live in a world where humans cause so much pain, oppression, hurt, and violence, not only to each other but to the Earth and other nonhuman creatures that inhabit it? Do we really want to live in a world ruled by misogyny and antiqueerness? While the downfall of humanity might seem like a pessimistic development to us for obvious reasons, would this not present a sense of hope and optimism for the planet and the creatures that we hurt, control, and oppress on an everyday basis? I'm obviously not calling for the end of humanity or the end of the world, but rather, I'm pushing us to consider how queer YA rewrites the script and uses the apocalypse to emphasize the harm and hurt humanity has and will continue to generate. It connects us to these histories and holds us accountable for them.

The novel's final pages convey the hope and utopic possibilities instigated by the end of the human world. As Austin and Robby head out of the silo to gather supplies and explore the outside environment, they encounter a vast herd of North American Bison. Creatures that have constantly been on the verge of extinction due to human hunting practices, creatures that once existed in the tens of millions and have been reduced to thousands thanks to human intervention, now roam the fields in staggering numbers after the end of the human world. Bison are no longer reduced to a human aesthetic representation on cave walls. The apocalypse has enabled bison to flourish, to grow collectively, and to escape the violent and ideological human practices that threatened their lives on an everyday basis. If "stupid rules" led humans to paint bison on the wall, then the obliteration of these rules allows the bison to break away from the wall on which they are painted. As the remaining New Humans stare in awe at the colossal herd of animals in front of them, they come face-to-face with the mesh: the boundaries between species, living creatures, and the environment have become delightfully messy and blurry.

Unlike Katniss, Austin doesn't find himself in a position where he needs to look back and remember acts of goodness to cope with his current conditions, nor does he need to look forward to live in service of a time that's yet to come. With the obliteration of the sociocultural blueprint used to uphold the rules of the human world, Austin embraces a state of confusion while remaining "wide-eyed about the next thing that will pop up" (Smith 383). Austin and other New Humans are uncertain whether they will continue to thrive as a species in the future—but despite this uncertainty, Austin can *explicitly* proclaim that he's "very happy" (383). Unlike Collin's *Mockingjay*, Smith's *Grasshopper Jungle* unequivocally demonstrates that comfort, queerness, and hurt can coexist if we refute normative standards and narrative templates.

Better Games to Play?

Grasshopper Jungle presents a fictional world that questions whether "essential" human values can or should be preserved. Whereas Sambell questions the possibility for YA novels to present disconsolate truths while still instilling a sense of hope in the reader, I suggest that despite their pessimistic "truths," (post)apocalyptic YA with overt queer themes and characters pave the way for alternative narratives to thrive. Ironically and devastatingly hopeful narratives where societal collapse allows queer teens to perceive and embody nonnormative and generative forms of kinship, love, and relationality. Dystopian and post-apocalyptic novels such as *Grasshopper Jungle* accomplish this by challenging and dismantling the normative and affective goals of the YA epilogue: instead of providing readers with traditional "happy endings," these queer narratives provide closures that frustrate rather than comfort, that challenge normative conceptions of what kinship, happiness, and a "good life" entail.

Wendy Gay Pearson, Veronica Hollinger, and Joan Gordon point out that queer theory possesses "both utopian and science fictional [qualities], in the sense of imagining a future that opens out, rather than forecloses, possibilities for becoming real, for mattering in the world" (5). Collins' *Mockingjay* forecloses the fluidity of gender performance and identity, limiting what bodies and their performances can mean through the forces of patriarchy and reproductive futurism. When analyzing the conclusion to the *Hunger Games* series, we must ask ourselves: *does* Katniss matter in her world? Do her desires matter? Does she have a life that enables rather than hinders queer potentiality? Maybe Katniss was right in stating, "there are much worse games to play," especially when it comes to coping with trauma. However, I suggest that there are better games to play, games that avoid repetitiveness, stasis, and roundaboutness—open-ended, changeable, and downright challenging games. *Grasshopper Jungle* ultimately *attempts* to offer us such a game. Imperfect at its core, feelings of bleakness, misogyny, disgust, and despair saturate this game. It messes with your head and pushes you to confront contradicting possibilities and rules designed to be broken. It explores avenues for living during bleakness and chaos in that queer people, non-monogamous people, and non-human creatures finally matter in the world. Indeed, we're presented with a human world destined to end—but despite this ending, the epilogue does not undo the queer comforts that people have access to, even if such comforts are fleeting.

If epilogues exist to reassure readers that happiness "sticks," then endings and epilogues that don't make these assurances and that don't guarantee that its characters will live long and comfortable lives perhaps allow readers to, as Austin puts it, "remain confused and wide-eyed." *Grasshopper Jungle* queers the affective aims of the epilogue, using it not to instill a normative sense of comfort and happiness, but rather, to make us question the harmful realities of our world and our practices. It celebrates negative and positive feelings, pushing us to interrogate how we prevent other people and beings from mattering and feeling. Personally speaking, it makes me *deeply* uncomfortable for all the reasons mentioned above, but I also feel an ironic and twisted sense of hope. At least we won't have to deal with people who made Austin and Robby's life a living hell anymore—and we especially won't have to deal with people like Austin.

Whether the New Humans we encounter in *Grasshopper Jungle* will endure the hardships and trials of their new world rests in speculation. However, perhaps we can find comfort in the fact that these characters lived in a queer place and time, where queer modalities and positive affect could coexist. They didn't have to follow all the rules, they were closer to touching queerness, they could love more than one person simultaneously, binary choices became less imperative, time collapses and no longer regulates their bodies, and bison finally, *finally* roam free.

Notes

1. See Gina Gwenffrewi's "J.K. Rowling and the Echo Chamber of Secrets" for a more in-depth examination of J.K. Rowling's alignment with antitrans discourses.
2. Thomas' reading explores the racial politics behind Rue's representation, and how this informs the ways in which we interpret her relationship with Katniss. Thomas also explores the logics of race, spectacle, and innocence that are mobilized through these characters' interactions.
3. Freeman approaches chrononormativity as "the use of time to organize individual bodies toward maximum productivity" (3). Thus, it combines the elements of time, sexual identity, and capitalist production.
4. M.M. Bakhtin broadly characterizes the chronotope as "the intrinsic interconnectedness of temporal and spatial relationships that are artistically expressed in literature" (15).
5. Patient Zero is a medical term for the first person diagnosed with an epidemiological disease. Wald has discussed the case of Gaëtan Dugas, a gay flight attendant who was irresponsibly dubbed by media and medical practitioners as the Patient Zero for HIV—a move that animated discourse on HIV in the public imagination and "loosed the specter of a willful scourge" by humanizing the virus (215).
6. It's not a coincidence that Austin alludes to Warsaw during this contemplation. In addition to the novel's central tensions, *Grasshopper Jungle* also depicts a narrative of immigration in that Austin writes a fabricated history of how his great-grandfather traveled from Europe to the United States. In this fabricated history, Austin shares how his great-grandfather used to be in a relationship with a Jewish male refugee. Austin creates this narrative as a way of trying to develop a history for his own emergent queerness, although a complete discussion of this matter is beyond the scope of this chapter.
7. Although the love triangle has been a prevalent dynamic in YA literature and culture for quite some time, it was immensely popularized by Stephenie Meyers'

Twilight series—to the point where many deem that including this device will contribute to a work's success. While some quickly dismiss the critical importance of the love triangle in the field, some scholars have pointed out its narrative and literary merits. In his discussion on the classical roots of *The Hunger Games,* for instance, Barry Strauss points out that although Katniss, Peeta, and Gale form an expected love triangle, "they also represent, from the point of view of the ancients, an aroused citizenry banding together and fighting for freedom against an evil empire" (WSJ). Along these lines, the love triangle in *Grasshopper Jungle* serves a narrative purpose that transcends the characteristic romantic and sexual tension typically found in YA cultural productions.

6 The Limits of Repair

Taking place in a fictional universe where humanity has colonized other exoplanets through the use of fish-shaped spaceships, Tillie Walden's webcomic (and later graphic novel) *On a Sunbeam* (2016–2017) explores a future astronomically removed from our current place and time. Characteristic of many queer YA texts, this webcomic messes with chrononormative understandings of time, presenting us with an imagined world where traditional notions of masculinity are virtually extinct.[1] Many of the rules and structures in our present world are seen as quaint, or are entirely forgotten. The story oscillates between the past and present, compressing time and pressuring linear and normative trajectories of development seen in various YA cultural productions. The novel implements (and challenges) coming of age and school narrative tropes, channels both the glamor and spectacle expected of a space saga, and focuses extensively on the queer development of Mia and Grace's relationship. Here, I'm less interested in exploring the representation of this relationship throughout the webcomic, and instead, more invested in how this text visualizes and structures the processes of history, repair, time, and (re)construction often centralized in narrativizations of queer YA. Walden's graphic narrative implements motifs of building, constructing, and recycling and connects them to the broader dynamics of repair explored in this book. Given the impossible distance that exists between our time and the temporal frame of the text, *On a Sunbeam* invites us to consider how repair and healing manifest in a time so disconnected from the past—so removed from history.

The webcomic represents Mia's positionality as a child and as an adult throughout the narrative. These temporalities aren't divided by chapters, but rather, they bleed into each other through the narrative's chaotic temporality and clever use of visuals, leading the text to combat the normative and "harmful effects of categories of age" while highlighting the complexities, continuities, and multiplicities that characterize teen personhood (Owen 148). As adults, Mia and Grace are no longer together. Mia now works for an intergalactic construction crew focused on repairing

DOI: 10.4324/9781003038627-6

This chapter has been made available under a CC-BY-NC-ND license.

crumbling buildings and structures peppered throughout the galaxy—fixing their flaws and weaknesses so they can be renovated into apartment complexes, offices, and other hallmarks of industrial development. Mia and her crew travel to different long-abandoned settlements and work on repairs over the span of days—replacing tiles, filling in cracks in the walls, and reinforcing the foundations of these mysterious structures.

In the webcomic's introduction, the crew lands their ship on a grand floating structure that resembles cathedral-like architecture. These dilapidated ruins covered in unknown symbols and imagery drown in the vegetation and overgrowth covering the walls. Ancient and lost to time, its grandiose and imposing presence is now but an echo of what used to be a culturally significant establishment connected to a larger institution. As Mia and her crewmate discover a hidden chamber located in the ruins—ostensibly used for meditation, study, or prayer—they note that the floating structure stands as a relic with no past, no history. As Char comments when examining the mysterious chamber and reflecting on the cultures who used to dwell there, "It wasn't just old, it was *forgotten*. Almost all records of this place have been lost or destroyed" (Walden, Chapter 2, emphasis in original). When looking at the various chambers and structures that comprise the construction site and paying attention to the imagery carved into wood and stone, Char—the crew's resident historian—points out how the institution's ideologies can be traced in the remnants of the site's architecture:

> The central belief was all about finding this one object. They thought that holiness was tangible, and that the founder had hidden it somewhere in this complex. That's why this whole place is full of tricks. Hidden rooms, stairs that lead nowhere.
> (Walden, Chapter 2)

The site was designed to prevent access to certain knowledges, to make answers impossible to find. Char discloses that many people spent their lives in search of this undefineable and unknowable object, and some even died in their efforts to uncover it. Was their search done in vain? What fears, hopes, expectations, and failures continue to echo through the walls of this structure?

Although this intergalactic relic connects to institutions and an unknown ideological system, how it stands in as an allegory for the history of queer representation and narrative intrigues and compels me. In many Western and colonized contexts, the histories and legacies of queerness and gender variance have often been suppressed, omitted, and destroyed. Kyla Wazana Tompkins has pointed out how the violent histories of colonization focused on the purposeful destruction of existing kinship networks, and the imposition of "disciplinary regimes" that punished nonnormative forms of gender expression and sexuality (174). Other scholars such as Sarah Ngu approach queerness as a white invention, in that it often erases broader histories of gender variance and sexuality that existed prior to the 20th Century—when the word "queer" became associated with deviance in Western contexts:

> The historical records suggests that early modern (16th century onwards) Southeast Asia was a region that encouraged societal tolerance, even respect, of gender and sexual fluidity and that such a tolerance was eroded by the forces of modernity and European, Christian colonialism.
> (81)

As Mia and Char examine the chamber, we're invited to reflect on the histories that have been forgotten—and destroyed—by human intervention and the passage of time. Mia and Char are left with nothing but imagination and speculation to fill in the blanks.

Akin to the giant floating structure in *On a Sunbeam*, histories of queerness are often suppressed and forgotten. Records, artifacts, and texts that document our lives and stories were crushed, burnt, destroyed, or erased—reinforcing the faulty understanding of heterosexuality and cisgender embodiment as true, authentic, and natural. The development of our history relies on scavenging practices. We wander through staircases that lead to nowhere, get trapped in hidden rooms, and stand on cracked and incomplete foundations in our search of larger narratives to insert ourselves into. Darieck Scott and Ramzi Fawaz, for instance, have disclosed that the processes of erasure that haunt queer representation have pushed us to shape histories using alternative texts and artifacts such as comic books, going as far as to approach comics *as* queer history rather than a supplement to it. Comics thus became an "archival visual history" that illuminated dynamics of gender and sexuality in ways that historical records, and historians, often refuse to acknowledge (211). Given that queerness was often excluded from larger historical and narrative imaginings, comics helped to address this epistemological gap—and the same can be said about queer YA culture, and how it helps us in constructing alternative, countercultural histories that address the omissions and inconsistencies that haunt us today.

But queerness, in other ways, manifests through the organization and composition of this floating structure that the crew repairs. The structure and its markings pose a question that can never be answered; it conceals an object of great truth and meaning that can never be found. One can never truly understand or map the place. Similar to the composition and architecture of the underworld in *Hades*—which I explored with more nuance in Chapter 4—the building, even though on the verge of collapse, "dominates

158 *The Limits of Repair*

the (heterocentric) norm, the dominant social narrative of the landscape" (Désert 21) and deliberately provides a sense of disorientation that challenges linear and straightforward orientations. This sense of displacement and orientation can be observed as Mia walks into a restricted and condemned section of the building that hosts a central chamber (Walden, Chapter 4, see Figure 6.1). Trees burst through the building's architecture. Empty doors, chambers, and staircases have no clear destination. The space defies normative forms of organization, it resists being decoded or navigated in a singular way, and it's built with the purpose of concealing an object that can never be found. The building's structure embeds

Figure 6.1 Mia stands on the fragile foundations of the ancient queer structure floating in space (Walden, Chapter 4). Every effort has been made to contact copyright-holders. Please advise the publisher of any errors or omissions, and these will be corrected in subsequent editions.

an answer within, making the object an aspiration that's always out of reach. This echoes Muñoz's approach toward queerness and futurism, in that the building itself was constructed around the premise of the "not yet here but nonetheless always potentially dawning" (Muñoz, *Cruising Utopia* 187). However, if queer futurism relies on a relationship to the past, and if the past enables "utopian imaginings of another time and place that is not yet here but nonetheless functions as a doing for futurity" (106), what do we make of the processes of (de)construction that we observe in *On a Sunbeam*? How can the past push us to work towards futurity when it's nothing but a crumbling structure floating in space, disconnected from reality, history, and memory? Is this what we crave? For remnants of queer hurt to be unrecognizable and disconnected from the passage of time? Matters become even more pressing when we realize that the people and cultures who dwelled in this structure are no longer present, and that the object they searched for never came to fruition. In a sense, the building memorializes failure.

The webcomic amplifies the gravity of these questions and issues in intriguing ways. As Mia ventures through the central chamber surrounded by aimless doors and staircases, she stands in the middle of the floor and notices how it begins to crack underneath her. This building, this relic of the past, structured by an unknown history, was ultimately unable to sustain her. Mia's crew rescues her from the abyss, holding onto her hand tightly and returning her safely to the crumbling structure. Here, pressing questions emerge, especially if we continue to approach the crumbling building as a stand-in for queer history and the imagination. There's much to be said about how a foundation built by past generations can't sustain a queer young adult and keep her safe. We can say even more about Mia and her crew's efforts to repair this fractured and collapsing building—and the fact that this repair is ultimately done to mobilize the spread of capitalism, and to accommodate the dwelling of bodies who are completely disconnected from the original design and function of this space. The ghosts of regret and displacement haunt this antique structure.

What does it mean to repair something that has no documented history or past? What materials do we select in our efforts to repair a structure, replace its tiles, and fill the cracks in the walls? What or who are we repairing in service of? What happens when history collapses under our feet and we have nobody to rescue us? Mia and her crew approach historical buildings of all kinds and reconfigure them to suit the needs of present generations. When Mia and her crewmate walk around another jobsite—a dilapidated building full of offices—she highlights how these spaces are "going to be turned into apartments" (Walden, Chapter 5). The ways in which this echoes the neoliberal instrumentalization of queer representation and YA criticism is eerie. The tools of repair can strip away the burdens of history to provide

160 *The Limits of Repair*

protection, sustenance, and purpose. But they're also powerful enough to convert a structure into something entirely different—wholly removed from the forces and bodies that created and shaped its foundation.

In this volume, I've attempted to trace a reparative impulse present in the creation and reception of contemporary queer YA literature and culture. I've shown how texts try to establish a connection to a past of hurt, the ways in which critical sensibilities and demands shape the emotional and narrative contours of queer YA, and how we can implement underexplored ways of reading and interpretation to challenge normative understandings of happiness, hope, success, and futurism. In my readings, I've tried to consistently connect texts to broader cultural and affective systems, and even more so, I've shown how time, feeling, and genre affect our critical moods and dispositions toward queer YA cultural productions. These elements also affect whether we approach a text with a mind for generosity or a mind for scorn. In this concluding discussion of this volume, I want to take the issues of history and repair highlighted in *On a Sunbeam* and apply them to an existing conversation on queer YA and reparative approaches. I'm interested in determining what can potentially be lost in our efforts to repair, and even more so, how reparative readings that are removed from a text's history and context can promote cruel forms of optimism, and forms of reading that console rather than challenge.

More specifically, I want to further explore Benjamin Alire Sáenz's *Aristotle and Dante* series, and its overall exploration (or lack thereof) of HIV and AIDS. Set primarily in El Paso, Texas, during the late 1980s, many critics were surprised that the first novel in the series, *Aristotle and Dante Discover the Secrets of the Universe* (2011, henceforth *Secrets of the Universe*) completely ignored the larger history and ramifications of HIV and the AIDS pandemic. Critics were quick to label this omission as a problem or a critical mistake, leading to an influx of both suspicious and reparative interpretations of the text. The lack of AIDS discourse in the first novel becomes even more compelling when considering that its sequel, *Aristotle and Dante Dive into the Waters of the World* (2021, henceforth *Waters of the World*), includes HIV and AIDS as central themes. In the remainder of this chapter, I examine how this series had to negotiate the reparative demands and expectations of queer YA criticism, and I want to scrutinize the methods of repair used to examine narrativizations of AIDS in queer YA. More critically, I use this case study to highlight the limits that sometimes come with reparative reading, and the importance of centering history and intersectional thinking in our efforts to repair and rebuild.

AIDS in the *Aristotle and Dante* Series

Benjamin Alire Sáenz's *Aristotle and Dante* was a text that originally inspired this book, which in its early stages started out as an exploration of hope and optimism in queer YA. I was taken aback by the quietness of this novel, and even more so, how the text illuminated issues that I myself experienced as a teen. Witnessing protagonist Ari negotiating his own queerness vis-à-vis his Latinidad dragged out feelings I experienced and negotiated growing up as a queer teen in Puerto Rico. Although I was an adult by the time I read that text, it touched me in a way that few other texts have prior to that moment.

Part of the reason I was so drawn to the novel is that Sáenz has been pretty upfront about the novel's reparative aims. In a sense, the text became a way for him to process the implications and ramifications of growing up queer and Latine without having a language, framework, or queer history to express his desires and yearnings. Like Aurora Guerrero, who used *Mosquita y Mari* as an opportunity to visualize an undefinable relationship between two Latina girls (see Chapter 2), Sáenz's approached writing as a way of negotiating and understanding his own queer becoming. As Sáenz himself discloses, "I was more than a little afraid of writing the novel because I didn't feel comfortable coming out in the literary world in such a public manner. I almost told myself to 'forget it'" (R.J. Rodríguez 258). Sáenz's apprehensions stem from the fact that he came out in his 50s, and was a student of theology and a Roman Catholic priest for a short period (254). In structuring this novel, Sáenz admits that there was a lot of wish-fulfillment that went into crafting the text, and he explains that it was written with an agenda focused on healing and repair: "I wrote this book as a gift to myself. To heal myself. The inspiration for Ari and Dante, in the end, was my own hurt" (259). The novel wasn't imagined as a way of erasing the hurt of the past, but rather, as a way of confronting it. The product of an author who struggled with his sexuality for decades, we can't deny the fact that the text was written vicariously—it helped Sáenz to imagine a queer teen life that was impossible to him due to his Latinidad, his cultural and historical context, and his attachment to religious institutions. In this sense, Sáenz exploits the narrative irony of YA fiction to explore ideas on adolescence that were unfamiliar and inaccessible to him as he came of age, thus explaining why the novel is set during the late 1980s rather than our current moment.

This ironic narration doesn't have to be a problem. Critics such as Brian McHale have pointed out how all novels that take place in the past "typically involve some violation of ontological boundaries" (16) and oftentimes attempt to conceal the divide "between fictional projections and real-world facts" (17). McHale points out that when a text goes against an established expectation of narrative or genre, it's because it has some investment in becoming "a medium for raising ontological issues" (17) regarding the genre, its characters, or its setting. Given the fact that Sáenz so deliberately infuses his current ideologies and sensibilities in constructing a representation of queer Latine youth, we can see that the novel aims less to be an accurate representation of queer Latine life and more of a project aimed at repair, at conjuring impossible histories, and imagining the past as one that makes room and space for queer life to thrive. But if fiction set in the past should conceal the seams between fiction and historical facts, and if going against an established representative tendency purposely raises ontological issues, what do we make of the absence of HIV and AIDS in *Secrets of the Universe* given that it takes place in the late 1980s and centers on the experiences of queer boys? Is this omission wrong? Was Sáenz irresponsible in refusing to mention HIV or AIDS in this narrative? What do we make of this violation of the ontological boundary between the realm of the text and the worlds we inhabit? I don't believe the absence of AIDS in this text necessarily has to be framed as an issue. Doing so involves the very processes of suspicion that Sedgwick and Felski interrogate in their oeuvre. As I've discussed in Chapter 3, part of the representative politics of AIDS literature often involved refusing to name the disease by its name or to avoid any references to the disease in order to avoid summoning the cultural baggage associated with it (see Jones 240). But what happens when this lack of representation draws critical ire or suspicion? Do we need to read this novel reparatively to draw emotional sustenance from it despite its omission of the AIDS crisis?

Secrets of the Universe has received countless accolades—including the 2013 Pura Belpré Narrative Medal for Latino Fiction and the 2013 Lambda Literary Award for LGBTQ Children's and Young Adult Literature. Despite the awards and praise the novel received in its representation of the overlap between queerness and Latinidad, Sáenz was pushed to reckon with all the content he barred from this book—in particular, the exclusion of any discourse on HIV or AIDS in a YA novel set during the 1980s. As he discloses in an interview published shortly after the sequel was released,

> I couldn't quite forgive myself for not having included the AIDS pandemic. It was personal. [...] And I felt, too, that the [first] novel was turned inward. I wanted very much for the novel to turn outward, for Ari and Dante to turn toward the world in which they lived to make sense of their lives.
>
> (Schulman)

Sáenz's disappointment was also partially driven by critiques that circulated in pedagogical and scholarly circles regarding the lack of any discourse about HIV and AIDS in the first novel. This is especially true when considering that HIV and AIDS had significant effects over how queer people framed their lives and practices in the United States during this decade.

Criticism of the lack of AIDS discourse in the first novel reached its peak with the publication of Michelle Ann Abate's article "Out of the Past" in 2019, which addresses the problems of a culturally significant queer YA novel set in the 1980s failing to acknowledge the pandemic. Abate sets up the discussion by questioning whether the novel can or should "be viewed as a positive portrayal of queer identity when it fails to engage with one of the biggest challenges to, as well as catalysts for, the LGBTQ community" (2). While Abate situates the first half of this critique in the hermeneutics of suspicion, addressing the historical, literary, and political implications of this omission and its effects on how we interpret the novel, the later part of this reading pivots to reparative critique to redeem the novel from its representative faults. To accomplish this, Abate rethinks *Secrets of the Universe*'s genre, thinking of it not as a form of historically oriented queer teen fiction, but as a form of speculative and hopeful literature that *reimagines* a history of hurt:

> The YA novel revisits one of the most tragic periods in LGBTQ[+] history. But it does not go there to wallow in the sadness or rage over the injustice—reactions and emotions that have been explored in many previous works about AIDS. Instead, the novel returns to this era to depict the wonder that was denied, the splendor that was stifled, and the joy that was missed.
>
> (Abate 18)

In simpler terms, Abate frames *Secrets of the Universe* as an exercise in utopian and ahistorical thought in its attempts to envision what queer boyhood would look like in the 1980s without dealing with the deathly connotations associated with the AIDS pandemic. Rather than framing this omission as a critical fault or product of authorial intent, Abate reconfigures our understanding of this narrative gap in search of hope and joy. While such a reading allows us to be comfortable with the text's omission, what else is gained (and lost) through such efforts at repair? To what extent does this repair engage in the processes of joywashing raised in Chapter 2 of this volume?

While this utopian approach pushes us to reimagine the novel's scope and view it through a different lens, matters of history and cultural context compel us to acknowledge the limitations of such a reparative gesture. To what extent do queer novels set in the 1980s have an obligation to address the AIDS crisis? Why do some readers feel hurt by the first novel's omission of the AIDS pandemic, and why do they go to such great lengths to salvage the book from its ambiguities and omissions? These questions become even more overloaded when we consider the state of queer Latine literature in the early 2010s and how *Secrets of the Universe* needed to carve out representational space to circulate the intersection of queerness and Latinidad on such a large and mainstream scale. In my previous work on the first novel, I discussed how *Secrets of the Universe* deliberately focused on subverting tropes often found in queer Latine YA, not only in its implementation of future-oriented thinking but, even more so, in its "attempts to imagine a historical moment in which Latin[e] parents cultivate, rather than encumber, their child's queerness" (Matos 45). The novel aims at disrupting some of the ties between machismo, patriarchal values, and queerness, not to mention that it also attempts to disrupt monolithic approaches toward Latine communities and practices—it wasn't written nor framed as an AIDS novel.

To further compound these issues, note that a utopian approach towards *Secrets of the Universe* opposes the ideological scope of new-wave YA novels focused on AIDS, which Gabriel Duckels describes as texts focused on the politics of memorialization—texts that synergize queer *cultural history* and the representation of queer sexual futures (436, "From Heterosexualization..." emphasis mine). Indeed, a sense of ahistoricism must come into play when approaching *Secrets of the Universe* as an aesthetic attempt to envision a queer life trajectory devoid of the pressures and cultural hurt attached to AIDS. This approach to the text does carve a sense of futurity and hope for readers, but it does so at the cost of a cultural, and more specifically, queer Latine history that stands in opposition to the grand narratives of queerness commonly circulated in the United States. Through this approach, we witness a utopic coming of age narrative that forecloses opportunities for memorialization and for readers to come to terms with the strategies of survival our queer Latine ancestors have used throughout history.

The stakes of reading *Secrets of the Universe* as an exercise in utopian thinking have been intensified with the publication of *Waters of the World* and its meaningful focus on the AIDS crisis—centering on its impact on the protagonists' psyches and sense of wellbeing as young queer Latine men growing up together with an uncertain future ahead. *Waters of the World* aligns itself with the new-wave of AIDS YA literature in its attempts to offer a historically oriented sense of futurism that "retrospectively remed[ies] the otherization of stigmatized people" (Duckels, "From Heterosexualization" 436). Approaching the first novel's omission of the epidemic as an optimistic opportunity to rewrite and redeem the past becomes increasingly untenable when considering the content of the sequel, which serves as a text that reminds young readers of the effects of the AIDS crisis and its lasting impact on contemporary queer life. It further harkens back to the differences between repair and revision discussed in previous chapters.

With the overt inclusion of HIV and AIDS discourse, and by exploring the ramifications of the pandemic in the lives of Latine youth, *Waters of the* World informs and transforms our understanding of the absence of HIV and AIDS in *Secrets of the Universe*. The sequel uses the motif of silence to disrupt the politics of legibility and visibility present in many YA texts, and that were especially present in the lives of young Latine folk during the peak of the AIDS pandemic. The first novel's treatment of HIV and AIDS as a speculative, hopeful gesture only becomes justifiable when stripping the novel of the cultural and historical frameworks central to Sáenz's reparative and healing aims. Such forms of reparative reading rely on logics and dynamics similar to those present in whitewashing, in that they disregard how the historical and current conditions of Latine life's impact what can (or can't) be articulated—and at times, what can or can't be *felt*.

Silence = Death?

The drive to redeem texts despite their issues, gaps, and anxieties draws from the frameworks of reparative reading, a method that pushes people to acknowledge how texts can still be helpful, influential, and emotionally sustaining for specific reading communities despite their issues, gaps, or representative tendencies. The introduction of this book delves more deeply into the topic of reparative approaches, but for the sake of this chapter, recall that they've traditionally centered around the redemption of texts featuring problematic features and elements—in pushing readers to "feel good" about their emotional and critical relationship with a text. These approaches aim to demonstrate how readers find comfort and solace in such texts despite their problematic elements, omissions, and associations of queerness with death and violence.

In the fields of children's and YA literary studies, reparative approaches have slowly but surely surfaced in research that explores the intersections between youth literature, theory, and activism in queer contexts—with said approaches implemented heavily in my own work and in the scholarship of other colleagues such as Jon M. Wargo, Joshua Coleman, Cristina Rhodes, Michelle Ann Abate, Shane T. Moreman, and countless others. Such approaches have been helpful in identifying strategies that readers use to develop relationships with texts generated and distributed in oppressive, violent, and capitalist contexts. However, such approaches, when handled recklessly, can come off as ahistorical, apolitical, and contribute little to disrupt the very powers that limit our bodies, practices, and desires. While reparative approaches are often implemented in the field to challenge the overwhelming presence of homonormative panic narratives in the field (see Jennifer Miller), we must consider the extent to which such readings can unintentionally realign our scholarship with the logics of panic and suspicion that dominate the study of youth cultural productions. What if we think of the omission of HIV and AIDS not as an exercise in utopian thinking, but rather, as an honoring of the codes of silence that Sáenz experienced while growing up in the 1980s? How does this approach push us to identify reparative engagements with texts that are informed by history and culture?

A reparative approach to *Secrets of the Universe* focused on examining the text through a utopic, ahistorical lens becomes unsustainable once we politicize and historicize the text. The stakes of reparative approaches to this series become increasingly palpable when interpreting it through an intersectional lens that considers notions of ethnicity and culture that are frequently ignored in these analyses. I want to think more carefully about HIV and AIDS from a Latine context, and even more so, I want to address the role of silence and omission in narrativizations of AIDS in Latine and Chicane literature. In doing so, we not only reckon with the expectations of normativity and assimilation that constantly inform queer YA criticism, but we also think deeply about what we desire, and what we wish for, in our efforts to heal and repair. We also complicate the histories of queerness that are normatively superimposed over YA texts.

For instance, *Waters of the World* invites readers to understand the difficulties and challenges of discussing AIDS in Latine youth contexts, and how many of the ideas upheld by activist groups at the time opposed the normative demands of Latine, particularly Chicane communities. In critiquing the absence of AIDS discourse in *Secrets of the Universe*, Abate invokes the fact that the AIDS Coalition to Unleash Power (ACT UP)—a radical group of activists focused on publicly demystifying the stigma of AIDS and addressing issues of inequality in healthcare—was formed in 1987, months before the first novel takes place. Known for their now famous slogan "Silence = Death," Abate claims that the first novel "does not heed this advice" and that it ultimately "disregards this well-known slogan from the history of the LGBTQ[+] movement," reinstating the silences and omissions that the activist group fought so hard to disrupt (11). This reading, while highlighting a disjuncture between mainstream AIDS activism and Latine contexts, unfortunately, ignores the exceptional ways in which silences, absences, and omissions operate within Latine families with queer children and, even more so, the extent to which members of ACT UP were aligned with practices that reinforced frameworks of ideological whiteness that shut down opportunities for coalition across different demographics.

Deborah B. Gould has pointed out that racism was quite palpable in the everyday operations of ACT UP. Several conflicts arose during meetings during the late 1980s and early 1990s, especially when it came to the role of collectivity and intersectional thinking in their activism. Although the organization assumed a universalizing agenda focused on advocating for all people with AIDS, many white participants refused to engage in activist practices focused on overlapping forms of oppression, and focused on activism that privileges "the concerns of white, middle-class, gay men over those of others with HIV/AIDS" (57). ACT UP's internal conflicts and tense relationship with nonwhite queer communities became increasingly convoluted as many participants sidelined the political dimensions of ACT UP's activist agenda to focus exclusively on financial, capitalist, neoliberal concerns. This was particularly true when seeing how the organization's later activism focused almost exclusively on expediting AIDS drug research. Many of ACT UP's early members thought that a focus on other interconnected axes of identity and power, such as race, ethnicity, or gender, would derail focus from their overarching goals (Gould 57).

Alexandra Juhasz has further highlighted how logics of whiteness are partially responsible for the visibility of ACT UP's activist agenda and that, for the most part, ACT UP was "thought to be the home of white men." Thus, the activist endeavors of queer people of color were often overshadowed or invisibilized by the more confrontational, "in your face" methods used by white members (Juhasz 71–72). Furthermore, we must also recognize that many people—including undocumented people and people of color—frequently couldn't afford to engage with the visible and public activism typically practiced by the affluent and white members of ACT UP. Given that the organization was so focused on concerns that affected the lives of primarily upper-class, white gay men, it becomes questionable whether their activist practices had much circulation in Latine contexts and communities, and particularly the consciousness of queer Latine *teenagers* in the 1980s, who were still coming to developing understandings of their sexualities, identities, and sense of national belonging in a normative, deeply antiqueer context. We can't succumb to the pressure of overgeneralizing how queer teens in the 1980s felt about their queernesses vis-à-vis HIV and AIDS, especially given the obvious fact that not all communities or contexts have access to the same knowledges or resources.

Silences, gaps, and omissions are often approached with suspicion in YA texts, especially since they are viewed as "detrimental" to marginalized readers. M. Roxana Loza, for instance, has argued that YA novels, even when centered on Latine experiences, approach silence as oppressive, and these texts ultimately achieve a sense of narrative closure through a dismantling of different forms of trauma induced by the breaking of silence (7). But when looking at the role of silence within a larger tradition of queer Latine and Latin American writing, matters are anything but simple—and the silences present in this literary strand are anything but a matter of unknowing of ignorance, nor do they always lead to violence and oppression. As Ben Sifuentes-Jáuregui has suggested, silence arises from "a conscious position of unspoken knowledge, an assertive refusal to name that desire—and to link it with an identity" (5). Sifuentes-Jáuregui urges us to approach silence as a trope that can "make certain sexualities possible" and to think critically about how specific identifications manifest even when they aren't explicitly voiced (133). This is especially true in many Latine contexts—where there are different understandings and dynamics of secrecy and exposure that don't necessarily mirror those found in other queer contexts.

The stakes of silence in *Waters of the World* increase as Ari grapples with the implications behind ACT UP's "Silence = Death" slogan and how it feels contradictory to his sense of identity: "The men who are dying of AIDS have a poster that says *SILENCE = DEATH*. I think I know what that means. But for a guy like me, silence can be a place where I am free of words" (Sáenz, *Waters* 153). Here, Ari reflects on the self-determination that silence grants him, in that it allows him to think and feel beyond the parameters of language and to acknowledge how words can lock us into specific ways of being and feeling. Silence pushes Ari to process his identification with Dante without resorting to the use of predetermined concepts and approaches to the world, and to grapple with the repercussions of being a queer teen developing during the peak of the AIDS crisis. Similar to Austin's explorations of the follies of representation explored in the previous chapter, Ari's framing of silence channels a politics of opacity that challenges the compulsory visibility often demanded by critics of queer YA. Ari's process of disidentification with this slogan becomes imperative not only for his positionality as a queer Latine teen, but for his very survival.

Throughout the novel, the reiterative invocation of ACT UP's slogan becomes a compulsive motif within the text, and Ari continues to negotiate his own identity vis-à-vis the disruption of silence called for by mainstream, white, and visible forms of activism. During a particularly moving moment in the novel in which Ari comes out to his friend Cassandra, he reveals that he's only disclosed his sexuality to a small group of people: "I know that all the gay activists are saying that silence equals death, but my silence, at least right now, equals my survival" (184). Ari's contemplation of silence vis-à-vis the declaration of ACT UP's slogan exudes complexity. First and foremost, Ari's engagement with the slogan is a process of disidentification with mainstream forms of queer activism. José Esteban Muñoz approaches disidentification as the "survival strategies the minority subject practices to negotiate a phobic majoritarian public sphere that continuously elides or punishes the existence of subjects who do not conform to the phantasm of normative citizenship" (*Disidentifications* 4). Ari's disidentification with the slogan emphasizes the negotiations and compromises that his embodiment as a brown, Latine teenager invokes within the dominant culture. His relationship to silence also further demonstrates how ACT UP's demands were aligned with dimensions of class and race that excluded people who look, act, and talk like him.

Ari understands how silence is a double-edged sword. While he recognizes the oppressive practices and beliefs it mobilizes, he doesn't let this create a universalizing and totalizing narrative about silence and its effects on queer life. Ari consistently reflects on the importance of speaking out and making his feelings and thoughts known to others, but he also basks in the queer potentialities induced by the absence of language and words. Near the conclusion of *Waters to the World*, Ari and Dante visit a desert in El Paso, Texas, a place where Ari and Dante cemented their relationship. As the two boys stare at the open environment and breathe in the fresh air, Ari takes a moment to show appreciation for the desert's quietness:

> A walk in the desert in the quiet. Sometimes, the silence of the desert was a kind of music. Dante and I, we shared a silence between us that was a kind of music too. The desert didn't condemn Dante and me for holding hands.
>
> (435)

Toward the novel's ending, Ari goes as far as to characterize silence as "rare and so sacred" (514). Silences, gaps, and omissions aren't always represented as sources of tension for these characters, but rather as moments of queer potentiality and moments of identification and filiation that elude words and the control of language.

Engagements with silence have been vital in constructing fictional Latine worlds inhabited by queer youth, where queer Latine teens had little language, experience, and knowledge to articulate their queerness, much less their fears and apprehensions regarding HIV and the proliferation of the AIDS epidemic in the 1980s. We've seen this in other explorations of queer Latinidad such as *Mosquita y Mari*, in that the film engages in similar dynamics of silence to identify alternative structures of belonging and imagining (see Chapter 2). Ari acknowledges how he and Dante are engaging in new and challenging worldbuilding processes with little language, representation, history, or assistance from other people or from their culture:

> It seemed that we *had* actually become cartographers of a new world, had mapped out a country of our own, and it was ours and only ours, and though we both knew that country would disappear, almost as soon as it had appeared, we had full citizenship in that country and we were free to love each other.
>
> (*Waters of the World* 101, emphasis in original)

Imagery connected to mapping and cartography is vital in understanding the relationship between these boys and the world they inhabit. Juana

María Rodríguez has explored the affective contours of maps, in that they offer a tangible "promise of reaching the end of the journey. Maps are useful guides, but they are site-specific ideological constructions and are quickly dated by the earthquakes of history" (*Queer Latinidad* 39). What's so compelling about the map that Ari and Dante chart is that they're aware of this ephemerality, of how this map is limited in its capacity to guide in the future, when claiming that their country will eventually "disappear." *Waters of the World* doesn't provide readers with a map, but rather, it narrativizes a process of charting and mapping that doesn't have an end goal in sight—that resists a specific destination and outcome. Their feelings for each other and the pathways they walk together are what ultimately help them to continue wading through the waters of the world. Wherein lies the stakes of holding Latine teen characters accountable for articulating their relationship with HIV and AIDS discourse as they're attempting to chart out their lives with little knowledge or experience with the broader queer world? Why are we trying to make Ari and Dante's story fit within broader, more general narratives connected to mainstream stories of queerness? The stakes of these questions become even more charged as we see that the boy's attempts to map and chart their country are frequently disrupted by heteronormative and supremacist forces. They continuously deal with the pressures of racism, homophobia, violence, and assimilation in their attempts to trace the contours of their own private nation.

Saénz has explained that the COVID-19 pandemic pushed him to realize that his "readers could draw their own parallels between the AIDS epidemic and the pandemic they are living through" (Turner), thus prompting him to pen the sequel. However, we must acknowledge that Saénz was aware of the criticism regarding AIDS and its omission in the first *Aristotle and Dante* novel. Just like his first novel, *Waters of the World* is first and foremost a gesture toward repair. The stakes of these reparative aims were relatively high for Saénz, especially since the effects and ramifications of the epidemic led to many losses in his personal and professional life:

> I lost my mentor Arturo Islas, a writer and professor at Stanford. I lost my older brother, Donaciano Sanchez, and I lost one of my closest friends, Norman Campbell Robertson. And the U.S. government didn't give a damn. Never has the gay community been more hated because they were afraid [of us].
>
> (Sánchez Torres)

In a sense, *Waters of the Word* was a grieving process for Saénz in that he had to reckon with the losses that AIDS has caused in his life. But even more so, it was a way for Saénz to partially disrupt his own silence and bear witness to a difficult moment in queer Latine history that was incredibly personal to him. Does Sáenz owe readers this history? To what extent do we, as reading audiences, push people to exploit their own difficult histories in an effort to show us a more utopic world? Sure, we can approach *Secrets of the Universe* as a text that imagines a past without AIDS, but why are we attempting to engage in such processes of repair? I'm curious as to what drives the impulse to reconfigure a text's genre in an attempt to fix its issues, an issue that solely exists because critics enter the text with a preexisting understanding of what a queer YA text set in the 1980s *should* accomplish and *should* represent. It says much about our engagements with queer YA culture, and how we think about the broader political work this field mobilizes. It says even more about the challenges of doing queer work in a field so focused on normative understandings of what is correct, positive, and true.

The parallels between Sáenz's work and that of his late mentor, Arturo Islas, are uncanny. Islas was a Chicano writer who explored themes of queerness and sexuality in his groundbreaking semi-autobiographical novel *The Rain God* (1984). In his examination of the themes of sexuality and illness in Islas' novel, Manuel De Jesús Vega discloses how AIDS connects profoundly to *The Rain God* even though it never appears explicitly in the text. The logics of silence often frame the representation of illness within the novel, and Islas resorts to intricate forms of queer coding and "complex metaphor" to confront the issues decay and the body within the scope of the text—it implements the motifs of monstrosity, the desert, and Pre-Columbian deities to symbolically discuss illness (112). De Jesús Vega highlights how Islas' coded approach toward illness in *The Rain God* can be partially attributed to the "social climate of the early 80s, along with the homophobia prevalent in the Chicano community" (117), but I'm interested here in how Sáenz drew from the same representative tendencies as his mentor to craft a queer Latine narrative. The significance of Islas' silences and coding gains even more traction when acknowledging his complicated relationship with AIDS. Not only did Islas lose a lover and various friends during the height of the epidemic, but he consistently and openly shared fears and anxieties about AIDS in diary entries. Islas, for instance, would disclose how these fears further deepened his "own sense of a deformed body and his already acute sense of his own mortality" (Aldama, *Dancing* 120). If Chicane authors had a difficult time in terms of directly articulating the ramifications of AIDS in their lives and communities, wherein lies the narrative and ideological stakes of holding *imagined* Chicane *teens* accountable for dealing with these tensions?

Why must we read this silence as a fault rather than reading it as a *wound*? These silences come from a place of hurt. They are designed to channel pain. So many people are uncomfortable with the generative potentialities that hurt and pain can summon, which thus presents an urgency for repair. But when we sideline hurt entirely in an effort to celebrate progressive and comforting stories and possibilities, we foreclose opportunities to think about how the "crossroads of trauma and injury" can lead to "the potential for material transformation and healing" (Green and Ellison 223). The overt presence of AIDS in *Waters of the World* pressures the ability to read the first book as a utopian fiction that imagines a queer history devoid of AIDS, and also pushes us to think more carefully about whether the absence of AIDS discourse in *Secrets of the Universe* was a gross oversight. The consistent use of motifs of silence and absence in *Waters of the World* aligns with the broader expectations of Latine AIDS narratives, which Alberto Sandoval Sánchez celebrates for their potential to "give voice to experiences" and help us to "bear witness and testimony" to break the silence tethered to queerness in Latine contexts (172). Latine texts that focused on queerness and AIDS highlighted how the pandemic helped characters to construct a subjectivity and purview "that allows for the questioning of sexual taboos and the breaking of silence at home on homosexuality and AIDS" (Sandoval Sánchez 172). And while I don't want to underplay the importance of breaking these silences and the labor that early Latine AIDS novels went through in materializing queer Latine subjectivity, we must also recall that the impulse to make things transparent, visible, and palpable is very much couched within the confessional demands of Western thought. Not to mention that this pattern also connects to YA critics' tendency to prefer narratives focused on namable and coherent sexual and gender identities (see Mason, *Queer Anxieties* 18).

In a discussion on the critical value of "opacity," Édouard Glissant argues that in Western cultures, "to understand and thus accept you, I have to measure your solidity with the ideal scale providing me with grounds to make comparisons and, perhaps, judgments. I have to reduce" (190). Glissant critiques the Western obsession with "understanding" and transparency precisely because of their normalizing and assimilative tendencies, and focus on making any experience or feeling consumable and interpretable to a broad audience. This obsession is definitely apparent in the study of youth literatures, especially when concerning matters of representation and diversity and its attachment to neoliberal frameworks of visibility. You can't go to a youth literature conference without a scholar *uncritically* summoning Rudine Sims Bishop's framework on windows, mirrors, and sliding glass doors, focusing solely on optics and visibility rather than thinking about the larger systems of oppression that are at play in the creation and critique of youth cultural productions. I'm in no way contesting the value or importance of Bishop's framework and how it promotes a more thoughtful and creative representation of marginalized bodies and experiences. And cultural mirrors, as S.R. Toliver has pointed out, are vital in identifying the shattered mirrors "that marginalized children were often forced to look through as they searched for themselves in literature" and the ways in which certain narratives misrepresented marginalized lives and communities (2).

But just as we should have the right to see our lives, communities, practices, and experiences reflected on the page and screen, we should also have the right *not* to disclose certain parts of ourselves, especially when this disclosure is structured by normative expectations of what counts as good, successful, possitive, or healthy. At the end of the day—and regardless of the emancipatory promises present in a text—YA literature and media are first and foremost industries. Books are expected to sell, especially when curated and distributed by major, mainstream presses. An adult's thoughts are disguised using a teen's constructed voice and perspective, packaged in an alluring and attractive cover, filtered through the consciousness of capitalist-driven adults and institutions, and sold to a mass market. I absolutely understand the importance of representation—and I also know that representation can *never* truly reflect reality, but rather, imagine it and construct it. The reason the absence of AIDS seems so problematic in *Secrets of the Universe* is because readers are hurt that a fictional representation doesn't mirror the logics and organization of the world we inhabit. They delve into a text with a suspicious, predetermined set of ideas regarding what a queer YA novel should be, what affects and emotions it should address, and even what historical events it should include or exclude. This harkens back to Toliver's views on the tyranny of realism in representing marginalized bodies and experiences in youth literature raised in Chapter 4, and how demands for authenticity and reality leave little room left to imagine, speculate, dream, and transgress.

What were to happen if we approach the absence of AIDS in *Secrets of the Universe* as a project focused on the logics of opacity? What if the series wasn't designed to provide transparency and clarity to readers, but rather, to emphasize the cultural limitations of our knowledge and our inability to fully represent specific ideas and complete worlds? To what extent do queer Latine subjects have a right to opacity, the right to limit how much transparency and access is given to a broader, potentially non-queer and non-Latine audience to understand the intersections between queerness and Latinidad? Juana María Rodríguez has approached queerness as a practice that refuses explication in that it pushes readers to "read against your preconceived notions of academic disciplinarity, research, language, and scholarship to reimagine the practice of knowledge production" (3). What if we were to approach *Secrets of the Universe*'s lack of AIDS discourse not as an oversight but as a queer attempt to refuse explication, to pay tribute to the logics of silence that have saturated a queer past and present—to go against the whims and normative moods that come with queer YA narrativizations? Unless, of course, we're trying to remove the text from this past entirely. What if we refuse to view this absence as a gap to be filled and instead viewed it as an opportunity to rethink how knowledge is generated, circulated, challenged and foreclosed in queer Latine texts? There's no need to reconfigure the genre of this novel to make it fit a broader narrative of progress—history and context already give us plenty of material for deconstructing and repairing it.

Waters of the World can be viewed as a disruption of Sáenz's own silence when it came to the representation of HIV and AIDS in a 1980s Latine context, but it doesn't entirely reject the disruptive and queer potential that silences can offer. Silence remains sacred in the series, even after confronting the realities of HIV and AIDS. Rather than falling into the normative practice of approaching silence or omission as problematic or ideologically faulty, *Waters of the World* pushes us to witness how silence carves out moments of possibility and narrative resistance. It presents readers with moments in which queer Latine characters don't have to frame their identities or histories according to white, neoliberal, and normative standards of livability, activism, visibility, and survival. The absence of AIDS in *Secrets of the Universe* can best be understood as a queer form of opacity or as a refusal to explicate—one that highlights the impossibility of distilling certain feelings, experiences, and cultural practices in ways that can be easily digested and fully "understood" by readers. By centering the historical and cultural dimensions of silence in Latine contexts in our interpretation of the series, we're better able to understand why AIDS discourse was absent from the first novel, and the cultural significance behind the novel's omissions, without resorting to versions of utopianism that lack historical grounding and that are fundamentally distanced from the hurt that haunts queer Latine readerships.

On Our Messy Relationship with Queer YA: A Provocation

Reparative readings are often a compromise: they push us to feel comfortable with a text, but this sense of solace and relief always comes at a cost. In an examination of processes of repair and teacher identity, James Joshua Coleman succinctly argues that "narrative repair is a process, not a panacea" and how realizing queerer futures involves attending "to histories that hurt within our field" (10–11). These aims resonate with the reparative practices implemented in literary and cultural studies, and frame repair not as a quick and easy solution, but as a difficult, sometimes painful experience of witnessing, reckoning, and moving. As we grapple with different and emerging forms of interpreting youth literature, we must be especially mindful of the cultural and personal expectations that come with other modes of critique. If the lack of HIV/AIDS in *Secrets of the Universe* bears such significant consequences in how we read and connect to the novel, why isn't it sufficient to conduct an examination couched in the hermeneutics of suspicion: one that exposes the problem and brings awareness to the topics imbued within this absence or one that tries to examine this silence from the perspective of Latinidad? What drives the impulse to find a sense of ease and acceptance with the literature we consume? Does this impulse arise from a duty to uphold the reputation of celebrated works or a desire to uncover flaws lurking in the (sub)text? These questions connect to more extensive conversations on the limits of reparative reading and how this critique sometimes reinforces rather than dismantles hegemonic powers.

As discussed in the first chapter of this volume, Patricia Stuelke argues that many forms interpretation fixated on being generous with problematic texts have oftentimes reinforced the status quo. Stuelke suggests that reparative criticsm pushes us to accept the world as it's currently structured, rather than offering us opportunities to break with the world as it is "and rebuild it from the ground up" (29). When applying this framework towards criticism surrounding AIDS and the *Secrets of the Universe*, we must be upfront about what a reparative reading should accomplish and the stakes of conducting one. If we take seriously Marilisa Jiménez-García's claim (and we should) that contemporary Latine YA literature "serves as a window into how authors narrate the promises and failures of cultural nationalism" in efforts to destabilize the American canon, (231) then we must be wary of interpretations that attempt to offer a reparative approach to a queer Latine text by sidelining the cultural, aesthetic, and ideological elements that prompt these destabilizations. Lázaro Lima has further argued that queer Latine texts serve as "narrative acts against oblivion. It is the name we give to an archive of feelings, traits, desires, urges, behaviors, and aspirations in 'American' literary vernacular that can apprehend our relationship to the worlds we inhabit through our collective agencies" (8–9). In due course, we could implement a reparative approach to *Secrets of the Universe* that reconfigures its genre to make it seem more utopian and progressive, but to do so requires a willful ignorance of the very traits, feelings, and desires that define queer Latine narrative in the first place. Reframing the absence of AIDS as a site of joyful and hopeful possibility, after all, undermines the critical value of silence and omission in disrupting the oppressive dimensions of words and, even more so, how Latinidad invites us to interpret silence as a strategy of resistance and survival. It further undercuts the logics of opacity that are at work in this book—logics that carry even more weight given the fact that Sáenz experienced personal losses directly connected to AIDS, and that highlight a series of ethical questions about what knowledges and feelings queer Latine authors "owe" their audiences.

Shedding a novel of its historical and Latine cultural contexts to accommodate it into a broader utopian narrative of progress contradicts the pillars of queer thinking and potentially embraces assimilative and colonizing logics. It fails to encourage us to acknowledge—and more important—witness the harsh truths of knowledge and representation present in society. It reinforces a limited outlook that upholds existing power dynamics and overlooks the complexities of intersecting identities. It prioritizes a sense of ease, of "feeling good," striving for a present and future that ignores the realities of our current sociocultural climate. Heather Love has pointed out how contemporary queer politics' focus on notions of forward-driven progress and optimism has made it "difficult to approach the past as something living," and even more so, how these notions of progress often happen "on the condition that one breaks ties with all those who cannot make it—the nonwhite and the nonmonogamous, the poor and the genderdeviant, the fat, the disabled, the unemployed, the infected, and a host of unmentionable others" (9–10). To read the absence of AIDS as a utopian reimagining in *Secrets of the Universe* involves approaching history and the past as dead. The absence of AIDS in *Secrets of the Universe* is an attempt to further explore queer Latine subjectivity and the specific sociocultural circumstances that affected what knowledges on queerness and AIDS could be circulated. The reframing of *Secrets of the Universe* as an exercise in historical revisionism focuses more attention on *feeling good* about this absence rather than thoroughly thinking through what this absence means and how it *moves* us. I'm skeptical, if not fearful, of what occurs when feeling good about the texts we read supersedes our ability to appreciate a text's penchant for disruption and deconstruction, for attempting to shift the paradigm, or for critiquing normative practices.

We can't sacrifice cultural and historical inquiry in favor of comfortable, progress-ridden readings. Cristina Rhodes, in her exploration of temporality in queer Latine literature, has pointed out how this corpus of texts offers us a unique space to reflect on the impossibilities of queer life in the present, and the many ways in which queer characters develop strategies for inhabiting in worlds that are antithetical to brown, queer being (7–8). A refusal to deeply consider the historical role of silence in Latine contexts when approaching the *Aristotle and Dante* books thus limits an understanding of the radical potentiality of silence in pushing people to resist normative narratives of nationalism and queerness that the novels critique. As Stuelke argues, history should "have some bearing in our reflexive assessments of what is ethical, not to mention what is radical, in our present" (30). By employing historical thinking that is attuned to a text's contexts, we're compelled to delve deeper into the realms of the unseen, the unspoken, the missing, and unrepresentable to understand what it wants us to feel and, more importantly, *why* it wants us to feel these things. We must differentiate between mere attempts to put a bandage on the wounds inflicted by queer Latine YA literature, and efforts that seek to scrutinize and dismantle the very powers, influences, and ideologies that repeatedly harm us and necessitate the creation of survival and reading strategies

I find reparative reading incredibly generative and alluring, but I also recognize that this method is sometimes limited in its capacity to change, move, and provoke. I've tried to make the case in this book, however, that repair becomes particularly generative, transformative, sharp, and politically viable when it's driven by a history of pain and hurt—a history that continues to mark queer teens, adults, and communities as lesser, insufficient, aberrant, out of place, and out of time. We're constantly inhabiting real and imagined worlds full of gaps and omissions. Incomplete histories haunt us, gaps in records make it difficult to situate our bodies and practices within larger narratives of feeling and desiring. Even now, over a decade after YA culture promised us that things were getting better, we find ourselves desperately scavenging for happiness, hope, reprieve, relief, belonging, fulfillment, and purpose. Sometimes we even end up enforcing happiness where it has no place. We continue living and dying in attempts to change what happiness, success, joy, and futurity could mean. Sometimes, the search for these feelings is too unbearable to even imagine. Over a decade ago, Kenneth Kidd highlighted how queer YA has become "more sophisticated and harder to characterize" due to the emergence of unconventional ways of exploring, narrativizing, and imagining sexual and gender identity ("Queer Theory's Children" 114). Queer YA has shown us, over and over again, how it continues to become increasingly complex and elusive in its efforts to shed light on the impossible, the unspeakable, the invisible, the visceral, and the tacit—a complexity that increases in voltage when considering the challenges of contextualizing scholarship and the differences in mood that we bring into our engagements with queer YA literature and culture.

Queer YA culture can offer an alternative to happiness scripts, to what is considered good, right, or correct. It's a powerful site for representing the unspeakable, for giving shape to feelings and outcomes excluded from the record, and for making the unbearable seem endurable. It can do much more than make us feel good about our current place and time. It can do so much more than normalize. It can *move* and *affect*. Much like the broader archive of queer cultural production, it can bend and twist words, images of youth, feelings, and time itself to pose a challenge to normalizing practices, attitudes, and beliefs. The queer YA archive can be an ever-changing, ever-expanding blueprint that helps determine what fractures need to be mended, what histories are buried in the structures of everyday life, what cultural foundations need to be reinforced, and what ideological staircases lead to nowhere. It weaves our minds and spirits into the broader quilts of queer history, memory, defeat, and refusal—revealing ever more *artful* and *moving* ways to delight us, frighten us, harm us, excite us, sustain us, inspire us, destroy us, teach us, and rebuild us.

Note

1 Leo Bersani criticizes heteronormative models of kinship because they are cyclical and inescapable. He argues that queer people should "resist being drawn into mimicking the unrelenting warfare between men and women, which nothing has ever changed" (218). In a sense, *On a Sunbeam* resists mimicking this warfare entirely by removing traditional representations of masculinity from this fictive universe.

References

Abate, Michelle Ann. "Out of the Past: *Aristotle and Dante Discover the Secrets of the Universe*, the AIDS Crisis, and Queer Retrosity." *Research on Diversity in Youth Literature*, vol. 2, no. 1, 2019.
Abate, Michelle Ann, and Kenneth Kidd. *Over the Rainbow: Queer Children's and Young Adult Literature*. U of Michigan P, 2011.
Abraham, Julie. *Metropolitan Lovers: The Homosexuality of Cities*. U of Minnesota P, 2009.
Acosta, Katie L. "Lesbianas in the Borderlands: Shifting Identities and Imagined Communities." *Gender & Society*, vol. 22, no. 5, 2008, pp. 639–659.
@AdamSilvera. Silvera, A. "I Will Forever Stand by *More Happy Than Not's* Rough Ending; It's Not Called *More Happily Ever After*. Life's Issues Aren't Resolved at 17." *Twitter*, 5 Jan. 2016.
Ahmed, Sara. *The Cultural Politics of Emotion*. Routledge, 2004.
Ahmed, Sara. *The Promise of Happiness*. Duke UP, 2010.
Ahmed, Sara. *Queer Phenomenology: Objects, Orientations, Others*. Duke UP, 2006.
Aldama, Arturo J. "Decolonizing Predatory Masculinities in *Breaking Bad* and *Mosquita y Mari*." *Decolonizing Latinx Masculinities*, edited by Arturo J. Aldama and Frederick Luis Aldama, The U of Arizona P, 2020, pp. 117–130.
Aldama, Frederick Luis. *Brown on Brown: Chicano/a Representations of Gender, Sexuality, Ethnicity*. U of Texas P, 2005.
Aldama, Frederick Luis. *Dancing with Ghosts: A Critical Biography of Arturo Islas*. U of California P, 2004.
Anderson, Benedict. *Imagined Communities: Reflections on the Origin and Spread of Nationalism*. Rev. ed., Verso, 2006.
Andiloro, Andrea. "Understanding Genre as Atmospheric Assemblage: The Case of Videogames." *Television & New Media*, vol. 24, no. 5, 2023, pp. 559–570. https://doi.org/10.1177/15274764231171076.
Anzaldúa, Gloria. "Foreword, 2001." *This Bridge Called My Back: Writings by Radical Women of Color*, edited by Cherríe L. Moraga and Gloria Anzaldúa, Third Woman Press, 2002.
Anzaldúa, Gloria. *Light in the Dark/Luz en lo Oscuro: Rewriting Identity, Spirituality, Reality*. Edited by Analouise Keating, Duke UP, 2015.
Austin, Sara. *Monstrous Youth: Transgressing the Boundaries of Childhood in the United States*. Ohio State UP, 2022.
Bakhtin, M.M. "Forms of Time and of the Chronotope in the Novel: Notes toward a Historical Poetics." *Narrative Dynamics: Essays on Time, Plot, Closure, and Frames*, edited by Brian Richardson, Ohio State UP, 2002.

Banks, William P. "Literacy, Sexuality, and the Value(s) of Queer Young Adult Literatures." *The English Journal*, vol. 98, no. 4, 2009, pp. 33–36.
Barthes, Roland. "Theory of the Text." *Untying the Text*, edited by Robert Young and Kegan Paul, Routledge, pp. 31–47.
Beauvais, Clémentine. *The Mighty Child: Time and Power in Children's Literature*. John Benjamins, 2015.
Bechdel, Alison. *Fun Home: A Family Tragicomic*. First Mariner Books, 2007.
Bennett, Alice. *Afterlife and Narrative in Contemporary Fiction*. Palgrave Macmillan, 2012.
Berlant, Lauren. *Cruel Optimism*. Duke UP, 2011.
Bernstein, Robin. *Racial Innocence: Performing American Childhood from Slavery to Civil Rights*. New York UP, 2011.
Bersani, Leo. "Is the Rectum a Grave?" *AIDS: Cultural Analysis/Cultural Activism*, vol. 43, 1987, pp. 197–222.
Bittner, Robert. "(Im)Possibility and (In)Visibility: Arguing Against 'Just Happens to Be' in Young Adult Literature." *Queer Studies in Media and Popular Culture*, vol. 1, no. 2, 2016, pp. 199–214.
Bittner, Robert, Cody Miller, and Summer M. Pennell. "We're Not Sick, We're Not Straight: Conversion Therapy and the Compulsory Body in Young Adult Literature." *The ALAN Review*, vol. 48, no. 3, 2021, pp. 27–36.
Boffone, Trevor. "Young, Gay, and Latino: 'Feeling Brown' in Emilio Rodríguez's *Swimming While Drowning*." *Nerds, Goths, Geeks, and Freaks: Outsiders in Chicanx and Latinx YA Literature*, edited by Trevor Boffone and Cristina Herrera, U of Mississippi P, 2020.
Boffone, Trevor, and Cristina Herrera, editors. *Latinx Teens: U.S. Popular Culture on the Page, Stage, and Screen*. U of Arizona P, 2022.
Bogost, Ian. "The Rhetoric of Video Games." *The Ecology of Games: Connecting Youth, Games, and Learning*, edited by Katie Salen, MIT, 2008, pp. 117–140.
Booth, Emily, and Bhuva Narayan. "Don't Talk About the Gay Character: Barriers to Queer Young Adult Fiction and Authors in Schools and Libraries." *English in Australia*, vol. 52, no. 2, 2018, pp. 40–48.
Bronski, Michael. *Pulp Friction: Uncovering the Golden Age of Gay Male Pulps*. St. Martin's Press, 2003.
Brown, Joanne, and Nancy St. Clair. *The Distant Mirror: Reflections on Young Adult Historical Fiction*. The Scarecrow Press, 2006.
Browne, Katelyn R. "Reimagining Queer Death in Young Adult Fiction." *Research on Diversity in Youth Literature*, vol. 2, no. 2, 2020, pp. 1–25.
Bushman, John H., and Kay Pars Hans. "Young Adult Literature and the Classics." *Using Young Adult Literature in the English Classroom*. 4th ed., Up Saddle River: Pearson Education, 2005, pp. 167–186.
Butler, Judith. *Gender Trouble: Feminism and the Subversion of Identity*. Routledge, 2011.
Butler, Judith. "Imitation and Gender Insubordination." *The Lesbian and Gay Studies Reader*, edited by Henry Abelove, Michéle Aina Barale, and David M. Halperin, Routledge, 1993.
Butler, Judith. *Precarious Life: The Powers of Mourning and Violence*. Verso, 2006.
Butler, Judith. *Undoing Gender*. Routledge, 2004.
Cadden, Mike. "All is Well: The Epilogue in Children's Fantasy Fiction." *Narrative*, vol. 20, no. 3, 2012, pp. 343–356.
Cadden, Mike. "The Irony of Narration in the Young Adult Novel." *Children's Literature Quarterly*, vol. 25, no. 3, 2000, pp. 146–154.

References

Campbell, Edith. "Grumpy Monday." *Cotton Quilts Edi*, 19 Aug. 2019, https://edicottonquilt.com/2019/08/19/grumpy-monday/. Accessed 11 Nov. 2022.

Cart, Michael. "Honoring Their Stories, Too: Literature for Gay and Lesbian Teens." *The ALAN Review*, vol. 25, no. 1, 1997. Web.

Cart, Michael. *Young Adult Literature: From Romance to Realism*. American Library Association, 2010.

Cart, Michael. "What a Wonderful World: Notes on the Evolution of GLBTQ Literature for Young Adults." *The ALAN Review*, vol. 31, no. 2, 2004.

Cart, Michael, and Christine A. Jenkins. *The Heart Has Its Reasons: Young Adult Literature with Gay/Lesbian/Queer Content, 1969–2003*. The Scarecrow Press, 2006.

Chasin, Alexandra. "Interpenetrations: A Cultural Study of the Relationship between the Gay/Lesbian Niche Market and the Gay/Lesbian Political Movement." *Cultural Critique*, vol. 44, 2000, pp. 145–168.

Chbosky, Stephen. *The Perks of Being a Wallflower*. MTV Books, 1999.

Chrisman, Alyssa, and Mollie V. Blackburn. "Interrogating Happiness: Unraveling Homophobia in the Lives of Queer Youth of Color with *More Happy Than Not*." *Engaging with Multicultural YA Literature in the Secondary Classroom*, edited by Ricki Ginsberg and Wendy J. Glenn, Routledge, 2019, pp. 83–92.

Chung, Sandy. "Request to Ban 'Two Boys Kissing' from Virginia High School Library Denied." *School Library Journal*, 29 Apr. 2014, www.slj.com/story/request-to-ban-two-boys-kissing-from-virginia-high-school-library-denied. Accessed 8 Dec. 2015.

Clark, Caroline T., and Mollie V. Blackburn. "Scenes of Violence and Sex in Recent Award-Winning LGBT-Themed Young Adult Novels and the Ideologies They Offer Their Readers." *Discourse: Studies in the Cultural Politics of Education*, vol. 37, no. 6, 2016, pp. 867–886.

Coats, Karen. "Young Adult Literature: Growing Up, In Theory." *Handbook of Research on Children's and Young Adult Literature*, edited by Shelby A. Wolf, Karen Coats, Patricia Enciso, and Christine A. Jenkins, Routledge, 2011, pp. 315–329.

Colborne, Adrienne and Vivian Howard. "Happiness at the End of the Rainbow: Exploring Happy Endings in Young Adult Literature with Queer Female Protagonists, 2009–2017." *The Journal of Research on Libraries and Young Adults*, vol. 9, no. 1, 2018, pp. 1–20.

Coleman, James Johua. "Narrative Repair in Teacher Education: Restorying Painful Histories and 'Damaged' Queer Teacher Identity." *Teaching and Teacher Education*, vol. 124, 2023, pp. 1–12.

Collins, Suzanne. *The Hunger Games*. Scholastic Press, 2008.

Collins, Suzanne. *Mockingjay*. Scholastic Press, 2010.

Consalvo, Mia. "Hot Dates and Fairy-Tale Romances: Studying Sexuality in Video Games." *The Video Game Theory Reader*, edited by Mark J. P. Wolf and Bernard Perron. Routledge, 2003, pp. 171–94.

Corbett, Emily. "Transgender Books in Transgender Packages: The Peritextual Materials of Young Adult Fiction." *International Journal of Young Adult Literature*, vol. 1, no. 1, 2020, doi: 10.24877/ijyal.32.

Corboz, Julienne, Andrew Gibbs, and Rachel Jewkes. "Bacha posh in Afghanistan: Factors Associated with Raising a Girl as a Boy." *Culture, Health & Sexuality*, vol. 22, no. 5, 2020, pp. 585–598.

Craddock, David L. *Dungeon Hacks: How NetHack, Angband, and Other Roguelikes Changed the Course of Video Games*. CRC Press, 2022.

Crisp, Thomas. "From Romance to Magical Realism: Limits and Possibilities in Gay Adolescent Fiction." *Children's Literature in Education*, vol. 40, 2009, pp. 333–348.
Crisp, Thomas. "The Trouble with *Rainbow Boys*." *Children's Literature in Education*, vol. 39, 2008, pp. 237–261.
Crowe, Chris. "Young Adult Literature: The Problem with YA Literature." *The English Journal*, vol. 90, no. 3, 2001, pp. 146–150.
De Jesús Vega, Manuel. "Chicano, Gay, and Doomed: AIDS in Arturo Islas's *The Rain God*." *Confluencia*, vol. 11, no. 2, 1996, pp. 112–118.
D'Emilio, John. *Sexual Politics, Sexual Communities: The Making of a Homosexual Minority in the United States 1940-1970*. 2nd ed., The U of Chicago Press, 2012.
Désert, Jean-Ulrick. "Queer Space." *Queers in Space: Communities, Public Places, Sites of Resistance*, edited by Gordon Brent Ingram, Anne-Marie Bouthillette, and Yolanda Retter, Bay Press, 1997, pp. 17–26.
Donovan, John. *I'll Get There; It Better Be Worth the Trip*. Harper & Row, 1969.
Duckels, Gabriel. "From Heterosexualization to Memorialization: Queer History and Moral Maturation in Young Adult Literature about the AIDS Crisis." *Mortality*, 2021, vol. 26, no. 4, pp. 424–438.
Duckels, Gabriel. "Melodrama and the Memory of AIDS in American Queer Young Adult Literature." *Children's Literature Association Quarterly*, vol. 46, no. 3, 2021, pp. 304–324.
Duggan, Lisa, and José Esteban Muñoz. "Hope and Hopelessness: A Dialogue." *Women & Performance: A Journal of Feminist Theory*, vol. 19, no. 2, 2009, pp. 275–83.
Durand, E. Sybil, and Marilisa Jiménez-García. "Unsettling Representations of Identities: A Critical Review of Diverse Literature." *Research on Diversity in Youth Literature*, vol. 1, no. 1, 2018, pp. 1–24.
Dyer, Richard. "It's Being So Camp as Keeps Us Going." *Camp: Queer Aesthetics and the Performing Subject*, edited by Fabio Cleto, The U of Michigan P, 1999, pp. 110–116.
Edelman, Lee. *No Future: Queer Theory and the Death Drive*. Duke UP, 2004.
Eng, David L. *The Feeling of Kinship: Queer Liberalism and the Racialization of Intimacy*. Duke UP, 2010.
Engelstein, Geoffrey. *Achievement Relocked: Loss Aversion and Game Design*. The MIT Press, 2020.
Erisman, Fred. *Boys' Books, Boys' Dreams, and the Mystique of Flight*. Texas Christian UP, 2006.
Eytan, Ted. "2012 AIDS Quilt DC 13792 – Ryan White and Pedro Zamora." *Flickr*, 13 Jul. 2012, https://www.flickr.com/photos/taedc/7559370758/.
Faris, Wendy B. "The Question of the Other: Cultural Critiques of Magical Realism." *Janus Head* vol. 5, no. 2, 2002, pp. 101–119.
Fawaz, Ramzi. *The New Mutants: Superheroes and the Radical Imagination of American Comics*. New York UP, 2016.
Fear, David. "Mosquita y Mari." *Time Out*, 31 Jul. 2012, www.timeout.com/movies/mosquita-y-mari.
Feeny, Nolan. "The 8 Habits of Highly Successful Young-Adult Fiction Authors." *The Atlantic*, 22 Oct. 2013. Web. 3 Feb. 2015.
Felski, Rita. *The Limits of Critique*. U of Chicago P, 2015.
Foley, Helene. "Choral Identity in Greek Tragedy." *Classical Philology*, vol. 1, no. 98, 2003, pp. 1–30.

Freeman, Elizabeth. *Time Binds: Queer Temporalities, Queer Histories*. Duke UP, 2010.
Fuoss, Kirk. "A Portrait of the Adolescent as a Young Gay: The Politics of Male Homosexuality." *Queer Words, Queer Images: Communication and the Construction of Homosexuality*, edited by R. Jeffrey Ringer, New York UP, 1994, pp. 159–174.
Garcia, Antero. *Critical Foundations in Young Adult Literature: Challenging Genres*. Sense Publishers, 2013.
Garden, Nancy. *Annie on My Mind*. Farrar, Straus, Giroux, 1982.
Gates, Brandon. "'The First to Die at the End' Could Be the Newest Adam Silvera YA Blockbuster." *NPR*, 4 Oct. 2022, https://www.npr.org/2022/10/04/1126537811/the-first-to-die-at-the-end-could-be-the-newest-adam-silvera-ya-blockbuster.
Genette, Gérard. *Narrative Discourse: An Essay in Method*. Blackwell Press, 1988.
Gill-Peterson, Jules. *Histories of the Transgender Child*. U of Minnesota P, 2018.
Glissant, Édouard. *Poetics of Relation*. Translated by Betsy Wing, The U of Michigan P, 1997.
Gordon, Avery F. *Ghostly Matters: Haunting and the Sociological Imagination*. U of Minnesota P, 2008.
Gordy, Douglas W. "Gay and Lesbian Theater." *The Facts on File Companion to American Drama*, edited by Jackson R. Bryer and Mary C. Harting, Infobase Publishing, 2010.
Gould, Deborah B. "ACT UP, Racism, and the Question of How to Use History." *Quarterly Journal of Speech*, vol. 98. no. 1, 2012, pp. 54–62.
Green, Kai M., and Treva Ellison. "Tranifest." *Transgender Studies Quarterly*, vol. 1, no. 1–2, 2014, pp. 222–225.
Gross, Melissa, Annette Y. Goldsmith, and Debi Carruth. *HIV/AIDS in Young Adult Novels: An Annotated Bibliography*. The Scarecrow Press, 2010.
Gross, Melissa. "What Do Young Adult Novels Say about HIV/AIDS?" *The Library Quarterly: Information, Community, Policy*, vol. 68, no. 1, 1998, pp. 1–32.
Gubar, Marah. "Risky Business: Talking about Children in Children's Literature Criticism." *Children's Literature Association Quarterly*, vol. 38, no. 4, 2013, pp. 450–457.
Gwenffrewi, Gina. "J.K. Rowling and the Echo Chamber of Secrets." *Transgender Studies Quarterly*, vol. 9, no. 1, 2022, pp. 507–516.
Hades. Written by Greg Kasavin. Supergiant Games, 2020. Nintendo Switch game.
Hakim, Danny, and Douglas Dalby. "Ireland Votes to Approve Gay Marriage, Putting Country in Vanguard." *The New York Times*, 23 May 2015. Web. Accessed 7 Jun. 2015.
Halberstam, Jack. *Female Masculinity, 20th Anniversary Edition*. Duke UP, 2018.
Halberstam, Jack. *The Queer Art of Failure*. Duke UP, 2011.
Haley Jr., John H., "Love Simon as a Modern, Gay Coming-of-Age Narrative: A New Point of Contention and Engagement for Queer and Popular Culture." *Cinesthesia*, vol. 9, no. 1, Article 2, pp. 1–14.
Hansen, Miriam Bratu. "Room-for-Play: Benjamin's Gamble with Cinema." *Canadian Journal of Film Studies*, vol. 13, no. 1, 2004, pp. 2–27.
HarperCollins Publishers. "Letter from John Donovan Submitting the Manuscript for *I'll Get There. It Better Be Worth the Trip*." *Inside the Archives*, 19 Jun. 1968, https://200.hc.com/inside-the-archives/letter-from-john-donovan-submitting-the-manuscript-for-ill-get-there-it-better-be-worth-the-trip/.

Harris, John. *Exploring Rouguelike Games*. CRC Press, 2020.
Hartinger, Brent. *Geography Club*. HarperCollins, 2003.
Hayn, Judith A., and Lisa A. Hazlettt. "Hear Us Out! LGBTQ Young Adult Literature Wishes Are Answered!" *The ALAN Review*, vol. 38, no. 2, 2011, pp. 68–72.
Henderson, Alex. "Otherworldly Bodies: Non-human Non-binary Characters in YA Fiction." *The Affictionado*. 26 Jan. 2023. Retrived from: https://theafictionado.wordpress.com/2023/01/26/otherworldly-bodies-non-human-non-binary-characters-in-ya-fiction/. Accessed 10 Oct. 2023.
Herring, Scott. *Another Country: Queer Anti-Urbanism*. New York UP, 2010.
Holland, Isabelle. *The Man Without a Face*. Laurel-Leaf Books, 1972.
Hulan, Haley. "Bury Your Gays: History, Usage, and Context." *McNair Scholars Journal*, vol. 21, no. 1, 2017, pp. 17–27.
Hurley, Nat. "The Perversions of Children's Literature." *Jeunesse: Young People, Texts, Cultures*, vol. 2, no. 2, 2011, pp. 118–132.
Hurtado, Aída and Mrinal Sinha. *Beyond Machismo: Intersectional Latino Masculinities*. U of Texas P, 2016.
Jain, Unnati. "Female Masculinity: Othering and Belonging: The *Bacha Posh* of Afghanistan." *Voices*, vol. 13, no. 1, 2023, pp. 138–144.
Jenkins, Christine A. "From Queer to Gay and Back Again: Young Adult Novels with Gay/Lesbian/Queer Content, 1969-1997." *Library Quarterly*, vol. 68, no. 3, 1998, pp. 298–334.
Jenkins, Christine A. "Young Adult Novels with Gay/Lesbian Characters and Themes, 1969-92: A Historical Reading of Content, Gender, and Narrative Distance." *Over the Rainbow: Queer Children's and Young Adult* Literature, edited by Michelle Ann Abate and Kenneth Kidd, U of Michigan P, 2011.
Jenkins, Christine A., and Michael Cart. *Representing the Rainbow in Young Adult Literature: LGBTQ+ Content Since 1969*. Rowman and Littlefield, 2018.
Jiménez, Laura M. "PoC, LGBTQ, and Gender: The Intersectionality of America Chávez." *Journal of Lesbian Studies*, vol. 22, no. 4, 2018, pp. 435–445.
Jiménez, Laura M. "Trans People Aren't Mythical Creatures." *Booktoss*, 24. Sept. 2018, https://booktoss.org/2018/09/24/trans-people-arent-mythical-creatures/.
Jimenez García, Marilisa. "En(countering) YA: Young Lords, Shadowshapers, and the Longings and Possibilities of Latinx Young Adult Literature." *Latino Studies*, vol. 16, 2018, pp. 230–249.
Jones, Cleve. "Prologue: A Vision of the Quilt." *Remembering the AIDS Quilt*, edited by Charles E. Morris III, Michigan State UP, 2011, pp. xi–xxxvi.
Jones, James W. "Refusing the Name: The Absence of AIDS in Recent American Gay Fiction." *Writing AIDS: Gay Literature, Language, and Analysis*, edited by Timothy F. Murphy and Suzanne Poirier, Columbia UP, 1993, pp. 225–243.
Juhasz, Alexandra. "Forgetting ACT UP." *Quarterly Journal of Speech*, vol. 98, no. 1, 2012, pp. 69–74.
Kermode, Frank. *The Sense of an Ending: Studies in the Theory of Fiction*. Oxford UP, 2000.
Kerr, M.E. *Night Kites*. Harper Keypoint, 1986.
Kerr, M.E. "Writing about AIDS for Young Adults." *Confronting AIDS Through Literature: The Responsibilities of Representation*, edited by Judith Laurence Pastore, U Illinois P, 1993, pp. 65–67.

Kidd, Kenneth. "Introduction: Lesbian/Gay Literature for Children and Young Adults." *Children's Literature Association Quarterly* vol. 23, no. 2, 1998, pp. 114–119.
Kidd, Kenneth. "Queer Theory's Child and Children's Literature Studies." *PMLA*, vol. 126, no. 1, 2011, pp. 182–188, https://doi.org/10.1632/pmla.2011.126.1.182.
Kohnen, Melanie. *Queer Representation, Visibility, and Race in American Film and Television: Screening the Closet*. Routledge, 2015.
Kushner, Tony. *Angels in America: A Gay Fantasia on National Themes*. Theatre Communications Group, 2003.
Latham, Don. "The Cultural Work of Magical Realism in Three Young Adult Novels." *Children's Literature in Education*, vol. 38, 2007, pp. 59–70.
Levithan, David. *Boy Meets Boy*. Random House, 2009.
Levithan, David. "Boy Meets Boy, Ten Years Later." *OUT*, 9 Apr. 2013. Web. Accessed 12 Oct. 2014.
Levithan, David. "My Books: Two Boys Kissing." *David Levithan*. Web. Accessed 4 Mar. 2016.
Levithan, David. *Two Boys Kissing*. Alfred A. Knopf, 2013.
Levithan, David. "A Word from the Nearly Distant Past." *How Beautiful the Ordinary: Twelve Stories of Identity*, edited by Michael Cart, HarperTeen, 2009, pp. 7–21.
Lewis, Barry. "Postmodernism and Fiction." *The Routledge Companion to Postmodernism*, edited by Stuart Sims. 3rd ed., Routledge, 2011.
Lima, Lázaro. "Introduction: Genealogies of Queer Latino Writing." *Ambientes: New Queer Latino Writing*, edited by Lázaro Lima and Felice Picano, The U of Wisconsin P, 2011.
Lodge, Sally. "Flux to Issue 40th Anniversary Edition of Seminal John Donovan Novel." *Publishers Weekly*, 10 Sep. 2009, www.publishersweekly.com/pw/by-topic/new-titles/adult-announcements/article/13959-flux-to-issue-40th-anniversary-edition-of-seminal-john-donovan-novel.html.
Lothian, Alex. *Old Futures: Speculative Fiction and Queer Possibility*. New York UP, 2018.
Love, Heather K. *Feeling Backward: Loss and the Politics of Queer History*. Harvard UP, 2007.
Love, Simon. Directed by Greg Berlanti, performances by Nick Robinson, Talitha Bateman, Katherine Langford, Alexandra Shipp, and Jorge Lendeborg Jr., 20th Century Fox, 2018.
Loza, M. Roxana. "'He Doesn't Talk:' Silence, Trauma, and Fathers in *Aristotle and Dante Discover the Secrets of the Universe* and *I Am Not Your Perfect Mexican Daughter*." *Label Me Latina/o*, vol. XI, 2021, pp. 1–10.
Mann, Thomas. *Death in Venice, and Other Stories*. Signet Classics (Penguin), 2014.
Mason, Derritt. "On Children's Literature and the (Im)Possibility of *It Gets Better*." *ESC*, vol. 38, no. 3–4, 2012, pp. 83–104.
Mason, Derritt. *The Queer Anxieties of Young Adult Literature and Culture*. U of Mississippi P, 2020.
Matos, Angel Daniel. "A Narrative of a Future Past: Historical Authenticity, Ethics, and Queer Latinx Futurity in *Aristotle and Dante Discover the Secrets of the Universe*." *Children's Literature*, vol. 47, 2019, pp. 30–56. Project MUSE, https://doi.org/10.1353/chl.2019.0003.
Matos, Angel Daniel, and Jon M. Wargo "Introduction: Queer Futurities in Youth Literature, Media, and Culture. *Research on Diversity in Youth Literature*, vol. 2, no. 1, 2019, pp. 1–16.

McCrea, Barry. *In the Company of Strangers: Family and Narrative in Dickens, Conan Doyle, Joyce, and Proust*. Columbia UP, 2011.

McKay, Steven West, Elizabeth L. Cohen, Jamie Banks, and Alan K. Goodboy. "It's All Fun and Games Until Somebody Dies: Permadeath Appreciation as a Function of Grief and Mortality Salience." *Journal of Gaming & Virtual Worlds*, vol. 14, no. 2, 2022, pp. 181–206.

McLemore, Anna-Marie. *When the Moon Was Ours*. Thomas Dunne/St Martin's Griffin, 2016.

McMahon, Laura, and Michael Lawrence. "Introduction: Animal Lives and Moving Images." *Animal Life and the Moving Image*, edited by Laura McMahon and Michael Lawrence, Palgrave, 2015, pp. 1–22.

Mercado-Lopez, Larissa M. "Queer Voids: 'Lacking' Plotlines, Feelings of Unease, and Ambiguous Endings in *Mosquita y Mari*." *GLQ: A Journal of Lesbian and Gay Studies*, vol. 29, no. 2, 2023, pp. 277–282.

Miller, Jennifer. *The Transformative Potential of LGBTQ+ Children's Picture Books*. U of Mississippi P, 2022.

Miner, Barbara. "When Reading Good Books Can Get Schools in Trouble: First of Two Articles." *Reading, Writing, and Censorship*, vol. 12, no. 3, 1998.

Ministère de la Culture/Centre National de la Préhistoire/Norbert Aujoulat. *The Shaft*, 2024 (shared under CC BY-NC-ND 4.0). https://archeologie.culture.gouv.fr/lascaux/en/mediatheque.

Mitchell, Jennifer. "Of Queer Necessity: Panem's Hunger Games as Gender Games." *Of Bread, Blood and the Hunger Games: Critical Essays on the Suzanne Collins Trilogy*, edited by Mary F. Pharr and Leisa A. Clark, McFarland Press, 2012.

Monaghan, Whitney. "Not Just a Phase: Queer Girlhood and Coming of Age on Screen." *Girlhood Studies*, vol. 12, no. 1, 2019, pp. 98–113.

Montaño, Jesus. "Confronting the Whitewashing of (My) History: The Reparative Value of Latinx YA Historical Novels and Testimonio." *The Lion and the Unicorn*, vol. 36, no. 1, 2022, pp. 58–76.

Montaño, Jesus, and Regan Postma-Montaño. *Tactics of Hope in Latinx Children's and Young Adult Literature*. U of New Mexico P, 2022.

Moreau, Julie. "Trump in Transnational Perspective: Insights from Global LGBT Politics." *Politics & Gender*, vol. 14, 2018, pp. 619–648.

Moreman, Shane T. "A Queer Futurity Autofantasía: Contouring Discourses of Latinx through Memory and Queer Youth Literature." *Text and Performance Quarterly*, vol. 39, no. 3, 2019, pp. 185–202.

Morton, Timothy. *The Ecological Thought*. Harvard UP, 2010.

Morton, Timothy. "Guest Column: Queer Ecology." *PMLA*, vol. 125, no. 2, 2010, pp. 273–282. Web.

Mosquita y Mari. Directed by Aurora Guerrero, performances by Fenessa Pineda and Venecia Troncoso, Sundance Film Festival, 2012.

Muñoz, José Esteban. *Cruising Utopia: The Then and There of Queer Futurity*. 10th Anniversary ed., New York UP, 2019.

Muñoz, José Esteban. *Disidentifications: Queers of Color and the Performance of Politics*. U of Minnesota P, 1999.

Muñoz, José Esteban. "Feeling Brown, Feeling Down: Latina Affect, the Performativity of Race, and the Depressive Position." *Signs*, vol. 31, no. 3, 2006, pp. 675–688.

NAMES Project Foundation. "The AIDS Memorial Quilt." *The AIDS Memorial Quilt*. 2011. Web. Accessed 20. Dec. 2014.

Navarro, Elena Levy. "Fattening Queer History: Where Does Fat History Go from Here?" *The Fat Studies Reader*, edited by Esther Rothblum and Sondra Solovay, New York UP, 2009, pp. 15–23.

Ness, Patrick. *More Than This*. Candlewick Press, 2013.
Ngu, Sarah. "Is Queerness a White Invention?" *Asian American Policy Review*, vol. 29, Spring 2019, pp. 79–85.
Office for Intellectual Freedom. "Top Ten Frequently Challenged Book Lists of the 21st Century." *The American Library Association*. Web. Accessed 2 Feb. 2016.
O'Neill, Patrick. *Fictions of Discourse: Reading Narrative Theory*. U of Toronto P, 1996.
Ott, Brian L., Eric Aoki, and Greg Dickinson. "Collage/Montage as Critical Practice, Or How to 'Quilt'/Read Postmodern Text(ile)s." *Remembering the AIDS Quilt*, edited by Charles E. Morris III, Michigan State UP, 2011, pp. 101–132.
Ostry, Elaine. "'Is He Still Human? Are You?': Young Adult Science Fiction in the Posthuman Age." *The Lion and the Unicorn*, vol. 28, no. 2, 2004, pp. 222–246.
Owen, Gabrielle. *A Queer History of Adolescence: Developmental Pasts/Relational Futures*. U of Georgia P, 2020.
Parker, Ian. "The Story of a Suicide." *The New Yorker*, 6 Feb. 2012. Web. Accessed 23 Oct. 2014.
Pastore, Judith Laurence. "Introduction." *Confronting AIDS Through Literature: The Responsibilities of Representation*, edited by Judith Laurence Pastore, U of Illinois P, 1993.
Pearl, Monica B. *AIDS Literature and Gay Identity: The Literature of Loss*. Routledge, 2013.
Pearson, Wendy Gay, Veronica Hollinger, and Joan Gordon. "Introduction: Queer Universes." *Queer Universes: Sexualities in Science Fiction*, edited by Wendy Gay Pearson, Veronica Hollinger, and Joan Gordon, Liverpool UP, 2010, pp. 1–11.
Pennell, Summer Melody. "Queer Cultural Capital: Implications for Education." *Race, Ethnicity, and Education*, vol. 19, no. 2, 2016, pp. 324–338.
Peters, Julie Anne. *Keeping You a Secret*. Little, Brown, 2003.
Phillips, Leah. *Female Heroes in Young Adult Fantasy Fiction: Reframing Myths of Adolescent Girlhood*. Bloomsbury, 2023.
Poirier, Suzanne. "Introduction." *Writing AIDS: Gay Literature, Language, and Analysis*, edited by Timothy F. Murphy and Suzanne Poirier, Columbia UP, 1993, pp. 1–8.
Pow, Whitney. "Reaching Toward Home: Software Interface as Queer Orientation in the Video Game *Curtain*." *The Velvet Light Trap*, vol. 81, 2018, pp. 43–56.
Primera Hora. "Solicitan relevo de agente investigador en asesinato de joven homosexual en Cayey." *Primera Hora*, 15 Nov. 2009, https://www.primerahora.com/noticias/policia-tribunales/notas/solicitan-relevo-de-agente-investigador-en-asesinato-de-joven-homosexual-en-cayey/.
Przybylo, Ela. *Asexual Erotics: Intimate readings of Compulsory Sexuality*. The Ohio State UP, 2019.
Puar, Jasbir K. "Coda: The Cost of Getting Better: Suicide, Sensation, Switchpoints." *GLQ: A Journal of Lesbian and Gay Studies*, vol. 18, no. 1, 2012, pp. 149–158.
Ramdarshan Bold, Melanie. *Inclusive Young Adult Fiction: Authors of Colour in the United Kingdom*. Palgrave Macmillan, 2019.
Rhodes, Cristina. "Imagining the Future: The (Im)Possibilities of Queerness in Two Latinx Speculative Young Adult Novels." *Label Me Latina/o*, vol. 9, 2021, pp. 1–10.
Rhodes, Cristina. "Processes of Transformation: Theorizing Activism and Change Through Gloria Anzaldúa's Picture Books." *Children's Literature in Education*, vol. 52, no. 4, 2021, pp. 464–477.

Robinson, Laura. "Queerness and Children's Literature: Embracing the Negative." *Bookbird*, vol. 1, no. 52, 2014, pp. v–x.
Rodríguez, Juana María. *Queer Latinidad: Identity, Practices, Discursive Spaces.* New York UP, 2003.
Rodríguez, Juana María. "Queer Politics, Bisexual Erasure: Sexuality at the Nexus of Race, Gender, and Statistics." *Lambda Nordica*, vol. 1–2, no. 21, 2016, pp. 169–182.
Rodríguez, Richard T. "'Filmmaking Found Me': A Conversation with Aurora Guerrero." *GLQ: A Journal of Lesbian and Gay Studies*, vol. 29 no. 2, 2023, pp. 262–268.
Rodriguez, Rodrigo Joseph. "'A Riot in the Heart': A Conversation with Author Benjamin Alire Sáenz." *Study and Scrutiny: Research on Young Adult Literature*, vol. 1, no. 1, 2015, pp. 254–275.
Rodríguez, Sonia Alejandra. "Conocimiento Narratives: Creative Acts and Healing in Latinx Children's and Young Adult Literature." *Children's Literature*, vol. 47, 2019, pp. 9–29.
Roof, Judith. *Come as You Are: Sexuality and Narrative.* Columbia UP, 1996.
Rowling, J. K. *Harry Potter and the Deathly Hallows.* Bloomsbury, 2007.
Ruberg, Bo. *Video Games Have Always Been Queer.* New York UP, 2019.
Ruffolo, David V. *Post-Queer Politics.* Ashgate Publishing Limited, 2012.
Ruiz, Ariana. "Queer Chicana Feelings, Longings, and Community through *Mosquita y Mari*." *GLQ: A Journal of Lesbian and Gay Studies*, vol. 29, no. 2, 2023, pp. 285–289.
Ryan, Hugh. "The Failure of Male Societies: Author Andrew Smith Tackles Monsters and Sex." *Vice*, 8 Mar. 2015, https://www.vice.com/en/article/xd5nxn/failure-of-male-societies-869.
Sáenz, Benjamin Alire. *Aristotle and Dante Discover the Secrets of the Universe.* Simon and Schuster, 2012.
Sáenz, Benjamin Alire. *Aristotle and Dante Dive into the Waters of the World.* Simon and Schuster, 2021.
Sambell, Kay. "Carnivalizing the Future: A New Approach to Theorizing Childhood and Adulthood in Science Fiction for Young Readers." *The Lion and the Unicorn*, vol. 28, no. 2, 2004, pp. 247–267.
Sammons, Jeffrey L. "The Bildungsroman for Non-Specialists: An Attempt at a Clarification." *Reflection and Action: Essays on the Bildungsroman*, edited by James N. Hardin, U of South Carolina P, 1991, pp. 26–45.
Sánchez, Alex. *Rainbow Boys.* Simon & Schuster Books for Young Readers, 2001.
Sanchez Torres, Daniel. "Aristotle and Dante Are Back." *Xtra**, 14 Oct. 2021, https://xtramagazine.com/culture/dante-aristotle-waters-world-saenz-210460. Accessed 22 Jul. 2022.
Sandercock, Tom. *Youth Fiction and Trans Representation.* Routledge, 2022.
Sandoval Sánchez, Alberto. "Breaking the Silence, Dismantling Taboos: Latino Novels on AIDS." *Journal of Homosexuality*, vo. 32, no. 3–4, 1998, pp. 155–175.
Sanna, Antonio. "Silent Homosexuality in Oscar Wilde's *Teleny* and the *Picture of Dorian Gray* and Robert Louis Stevenson's *Dr Jekyll and Mr Hyde*." *Law & Literature*, vol. 24, no. 1, 2012, pp. 21–39.
Savage, Dan, and Terry Miller. *It Gets Better: Coming Out, Overcoming Bullying, and Creating a Life Worth Living.* Penguin, 2012.
Schulman, Martha. "Q & A with Benjamin Alire Sáenz." *Publishers Weekly*, 5 Oct. 2021, www.publishersweekly.com/pw/by-topic/childrens/childrens-authors/article/87543-q-a-with-benjamin-alire-s-enz.html. Accessed 24 Jul. 2022.

Schwab, Katie. "Publishing Queer Literature: A Comparison Between the Adult and Young Adult Markets from the Cold War to the Present Day." *Publishing Research Quarterly*, vol. 39, 2023, pp. 249–262.
Scoppettone, Sandra. *Trying Hard to Hear You*. Harper & Row, 1974.
Scott, Darieck, and Ramzi Fawaz. "Introduction: Queer About Comics." *American Literature*, vol. 90, no. 2, 2018, pp. 197–219.
Sedgwick, Eve Kosofsky. "Axiomatic." *The Cultural Studies Reader*, edited by Simon During, Routledge, 1999, pp. 320–336.
Sedgwick, Eve Kosofsky. *Novel Gazing: Queer Readings in Fiction*. Duke UP, 1997.
Sedgwick, Eve Kosofsky. *Tendencies*. Routledge, 1994.
Sedgwick, Eve Kosofsky. *Touching Feeling: Affect, Pedagogy, Performativity*. Duke UP, 2003.
Sifuentes-Jáuregui, Ben. *The Avowal of Difference: Queer Latino American Narratives*. SUNY Press, 2014.
Silvera, Adam. *More Happy Than Not*. Soho Teen, 2015.
Silvera, Adam. *More Happy Than Not (Deluxe Edition)*. Soho Teen, 2020.
Slater, Katharine. "Here and Not Now: The Queer Geographies of *This One Summer*." *Research on Diversity in Youth Literature*, vol. 2, no. 1, 2019, article 2.
Sloan, Brian. *A Really Nice Prom Mess*. Simon Pulse, 2008.
Smith, Andrew. *Grasshopper Jungle*. Dutton Books, 2014.
Snediker, Michael D. *Queer Optimism: Lyric Personhood and Other Felicitous Persuasions*. U of Minnesota P, 2009.
Snorton, C. Riley, and Jin Haritaworn. "Trans Necropolitics: A Transnational Reflection on Violence, Death, and the Trans of Color Afterlife." *The Transgender Studies Reader*, edited by Susan Stryker and Aren Aizura, 2nd ed., Routledge, 2013, pp. 66–76.
Spencer, Leland G. "Performing Transgender Identity in The Little Mermaid: From Andersen to Disney." *Communication Studies*, vol. 65, no. 1, 2014, pp. 112–127.
Stamper, Christine N., and Mary Catherine Miller. "Arts-Based Approaches to Social Justice in Literature: Exploring the Intersections of Magical Realism and Identities in *When the Moon Was Ours*." *Engaging with Multicultural YA Literature in the Secondary Classroom*, edited by Ricki Ginsberg and Wendy J. Glenn, Routledge, 2019, pp. 171–179.
"Stephen Colbert - It Gets Better." *YouTube*, www.youtube.com/watch?v =BThRZbCs-p8&t=22s. Accessed 9 May 2022.
Stockton, Kathryn Bond. *The Queer Child, or Growing Sideways in the Twentieth Century*. Duke UP, 2009.
Strauss, Barry. "The Classical Roots of *The Hunger Games*." *The Wall Street Journal*, 13 Nov. 2014. Web. Accessed 4 Dec. 2015.
Stuelke, Patricia. *The Ruse of Repair*. Duke UP, 2021.
Sturm, Brian W., and Karin Michel. "The Structure of Power in Young Adult Problem Novels." *Young Adult Library Services*, vol. 7. no. 2, 2009, pp. 39–47.
Super Mario Bros. Nintendo, 1985. Famicom Game.
Taylor, Jodie. "Queer Temporalities and the Significance of 'Music Scene' Participation in the Social Identities of Middle-aged Queers." *Sociology*, vol. 44, no. 5, 2010, pp. 893–907.
Tóibín, Colm. *Love in a Dark Time, and Other Explorations of Gay Lives and Literature*. Scribner, 2004.

Toliver, S.R. "Imagining New Hopescapes: Expanding Black Girls' Windows and Mirrors." *Research on Diversity in Youth Literature*, vol. 1, no. 1, 2018, article 3.
"Teacher's Pet." *Buffy the Vampire Slayer: The Complete First Season*. Written by David Greenwalt, Dir. Bruce Seth Green. 20th Century Fox, 2002. DVD.
Testa, Nino. *Written in Blood: AIDS and the Politics of Genre*. Diss. Tufts University. UMI, 2013.
The Hunger Games. Directed by Gary Ross, performances by Jennifer Lawrence, Josh Hutcherson, Liam Hemsworth, Woody Harrelson, and Elizabeth Banks, Lionsgate, 2012.
The Hunger Games: Mockingjay Part 2. Directed by Francis Lawrence, performances by Jennifer Lawrence, Josh Hutcherson, Liam Hemsworth, Woody Harrelson, and Elizabeth Banks, Lionsgate, 2016.
The Matrix. Directed by Lana Wachowski and Lilly Wachowski, performances by Keanu Reeves, Carrie-Anne Moss, Laurence Fishburne, and Hugo Weaving, Warner Home Studio, 1999.
The Matrix: Reloaded. Directed by Lana Wachowski and Lilly Wachowski, performances by Keanu Reeves, Carrie-Anne Moss, Laurence Fishburne, and Hugo Weaving, Warner Home Studio, 2007.
Thomas, Angie. *The Hate U Give*. Balzer + Bray, 2017.
Thomas, Ebony Elizabeth. *The Dark Fantastic: Race and the Imagination from Harry Potter to the Hunger Games*. New York UP, 2019.
Tompkins, Kyla Wazana. "Intersections of Race, Gender, and Sexuality: Queer of Color Critique." *The Cambridge Companion to Gay and Lesbian Literature*, edited by Scott Herring, Cambridge UP, 2015, pp. 173–189.
Torres, Justin. *We the Animals*. Houghton Mifflin Harcourt, 2011.
Tribunella, Eric L. *Melancholia and Maturation: The Use of Trauma in American Children's Literature*. U of Tennessee P, 2010.
Trites, Roberta Seelinger. *Disturbing the Universe: Power and Repression in Adolescent Literature*. U of Iowa P, 1998.
Turner, Molly Catherine. "Benjamin Alire Sáenz: 'I am the luckiest.' On Writing Aristotle and Dante Dive into the Waters of the World." *Lambda Literary*, 15 Nov. 2021, https://lambdaliteraryreview.org/2021/11/benjamin-alire-saenz-i-am-the-luckiest-on-writing-aristotle-and-dante/. Accessed 5 Feb. 2022.
Turner, Parrish. "When Animals Are Used as Stand-Ins for Transgender Humans, People Are Diminished." *School Library Journal*, 22 Feb. 2021, https://www.slj.com/story/animals-substitutes-for-transgender-humans-is-diminishing.
VanderMeer, Jeff. "Introduction: The New Weird: "It's Alive?" *The New Weird*, edited by Ann VenderMeer and Jeff VanderMeer, Tachyon Publications, 2008, pp. ix–xviii.
Velasquez, Gloria. *Tommy Stands Alone*. Arte Público Press, 1995.
Vidal, Gore. *The City and the Pillar*. Vintage International, 2003.
Wald, Priscilla. *Contagious: Cultures, Carriers, and the Outbreak Narrative*. Duke UP, 2008.
Walden, Tillie. *On a Sunbeam*. 2016–2017, https://www.onasunbeam.com.
Walker, Lisa. *Looking Like What You Are: Sexual Style, Race, and Lesbian Identity*. New York UP, 2001.
"War of the Coprophages." *The X-Files: Season 3*. Written by Darin Morgan. Dir. Kim Manners. 20th Century Fox, 2009. DVD.
Wargo, Jon M., and James Joshua Coleman. "Speculating the Queer (In)Human: A Critical, Reparative Reading of Contemporary LGBTQ+ Picturebooks." *Journal of Children's Literature*, vol. 47, 2021, no. 1, pp. 84–96.

Warner, Michael. *The Trouble with Normal: Sex, Politics, and the Ethics of Queer Life*. Harvard UP, 2000.
Wayland, Nerida. "Representations of Happiness in Comedic Young Adult Fiction: Happy are the Wretched." *Jeunesse: Young People, Texts, Cultures*, vol. 7, no. 2, 2015, pp. 86–106.
We the Animals. Directed by Jeremy Zagar, performances by Evan Rosado, Raúl Castillo, and Sheila Vand, The Orchard, 2018.
White, Edmund. *A Boy's Own Story*. Vintage, 2000.
White, Hayden. "Introduction: Historical Fiction, Fictional History, and Historical Reality." *Rethinking History* vol. 9, no. 2/3, 2005, pp. 147–157.
Wickens, Corrine M. "Codes, Silences, and Homophobia: Challenging Normative Assumptions About Gender and Sexuality in Contemporary LGBTQ Young Adult Literature." *Children's Literature in Education*, vol. 42, 2011, pp. 148–164.
Williams, Raymond. *The Sociology of Culture*. Schocken Books, 1982.
Wittlinger, Ellen. *Hard Love*. Simon and Schuster BFYR, 1999.
Woloch, Alex. *The One Vs. the Many: Minor Characters and the Space of the Protagonist in the Novel*. Princeton UP, 2003.
Woods, Gregory. *A History of Gay Literature: The Male Tradition*. Yale UP, 1998.
Yampbell, Cat. "Judging a Book by its Cover: Publishing Trends in Young Adult Literature." *The Lion and the Unicorn* vol. 29, no. 3, 2005, pp. 348–372.
Yang, Gene Luen. *American Born Chinese*. First Second Books, 2006.

Index

A Boy's Own Story (White) 52
Abate, Michelle Ann 18, 163, 165–166
Acosta, Katie L. xv
affect 5–7, 16–19
Ahmed, Sara: children 129, 148; cultural politics of emotion 104–105, 120; good life 22–23; orientations 112; (un)happiness in queer fiction 39–40, 50–52
AIDS 1, 57; ACT UP 166–168; allegory 137–138; emergence in YA 59–60; in Latine contexts 167–169; Memorial Quilt 73–76; omission of 163–168
Aldama, Frederick Luis 57, 171
American Born Chinese (Yang) 90
Andiloro, Andrea 104, 108
Angels in America (Kushner) 69, 75
animals *see* nonhuman representation
Annie on My Mind (Garden) xv, 41–42, 58n1
Anzaldúa, Gloria 20–22, 30–31, 52, 59
Aristotle and Dante Discover the Secrets of the Universe (Sáenz) 160–174
Aristotle and Dante Dive into the Waters of the World (Sáenz) 164–174
aromanticism 123, 131
assimilation 35, 42, 50–52, 57, 90, 172
Austin, Sara 91
authenticity *see* realism

bacha posh 94–96
backward feelings *see* emotion
Beauvais, Clémentine 28
Bennett, Alice 71, 77, 79–80
Berlant, Lauren 42–43, 130

binaries 3, 42–43, 57–58, 91, 131
bisexuality 43, 140
Bishop, Rudine Sims 172
Bittner, Robert 37, 47
Blackburn, Mollie V. 16–17, 35, 46–47, 54
bodies 20, 37, 57–58, 90–94, 129, 153
Boffone, Trevor 35, 50
Bold, Melanie Ramdarshan 8
Boy Meets Boy (Levithan) 43–44
Browne, Katelyn R. 18, 51, 93, 97
bury your gays *see* tropes
Butler, Judith 29, 87, 104, 148

Cadden, Mike 15, 53, 68, 122, 130
Campbell, Edith 90
Cart, Michael xixn1, 16, 41–42, 46, 103
categories of age 5, 93–94, 155
censorship 40, 58n1
change *see* transformation
Chrisman, Alyssa 47, 54
chrononormativity 102, 148, 153
Clark, Caroline T. 16–17, 35, 46
coalition 4–5, 79–81, 118, 166
Coats, Karen 20, 28, 123
Colborne, Adrienne 17, 35, 46
Coleman, James Joshua 12, 165, 174
colonization 155–157
coming of age 36, 93
coming out 36, 47, 101, 161
Consalvo, Mia 103
Corbett, Emily xvii, 91
COVID-19 pandemic 16, 20, 138, 170
Crisp, Thomas 42–44
Crowe, Chris 54
cruel optimism *see* optimism

Index 193

De Jesús Vega, Manuel 171
Désert, Jean-Ulrick 107
disidentification *see* Muñoz, José Esteban
Donovan, John 40–41
Duckels, Gabriel 57, 61, 68, 164
Durand, E. Sybil 30

Edelman, Lee 127–128, 132, 148
emotion 46, 56, 145; feeling negative or backward 21–22, 81–83, 130; inexpressible 32–35; politics of 104, 120; in video games 108
Eng, David L. 18
epilogues 53–56, 122–124, 150–152

family 47–48, 50–51, 53; expectations 112; generations 72; heteronormative 61, 126; nuclear 118
Faris, Wendy B. 92
Fawaz, Ramzi 10, 92, 157
feeling *see* emotion
Felski, Rita 10–11, 31n4, 45, 142
forgetting 17–18, 46–47, 51–52, 82
Freeman, Elizabeth 72–73, 83, 102–103, 148, 153
Fun Home (Bechdel) xiv, 72
Fuoss, Kirk 68
futurism 12, 28–30, 36, 112–114, 149; and imagination 92; and people of color 37; queer 127–178, 159; in queer YA 12–14, 52–56, 164, 174; speculative 9–10, 132–133

gay conversion therapy 46–47
ghostly narration 61–80
Gill-Peterson, Jules 96
girlhood 32, 91, 94
Glissant, Édouard 172
Gordon, Avery F. 22, 65
Gould, Deborah B. 166–167
grand narratives 20, 62–63, 164, 169
Grasshopper Jungle (Smith) 133–153
Gross, Melissa 61, 64
Gubar, Marah 4–5
Guerrero, Aurora 32–37, 55
Gwenffrewi, Gina 153n1

Hades (Supergiant Games) 98–110, 119–120
Halberstam, Jack 24, 81, 106, 137–138

happiness 23–27, 42–45, 53–58, 128–133
Harris, John 104
haunting 22
healing 5–6, 25, 92, 161
hermeneutics of suspicion 8–11, 29–30, 45, 163
Herrera, Cristina 35
heteronormativity 21, 37, 42–44, 53, 131
history: and authorship 15–16; comics as 31n1, 157; and hurt 56; of loss 21–22; negative 57; and repair 11; and representation 143–144, 164–166
homonormative panic narratives 9, 15
hope 6–8, 12, 20, 56–57, 123–125, 152
Howard, Vivian 17, 35, 46
Hulan, Haley 18, 103
Hurley, Nat 56, 91

identity 5–6, 35–37, 45, 91–93, 163
I'll Get There. It Better Be Worth the Trip (Donovan) 40
imagination 1, 10, 22–24, 91–93
intimacy 17–19, 33, 85
Islas, Arturo 170–171
It Gets Better 14–17, 81

Jain, Unnati 94
Jenkins, Christine xvii, 16, 31n2, 41–42, 103
Jiménez, Laura M. 19, 89
Jiménez-García, Marilisa 30, 175
Jones, Cleve 74
Jones, James W. 64, 162
Jorge Steven López Mercado xvi
joywashing 46, 54, 58

Kidd, Kenneth 18, 177
kinship 4, 36, 109, 121

language 3, 32–35, 64, 145, 168
Latham, Don 92
Latine 92–93; characters in YA 35, 48–50, 163–166; definition xixn3; nationalism 175
Lima, Lázaro 175
livability 23, 44, 87
Lothian, Alexis 10, 68
Love, Heather K. 21, 51, 176

Love, Simon (Berlanti) 37–38
Loza, M. Roxana 167

machismo 48–50, 58n4
magical realism 91–95
marketing 5, 40, 54, 173
Mason, Derritt 7, 15–17, 61–62, 135, 148
Matos, Angel Daniel 56, 164
McLemore, Anna-Marie 89–98
memorialization 60, 63, 164
Mercado-López, Larissa M. 36–37, 56
metafiction, 113–116, 142
Miller, Jennifer 9, 15, 165
Mitchell, Jennifer 131
Mockingjay (Collins) 124–134, 147, 151
monogamy 23, 44, 117, 147–148
Montaño, Jesus 6, 25
mood 11–19, 23, 90, 160
More Happy Than Not (Silvera) 46–57
More Than This (Ness) 110–121
Moreman, Shane T. 12, 165
Morton, Timothy 143–144
Mosquita y Mari (Guerrero) 32–39, 55–56
Muñoz, José Esteban xv; affect 6; disidentification 168; privilege 37; queer futurism 12, 29, 57, 105, 134, 159

NAMES Project Foundation 73
narrative: closure 35–36, 67, 83, 112, 122–123; developmental 18, 81, 110–111, 155; mode 112–115, 133; progress-driven 15, 23, 39, 97, 175; structure 48, 61–64, 100
necropolitics 93–96, 99, 102, 107
negative emotions *see* emotions
Ngu, Sarah 157
Night Kites (Kerr) 60–61, 85
nonhuman representation 9–10, 89–91, 142–144
normalization *see* assimilation

On a Sunbeam (Walden) 155–160
opacity 168, 172–175
optimism 15, 42–44, 123–124, 176
Ostry, Elaine 132
Owen, Gabrielle 3, 28, 93, 155

paranoid reading *see* hermeneutics of suspicion
Pearl, Monica B. 62–63, 66–67
Pennell, Summer Melody 16, 47
permadeath 97, 104, 111, 119
permalife 97–98, 104–105, 107
Phillips, Leah 131
Postma Montaño, Regan 25
Pow, Whitney 100
power 22, 28–29, 35, 43
privilege 18, 29, 54; class 37, 48–50; white 15, 166
problem novels 41–42, 58
Przybylo, Ela 124, 126
Puerto Rico xiv–xvi
Pulse nightclub shooting xvi, 13

queer: definition of 2–4, 83; ecology 143–144; reclamation of term 2; scavenging methods 23–24; as a white invention 157

racism 8, 25, 90, 166, 170
Rainbow Boys (Sánchez) 42–43, 48, 63–64
realism 16–19, 68, 91–92, 108, 116
reparative reading 8–12, 23, 55, 163–166, 174–177
representation 57; diverse 172–174; in early queer YA 42; historical 144; limits of 45; neoliberal 159; nonhuman 142–145; queer Latine 34–36, 162–164; of women 146
Rhodes, Cristina 30, 53, 165, 176
Robinson, Laura 39
Rodríguez, Juana María 2–3, 24, 170, 173
Rodríguez, R. Joseph 161
Rodríguez, Richard T. 32
Rodríguez, Sonia Alejandra 16, 135
romance 18, 99–100, 126–129, 131
Roof, Judith 117
Ruberg, Bo 45, 97–98, 104–106
Ruiz, Ariana 36

Sambell, Kay 132–133, 152
Sánchez, Alex 42, 48, 64
Sandercock, Tom 4, 7, 92
Sandoval Sánchez, Alberto 172
Sanna, Antonio 33
Schwab, Katie 5–6
Scott, Darieck 157

secondary characters 116–117
Sedgwick, Eve Kosofsky xix, 8–12, 60, 86
sexual orientation 3, 31, 112, 121n2
Shaw, Adrienne 108
Sifuentes-Jáuregui, Ben 167
Silvera, Adam 46–57, 123
Slater, Katharine 36
space 79, 103–108, 135–136, 153n4, 157–158
speculative fiction 90–97, 123, 132, 163
Spencer, Leland G. 91
Stamper, Christine N. 92
Stockton, Kathryn Bond 19, 50
Stuelke, Patricia 11, 175–176
suicide 13, 47, 51, 95–98, 111–115
Super Mario Bros (Nintendo) 97
survival 3, 18, 23, 45, 93, 168
suspicious reading *see* hermeneutics of suspicion

Taylor, Jodie 109
testimonio *see* witnessing
The Hunger Games (Ross) 124–125, 129
The Perks of Being a Wallflower (Chbosky) xiii–xiv, 42, 75
Thomas, Angie 54
Thomas, Ebony Elizabeth 19, 23, 90–91, 126
Toliver, S.R. 91, 172–173
Tommy Stands Alone (Velasquez) 48
Tompkins, Kyla Wazana 156
Torres, Justin 48
trans: children 96; necropolitics 93–95, 119–120; nonhuman representation 10, 91–92; representation in YA literature 89–91; studies 5
transformation 5, 9, 30, 56, 93–96, 120
trauma 5, 25, 39, 103, 130, 167
Tribunella, Eric L. 4–5, 14
Trites, Roberta Seelinger 24, 35
tropes: B-horror 139; breaking the fourth wall 52; bury your gays 18, 103, 111; Greek chorus 70; mermaid imagery 89; queer endangerment 31n2; silence 32–36, 166–170
Two Boys Kissing (Levithan) 65–88, 109–110
Tyler Clementi 13, 87

universalizing narratives *see* grand narratives

video games 97–100, 103–107, 120

Walden, Tillie 155–159
Wargo, Jon M. 12, 56, 165
We the Animals (Torres; Zagar) 48–49
When the Moon Was Ours (McLemore) 89–110
whiteness 157; and comfort 37; in queer activism 15, 165–167; in speculative fiction 23, 126; in YA publishing industry 8
whitewashing 6, 165
Wickens, Corrine M. 11
witnessing 20, 29, 52, 72, 171–172
Woloch, Alex 116
Woods, Gregory 1, 101

Printed in the USA
CPSIA information can be obtained
at www.ICGtesting.com
LVHW011831041124
795688LV00004B/452